W9-BOB-514

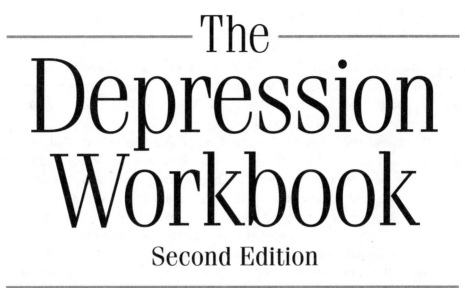

The Depression Workbook

Second Edition

A Guide for Living with Depression
and Manic Depression

Mary Ellen Copeland, M.S., M.A.

New Harbinger Publications, Inc.

Publisher's Note

This publication is designed to provide accurate and authoritative information in regard to the subject matter covered. It is sold with the understanding that the publisher is not engaged in rendering psychological, financial, legal, or other professional services. If expert assistance or counseling is needed, the services of a competent professional should be sought.

Care has been taken to confirm the accuracy of the information presented and to describe generally accepted practices. However, the authors, editors, and publisher are not responsible for errors or omissions or for any consequences from application of the information in this book and make no warranty, express or implied, with respect to the contents of the publication.

The authors, editors, and publisher have exerted every effort to ensure that any drug selection and dosage set forth in this text are in accordance with current recommendations and practice at the time of publication. However, in view of ongoing research, changes in government regulations, and the constant flow of information relating to drug therapy and drug reactions, the reader is urged to check the package insert for each drug for any change in indications and dosage and for added warnings and precautions. This is particularly important when the recommended agent is a new or infrequently employed drug.

Some drugs and medical devices presented in this publication may have Food and Drug Administration (FDA) clearance for limited use in restricted research settings. It is the responsibility of the health care provider to ascertain the FDA status of each drug or device planned for use in their clinical practice.

Warning: Anyone who experiences depression and/or manic depression needs to be under the care of expert health care professionals. Depression and mania are dangerous and can be life-threatening. The treatment strategies described in this book do not replace ongoing treatment. Do not abruptly stop other treatments in deference to the ones described in this book. Modify your treatment only after you have carefully considered it and discussed it with trusted health care professionals, and have put appropriate monitoring and support systems in place.

Originally printed by Peach Press, Brattleboro, Vermont.

Copyright 2001 © Mary Ellen Copeland
        New Harbinger Publications, Inc.
        5674 Shattuck Avenue
        Oakland, CA 94609

ISBN-10 1-57224-268-X
ISBN-13 978-1-57224-268-5

Cover design by Poulson/Gluck Design
Text design by Tracy Marie Powell
Back cover author photo © by G. Bolosky Perspectives

Distributed in Canada by Raincoast Books.

All rights reserved. Printed in the United States of America using recycled paper.

First edition printed from April 1992 to July 2001, totaling over 150,000 copies.

Second edition

19   18   17

30   29   28   27   26   25   24   23   22

This workbook is dedicated to

my mother, who served as a beacon of continuing hope and inspiration;

all the members of my support team—family, friends, coworkers, fellow travelers, counselors, and health care providers—who accompany, sustain, affirm, validate, nourish, and uplift me on this continuing journey to enhance my wellness, stability, serenity, and joy;

and the people from all over the country who shared so willingly of their experiences, from the deepest depths of depression to the wild fury of mania, from unspeakable tragedies to glorious triumph, so that their vast store of knowledge can be used to ease the way for others.

Contents

PART I
A Clearer Picture

Preface

This journal entry was written by a woman who has been a very close friend of the author for over 30 years. It was written when Mary Ellen was in the midst of what seemed to be an interminable depressive episode.

You were standing in the doorway when I drove into your yard. You'd seen my car go slowly down the road past your house and then double back, obviously lost.

And so we became friends quite by accident. We discovered that we had moved to Vermont within a few months of each other and that our husbands were both in public service professions. That was 30 years ago and we were just beginning to raise our families.

Over the years we have shared the usual (and the unusual) heartaches and pleasures that go with the territory of being wives and mothers. We did the PTA, band mothers, 4-H Club, ballet lessons, Little League route together. We survived our children's adolescence and our husbands' midlife crises. We supported each other through our own changes from divorce into new relationships and from housewives into more satisfying (and lucrative) careers.

Our annual New Year's Day sleigh ride became an event that marked the passing of time for us, just as large family gatherings must do for others. Years later I planned a "reunion sleigh ride," despite the fact that my son was in a "don't-call-me-I'll-call-you" phase and your daughter was equally unreachable in New Zealand at the time. Nevertheless, on New Year's Eve, as the full moon rose over fields covered with two feet of new fallen snow, all seven of our children were there, along with their spouses, partners, and children of their own.

The only person who didn't come was you, Mary Ellen. For three years you had been slowly withdrawing from us. Oh, you were there in body, but lost to the world around you—your friends, your colleagues at work, your family, and, ultimately, yourself.

The doctors called it bipolar disease (manic depression as it is more commonly known); we called it by other names, which gave expression to our anguish and bewilderment. They gave you medications and said, "This should ease your symptoms" ("cure" was never a word they used). We gave you love and support, not knowing if anything could halt your quickening slide into deep places of despair and isolation. They put you in institutions where you would be safe from harm (what they meant was safe from yourself). We sat up nights with you, facing together the demons that disturbed your sleep. They organized structures for you to fit into, to give a measure of normalcy to your life. We filled the hollow hours of your days with the familiar structures that were once your choices.

I stood by and watched as the friend I had known slowly disappeared. Gradually I learned to numb my feelings, to lower my expectations, and to settle for "reality." One by one I gave up such simple things as hearing your laughter, going for a walk, meeting for lunch, or carrying on a conversation of any length.

I remember the day I let you go—the vital, creative woman that you used to be—and mourned your death just as keenly as if you had actually died.

Ah, my friend, what does it mean? Could we have known it would come to this? All I know now is that I cannot leave this friendship. For someone must stand at the door, see you approaching on the road, and be there to welcome you back.

— Mary Liz Riddle

Introduction

The Origins of My Own Depression

I was born in 1941 and grew up outside of New Haven, Connecticut. My father worked for the railroad, a job that often took him away from home for extended periods of time and caused him to work very erratic hours, including holidays and other significant times in the life of his family. My mother had a degree in nutrition from Penn State and put her energies into raising five children, each born two years apart. I was the middle child, with an older brother and sister and two younger brothers.

My early years were not easy, marked by several severe traumas including being with a special friend when she was struck and killed by a car. I felt that, since her parents couldn't have any more children and my parents had "plenty," it was I who should have been killed.

To justify my existence, I tried to be the perfect child, always trying to do the right thing. But somehow I never seemed to be good enough. I felt responsible for everything bad that happened.

Ongoing sexual threats and molestation throughout my childhood by a cousin who lived next door turned me into a fearful child who was constantly on guard and afraid, never feeling safe. My perceptions of myself as a person and a woman were molded by these experiences. I continue to work diligently to overcome the severe damage this abuse caused to every part of my being.

In 1949, when I was eight years old, my mother went into a deep, agitated, psychotic depression. After being unsuccessfully treated with the various tranquilizers that were available at that time, as well as electroshock therapy, she was committed to a state institution. For the next eight years, her moods swung from deep psychotic depression to outrageous and uncontrollable mania.

Every Saturday we went to visit her. Sometimes she seemed fine, almost like her old self. At other times she would be extremely agitated, walking in circles and speaking continually in words we couldn't understand. During these periods she became very thin and made no effort to take care of herself. It was impossible to communicate with her. Sometimes when we went to visit she would take us around the place, introducing us to everyone, talking loudly and laughing uproariously at jokes only she could understand.

During my mother's visits home we couldn't relate to her; she was often completely out of control. I still remember what it was like when it came time to take her back to the hospital. Even though it seemed as if she was out of touch with reality, she resisted returning to the overcrowded, smelly institution that provided her with no support and little care. These horrible, violent scenes, trying to get her out of the house and into the car, shall live in a dark place in my memory forever.

I really missed my mother. And there was no one in those days who recognized the need to help a little girl work through such a profound loss. It was one of those unspeakable situations that everyone avoids talking about. No one ever says, "I'm sorry your mother is in a mental institution." That reality was something I did my best to hide from schoolmates. During the early years of my mother's illness, I was very depressed and withdrawn. I spent much of my time playing alone in the woods behind the house where we lived.

Life for me and my brothers and sister became a morass of sadness, pain, and confusion. Unfeeling caretakers came and went for a while; but before long we were taking care of ourselves while my father worked long hours to pay what must have been overwhelming hospital bills.

This went on for eight years—my mother in and out of the hospital, but mostly in and never well; five lonely children struggling to fend for themselves. The stigma of mental illness was so great at that time that we did our best to hide from others what was going on in our lives.

During this time I always felt that my mother's illness was my fault. I didn't know what I had done, but I was sure that if I could get my mother alone and say the right thing, it would all be over and she would be well again. The guilt I carried around with me was tremendous. My self-image and self-esteem dropped off the bottom of the scale.

Then I hit puberty. I suddenly became outgoing, gregarious, the "belle of the ball." But there was really no one around to notice and applaud this change. Although low self-esteem and issues related to my mother's illness continued to be a problem, I made my way through high school, experiencing some intermittent lows, but mostly flying high, getting good grades and having lots of friends.

After high school I studied home economics at the University of Connecticut for a couple of years. It was at this time that my mother got well. Her extreme mood swings ceased. She came home from the hospital and began her life over again. Her children were mostly grown by this time. Despite much disappointment and rejection caused by the stigma of her long hospitalization, she got a wonderful job as a dietician for a large school system. She revitalized and managed a hot lunch program, a job that she kept until her retirement 20 years later. Her story is one that gives us all hope. Through careful monitoring and management of all aspects of her life, she has maintained an enviable level of wellness.

I left college to get married to my high school sweetheart and had, in rapid succession, four children. In raising them I was determined that they would not have the kind of childhood I had. So we played, hiked, visited museums, read stories—whatever struck our fancy. I introduced them to the world. I had the childhood that I had missed. Although the marriage was not going well, this was mostly a delightful time. I had bouts of depression, but still managed to be a "super mom."

I had a compelling concern for less fortunate kids and an overwhelming conviction that I had to make everything in the world right for everyone. This led me to adopt an older child, take in foster children, and finish college with a degree in special education. I founded a private school for adolescents with learning disabilities and behavior problems and for four years directed that school and avoided addressing any of the feelings that had been bottled up inside me for so long.

Then the long festering wound burst, and in 1976 I suffered a bout of severe depression. I had experienced other depressive episodes, but I was able to "successfully" work through them by completely filling my days with taking care of others and not dealing with myself. I visited a psychiatrist when I couldn't bring this latest depressive episode under control by using all my usual evasion techniques. It was becoming impossible to get out of bed, much less to meet my overwhelming load of obligations to others. Based on my history and symptoms, the psychiatrist diagnosed me as manic depressive. On his recommendation I began what turned out to be long-term treatment with lithium and various antidepressants.

Through the next 10 years my life took various twists and turns. My children grew up and moved on. I left my husband of 20 years (the marriage had been over long before that). I quickly remarried someone who I felt was going to solve all my problems by giving me the attention and understanding I had longed for all my life, something I couldn't give myself.

This new marriage was a disaster. When my husband began drinking heavily and being emotionally and physically abusive, I started seeing a good therapist. With her help I began addressing important issues, including emotional, physical, and sexual abuse; my mother's illness; my very low self-esteem; my inability to do anything nice for myself or to see myself as worthy; my need to always be taking care of someone else, allowing others to define who I am and what I should be like; my inability to experience pleasure and intimacy, my workaholism, and on and on.

Thanks to the work of this therapist, I was able to leave my second marriage. I got my master's degree, had several very good, high-powered jobs, and was thankful for the hypomanic state that, although occasionally interspersed with deep depressive episodes, propelled me through those years.

The Beginnings of Recovery

In 1986 I found myself working in a space with no outside light, in a bleak classroom setting, trying to rehabilitate five high school boys whose emotional and educational needs had been neglected for years. As winter came on, I sank into a deep depression. This was the beginning of three years of severe, rapid cycling, during which I lost my job, was hospitalized many times, and made several suicide attempts. In short, my life was totally out of control. I was unable to concentrate or focus. My short-term memory was nonexistent. Friends drifted away or left abruptly. Some family members suggested that I "pull myself up by my bootstraps" and became extremely annoyed when I failed to do so. Life became a living hell; although I kept searching for answers, prospects for my future seemed quite dim.

In December 1988 I was suffering from a severe depressive episode. Somehow I dragged myself to a workshop on light therapy presented by Dr. Wayne London, a psychiatrist with a holistic and alternative view of mental illness. I listened intently and asked him afterward if light was safe for me to use, as I was diagnosed with manic depression. He suggested that I have a complete battery of thyroid tests. I was quite overweight at that time, my skin and hair were dry, my face was puffy, and I moved slowly.

I ignored his suggestion about the thyroid tests, erroneously assuming that they had been done during a previous hospitalization. I went home and tried the lights. The depression lifted somewhat, but the fog in my brain persisted. I kept meeting this doctor every time I walked down Main Street or at the local food cooperative. He kept saying, "When are you going to get your thyroid tested?" So finally I did, to satisfy him as much as anything.

Both Dr. London and the endocrinologist to whom he referred me were shocked at the test results. I was suffering from severe hypothyroidism, an illness that can cause mood swings. The screening tests that are routinely given in hospitals did not show this problem. A complete thyroid battery was necessary for diagnosis.

They started me on a very low dose of thyroxine, with the understanding that they would increase the dosage as my body got used to this amount. Within days of the onset of hormone replacement treatment, my mind started to clear. And then, very gradually, I got better and better. The severity of the mood swings decreased, until now they are a minor irritant in my life rather than a major crisis.

A Program for Wellness and Stability

I feel that I finally have my life back. I'm happier and healthier than I've ever been; and it has now been over ten years since I've had any severe symptoms of manic depressive illness. Through close personal monitoring of symptoms, and with the help of my support system, I've dealt effectively with the milder mood swings that are typical of anyone with a sensitive system and an active life.

I work constantly on a healthy lifestyle, cutting down on and dealing more appropriately with stress. I use many of the coping techniques suggested in this book. I've educated a wonderful group of people to be my support system. I meet with them regularly, keeping them honestly informed of how I'm feeling. I meet with several members of my support team for peer counseling on a weekly or as-needed basis. I'm an active member and regular participant in two support groups. I constantly monitor myself—my support team helps me with that—and take appropriate action when necessary. I have intervention plans for use by my support system in case I become depressed or experience symptoms of mania.

I've worked hard at developing positive attitudes and reducing the stress in my life. Through study and practice of various relaxation and meditation techniques, I enjoy deep relaxation which I use to feel better in general, to help me through the hard times, and even to put myself to sleep.

I do my best to eat right, get outside, and use a light box to get adequate light. Like many others, I've noticed a seasonal pattern to my mood cycles. Exercise is a critical part of my daily routine. Exposure to electromagnetic radiation from electric blankets and video screens seems to cause me to feel anxious: I've replaced my electric blanket with a fluffy comforter that I love, and gotten a radiation screen for my computer.

With a fine therapist, I continue to work intensively on issues that still plague me and limit my life potential and my enjoyment. I read every self-help book that looks like it might enhance my wellness, making regular visits to the library to check out new additions to the collection. I continue to search for and explore ways to maintain and increase my mood stability and overall health—ways that are safe, noninvasive, financially feasible, and effective. Currently, for me, these include homeopathy, body work, and working with a nutritionist who is also a medical doctor.

Initially, I was intensively involved in a vocational rehabilitation program, working to develop a career that takes advantage of my talents and allows me to take good care of myself. I have completed a study of coping strategies for 120 volunteers from around the country who have mood disorders, compiled the data, and sent it out to the project participants. In the spring of 1990 I began giving all-day and evening workshops based on the findings of the study. The workshops continue to be overwhelmingly successful. Now, ten years later, I have travelled all over the country, giving over 700 workshops to groups of people who experience psychiatric symptoms, their family members, supporters, and health care professionals. I am now focusing my energy on teaching others to teach the skills and strategies that have saved my life and improved or saved the lives of so many others. In addition, I am continuing to develop educational resources for people with mood disorders.

Since publishing the first edition of this book, I have written eight other books, two of them in collaboration with noted medical doctors. My book *Winning Against Relapse* (1999) describes a symptom monitoring and response system that is being used by individuals and in treatment centers all over the world.

This workbook is my gift to others who have experienced depression, mania, and other psychiatric symptoms, and to those people who love and care for them. It is my sincere wish that through this work, and the sharing of my own story, others may find the key to increased stability, long-term wellness, and happiness.

I know I will be working on maintaining and enhancing my wellness for the rest of my life; but it is the only path I can take. It is a gift I must give myself.

—*Mary Ellen Copeland*

Getting Started

At the present time, my mood has been stabilized for over a year. It would be unrealistic to think that I'll never have symptoms again; but at the same time, I don't want the anticipation of another episode to stop me from living and functioning right now. I just live with the security that if and when it happens again, I will handle it.

How to Use This Book

This workbook was born out of a study I made of the coping strategies and experiences of 120 people who experience depression and manic depression from around the country (only 25 percent of the surveyed participants had depression rather than bipolar illness).

As I began compiling the results of the study into a book, I found myself wanting to write personal notes to myself in the margins, compare my own experiences to those of the study participants, and commit myself to taking some action based on what I was learning. It became immediately clear to me that an interactive workbook format would be much more appropriate and useful than a merely factual report. To confirm the validity of my opinion, I shared drafts of the workbook with people in my support group, including others who have experienced mood swings, and with mental health professionals. There was a general consensus among us that an interactive format would work best. I hope you'll agree.

When depressed or manic, we are either going so fast or so slow that memory function is often impaired. Writing down your responses in the workbook will increase your ability to remember your thoughts, reinforce them, and subsequently allow you to take more effective action on your decisions. A written record allows you to refer back to your decisions at times when you are feeling less than decisive, or when your judgment is skewed. Use this book when you are well or when you are not feeling as well.

I recommend that you own your own copy of this book so that you can write in it. Some people may prefer to type or use a word processing system to print out their responses on a separate sheet of paper; this is also very effective. When you have completed all the exercises, save the book for handy reference when you are making decisions, and for periodic review.

Each one of you who experiences mood disorders is in a different place in your quest for achieving stability and wellness. You may have just experienced your first extreme mood swing or have just been diagnosed as having a mood disorder. Or perhaps you have been living and coping with these problems for years.

This workbook is designed to be used as a guide to achieving your maximum level of stability, and to enhancing your wellness in the years to come. Your family members, friends, co-workers, counselors, and health care professionals may also want to read this book to increase their level of understanding of what you are experiencing.

The material in this book is based on the findings of a study of 120 volunteers who have experienced depression or mania and depression. They come from all over the country, having responded to letters of appeal placed in several mental health newsletters and magazines. The response to the appeal was overwhelming, with over 1,000 people volunteering. Finances limited the study to the first 120 people who came forth. It's important to note that I made no effort to screen the volunteers. They comprise a random selection of people who felt comfortable responding to a study of this kind. They came from a wide variety of backgrounds and of experiences with mood disorders.

The thoughts, feelings, ideas, successes, and frustrations of the participants are quoted or summarized throughout this workbook, and provide the basis for a unique chronicle of wellness and stability. Whenever possible, I've quoted the responses of survey participants exactly as they were written. In some cases it was necessary to make slight changes for clarity, but I have made every effort not to change meanings.

I developed the three extensive questionnaires used in the study in consultation with mental health professionals, Vermont Vocational and Rehabilitation Services and, most importantly, other people who have experienced extreme mood swings.

Funds for implementing the study were secured from the Social Security Administration, through its Plan to Achieve Self-Sufficiency program. These funds are made available to people who receive Social Security disability payments and have developed a plan for becoming self-supporting.

The premise of this workbook is that by following a wellness program that includes simple, safe, noninvasive and inexpensive self-help techniques, combined with treatment strategies appropriate to the severity of the problem, extreme mood swings can at least be alleviated, and in many cases eliminated. This is not to say that any of this is easy. Nothing about this program is easy. It takes a lifelong dedication, persistence, and vigilance. But the payoff is well worth the effort.

Some parts of this workbook will be more relevant to you than others. But by working your way systematically through the various exercises, you'll discover new ideas and perspectives, gain a new respect for yourself and how you've handled your experiences, and come up with various plans for enhancing the quality of your life. Your goal in using this resource might be to discover the next most appropriate step or steps in your particular journey to physical and mental health.

Parts of this book will seem very appropriate to you right now. Other parts can wait until later. I recommend that you read through to the end before you begin writing. Then start from the beginning and do all the exercises (in writing) that seem most appropriate to you. Review your responses from time to time to remind yourself to keep up and to see how far you have come. When the time feels right, go back and complete those exercises that you left undone.

Be gentle with yourself. Don't rush the process. Just do what you can when you can. Don't forget to give yourself a pat on the back for everything you accomplish.

Many people lose hope when they are diagnosed as having a mood disorder. They may have been told by many health professionals that there is no cure for their problem and that they just have to learn to live with it.

In fact, there is hope. The majority of people in the study have been well for many years. My mother had no significant mood swings since she was 45; she died several years ago at the age of 82. After she got well, she worked at a wonderful job as a dietician until she retired. After her retirement she did volunteer work and enjoyed her many grandchildren and great-grandchildren. However, she continued to work very hard to maintain and improve her wellness.

I have not experienced any serious mania or depression in the last ten years. In those years I have compiled the data from the study, written this book, presented workshops, lectured all over the country, started a support group and a mood disorders hotline, and enjoyed wonderful times with family and friends. My health and sense of well-being have continued to improve. I know much more about mania and depression and other psychiatric symptoms now. I am confident that, using my symptom monitoring and response system, I can relieve symptoms when they first begin—before they become severe.

Your answers to these questions are for you alone. You may decide to share your responses with members of your support team or your therapist, but this is a very personal choice. You are not writing these things down for anyone but yourself—so be absolutely honest. This work is not to be judged by anyone; there are no right or wrong answers, just your answers. Don't worry about neatness, spelling, grammar, or composing complete sentences.

Some people find it easiest to do these exercises with their therapist or counselor, or someone in their support team. My mood disorders support group chooses an exercise to do together occasionally. Use whatever method works best for you, or makes you feel most comfortable.

It is advisable to set aside a certain amount of time every day to work on these exercises. I would suggest starting with 15 to 30 minutes per day. Some people prefer to work with the exercises when they first wake up in the morning. Others prefer a time in the early or late afternoon. Whatever schedule you choose, it's important to be consistent.

I plan to work on the exercises in the workbook every day from _____ to _____ o'clock.

Depending on where you are in the workbook, the length of time you spend on a given exercise may vary from day to day. This may also depend on how you are feeling and your ability on a particular day to focus on the work. Be gentle with yourself. If you find yourself feeling upset or very tired, put the book away until next time. Give yourself credit for whatever you do, whether it's a little or a lot.

Some questions—especially those in the sections on diet and light—require that you try something out for a couple of weeks before writing your responses. In those cases, you should continue working with subsequent questions until the experimental time has elapsed; then you can go back and answer the questions requiring a delayed response.

You might want to make a note on your calendar of the date when you'll be ready to answer the questions, and the page numbers on which they appear in the workbook.

Using simple relaxation and breathing techniques or exercising after doing this work will help relieve any tension you may feel (refer to the relaxation and exercise chapters).

Fifty people in the study have had times when they felt that their mood swings were over for good. These periods have lasted from one month to 25 years. Eighteen people in the study feel that they no longer have a problem with mood swings. I have not had a serious episode in many years.

Describe your own personal experience with mood swings and how they've affected your life. _____

_____

_____

_____

_____

_____

A frustrating aspect of this illness is how many difficulties it can impose on you as you try to meet life or career goals, in spite of an excellent education and exceptional abilities in many areas. The dramatic highs and lows, or the medication and treatment used to regulate them, often raise roadblocks that seem impassable. Although extreme mood swings can certainly make everything harder for you, they do not have to prevent you from doing what you want to in life.

Among the study participants, for instance, the educational backgrounds, interests, areas of expertise and achievements are simply amazing. Of the 120 people who participated in the survey, 12 had associate's degrees or two years of college, 34 had completed four years of college, 3 were doing graduate work, 14 had master's degrees, 5 had doctoral degrees, 2 were doing postdoctoral work, and 13 had completed various types of technical training.

What is your educational background? _____

_____

What are your future educational goals? _____

_____

How do you plan to meet your future educational goals? _____

_____

_____

In spite of having to deal with periods of mood instability, many people with depression and manic depression can boast of amazing accomplishments and lives that are the way they want them to be. Your life can be the way you want it to be. You can dream and you can achieve your goals. You are already on the way to doing just that. I dare you to make your life just the way you want it to be.

People in the study listed a wide range of interests. These included sports and recreational activities: art, including photography, film production, and theater; performing, understanding, and appreciating music; writing on all subjects (several having been published); extensive studying and teaching of the humanities and sciences; handcrafts, including crocheting, knitting, cross-stitch, needlepoint, sewing, carpentry, wood carving, woodworking, macramé, ceramics, calligraphy, paper making and flag making; technical skills, which include engineering, mechanics, and computer sciences; community service for the environment, children, the elderly, disabled, and handicapped; and work in the political arena.

What interests have you pursued? _____

_____

What other interests do you look forward to pursuing in the future? _____

_____

How do you plan to pursue these interests? _____

_____

_____

A sampling of the fields in which survey participants feel they are expert (something often very hard for a depressed person to do) includes:

consumer advocacy	addiction treatment
counseling	alternative counseling
child and adolescent psychology	psychology of women
all areas of education	community relations
public relations	customer service
working with the terminally ill	psychiatric social work
administration	management
negotiation	research
massage therapy	actuarial work
telemarketing	clerical work
plumbing	tool and die work
mechanics	paralegal work
sales and merchandising	political organizing
insurance	nursing
song writing	writing
baking	welding
music composition	computers

English	French
dancing	mathematics
history	library science
tropical fish	microbiology
spirituality	theology
nutrition	horticulture

What do you feel you are really good at? _____

_____

_____

What skills do you plan to develop further? _____

_____

_____

_____

How do you plan to further develop these skills? _____

_____

_____

Study participants feel their most significant achievements relate to long, happy marriages; successfully raising a family; establishing and maintaining long-term personal relationships; maintaining independence; surviving; coping with mood disorders and in many instances maintaining long-term stability; major contributions to the mental health movement; amazing progress in growth and development in spite of extreme mood swings; mental health advocacy work; achieving major eduactional goals of all kinds; recovering from other serious illnesses, including strokes and motor vehicle accidents; staying employed for long periods of time; writing and publishing.

I could fill this book with the achievements of the 120 people who participated in the study. The point of all this is that you can do what you want to with your life, in spite of extreme mood swings. Other people who experience depression and/or mania have done what they wanted with their lives and are continuing to do so. You can, too! It takes hard work, creativity, persistence, and patience. You may have a much harder time convincing others of your ability to meet your goals. But you can and you will if you are determined.

List your most significant achievements. Take your time. Include everything. Use additional pages if necessary. Be honest with yourself. _____

_____

_____

_____

_____

_____

_____

If your life could be any way that you wanted, what would it be like? Where would you live, who would you live with? What about your career and education? What hobbies and leisure interests would you pursue? Build yourself a dream and then begin working on it.

_____

_____

_____

_____

_____

_____

_____

_____

PART I

A Clearer Picture

1

An Overview of Depression and Manic Depression

The Depression Workbook is focused on how you can help yourself feel better if you have depression or manic depression (also know as bipolar disorder) and other troubling emotional or behavioral symptoms. While you may think of self-help as those things you do to help yourself, like going for a walk or avoiding alcohol, it also includes deciding what kind of assistance from others would be helpful in relieving these troubling symptoms. To begin that process it may help you to have the following information:

1. how clinicians (health care providers who can help you figure out how to relieve your symptoms) define depression and manic depression

2. how common depression and manic depression are

3. what's happening in your body

4. what affects your neurotransmitters

5. choices about relieving your symptoms

6. programs and services

7. holistic approaches

8. the trauma connection

9. the personal growth approach

10. the medical approach to relieving these symptoms

11. stigma and shame

12. good news

How Clinicians Define Depression and Manic Depression

If you have depression or manic depression, you know how you feel. In the chapters 3 and 4, "Experiencing Depression" and "Experiencing Mania," people like yourself who have experienced depression and/or mania tell what it feels like to them. You can write your own description of what it is like for you. However, you may be interested in knowing how doctors, psychologists, and other health care providers describe these conditions.

The medical perspective recognizes two main types of mood disorders: depressive disorders—characterized by one or more periods of major depression; and bipolar disorder, commonly called manic depression, which includes at least one period of extreme elation or mania and one or more periods of major depression.

According to the *DSM-IV*, the *Diagnostic and Statistical Manual for Psychiatric Disorders, Fourth Edition*, major depression is when you have at least five of the following nine symptoms for at least two weeks:

1. Depressed mood most of the day, nearly every day.

2. Diminished interest or pleasure in almost all activities of the day, nearly every day.

3. Significant weight gain or loss when not dieting, and decreased appetite nearly every day.

4. Insomnia or hypersomnia (sleeping too much) nearly every day.

5. Abnormal restlessness or a drop in physical activity nearly every day.

6. Fatigue or loss of energy nearly every day.

7. Feelings of worthlessness or excessive inappropriate guilt nearly every day.

8. Diminished ability to think, concentrate, or make decisions nearly every day.

9. Recurrent thoughts of death, or recurrent suicidal thoughts with a specific plan; or a suicide attempt; or a specific plan for committing suicide.

It also says that one of the first two symptoms (depressed mood or diminished interest) must be among the five symptoms you are experiencing—and that these behaviors must reflect a change from your ordinary behavior. In addition, the following must also be true:

1. The disturbance is not being caused by another illness (there are some exceptions, which are discussed later in this chapter under What Affects Your Neurotransmitters).

2. The disturbance is not a reaction to the loss of a loved one. (Author's note: If a person has lost a loved one and the period of deep grieving seems to go on and on, many of the same strategies used to address depression may be helpful.)

Dr. John Preston, as well as many bereavement experts, feels that the next revision of *DSM* will also include people who have suffered the loss of a loved one and also have symptoms of depression in this category.

How does the *DSM-IV* describe mania? In order to be considered mania, your mood must be elevated, expansive, or irritable. This mood must be different from your normal personality. The change must be unusually intense, and must last for a considerable period of time. While exhibiting this elevated mood, a person can become very expansive and grandiose. Sometimes the mood that is expressed may be irritated and angry, and the person may become arrogant and belligerent.

In addition, at least three of the following symptoms must have been present to a significant degree:

1. Inflated sense of self-importance.

2. Decreased need for sleep (for example, the individual feels rested after only three hours of sleep).

3. Unusual talkativeness.

4. Flight of ideas, or a subjective feeling that thoughts are racing.

5. Distractibility (the person's attention is too easily drawn to unimportant external stimuli).

6. Increase in goal-oriented activity (for instance social or sexual) or physical activity.

7. Excessive involvement in activities that bring pleasure but have a high potential for painful or harmful consequences (for example, the person engages in unrestrained buying sprees, sexual indiscretions, or unwise business investments).

In addition, the *DSM-IV* says that to be defined as mania, a mood disturbance must be severe enough to affect your job performance and participation in regular social activities or relationships, and that hospitalization may become necessary to prevent self-injury or injury to others.

The changing of moods is often referred to as "cycling." It would be useful if one could predict how long these cycles would last. However, this is not possible. While some people may see some consistency in their cycling, you cannot predict how long cycles will last. If the symptoms are not controlled in some way, a person can cycle often, occasionally, or seldom. When you switch often from one phase to the other, it is referred to as "rapid cycling."

Severe mania can be dangerous and life threatening. "Hypomania" is a term used to describe mild mania. It is often hard to distinguish between mild mania and an ordinary good mood where a person feels happy, outgoing, exuberant, and creative. However, it is important to make that distinction because hypomania can be your first sign of impending mania—a time when you may need to take some action to prevent the mania from becoming more severe. If you have had severe mania before, are taking an antidepressant medication that has mania as a possible side effect, other people in your family have experienced mania, and/or this good mood is accompanied by irritability, lack of expected fatigue, feeling like you can't stop what you are doing, and other unusual feelings, it is important to take action, like contacting your health care provider and reducing the stimulation in your environment, to prevent the symptoms from worsening.

As for normal good moods, your family members and friends may overreact at these times. I remember getting silly over something inconsequential with my daughter and being accused of being out of control by another family member. I really appreciated the support of my daughter at that time as she defended our fun time together.

How Common Are Depression and Manic Depression?

Statistics compiled by the National Institute of Mental Health indicate that major depression affects over ten million people in the United States each year and that over a lifetime between 10 and 15 percent of people will experience at least one episode of major depression. Rates of depression may be even higher in other areas of the world where issues related to poverty, poor diet, natural disasters, and environmental degradation may be factors. In addition, research has shown that two out of three people who experience depression are women. However, this figure may not accurately reflect male and female depression because in our culture it is generally considered to be more acceptable for women to talk about their feelings and show emotion. There may be many men with depression who are trying to "tough it out" without telling anyone about it.

Bipolar illness or manic depression is thought to affect between 1 and 2 percent of the population, with equal numbers of men and women receiving this diagnosis. Again, these statistics may be affected by a person's willingness to disclose—although, due to the bizarre behaviors that sometimes characterize the mania phase, it is often apparent to others.

Experiencing extremes of moods is very costly to the individual. It can wreak havoc on both your personal and professional life. It affects your quality of life and that of family members and others with whom you are closely associated. You may have lost the ability to support yourself. Your health care costs may be very high.

In addition, these disorders are very dangerous. Fifteen percent of people who have been diagnosed with either depression or manic depression end their lives by suicide. This figure does not take into account the many people who experience these symptoms and have not received a diagnosis.

The good news is that if you have these symptoms, you can recover. There are many things you can do to help yourself to feel better, and there are various approaches and treatments that may be helpful to you. You can be one of the many people who have had one of these disorders and who have found ways to relieve their symptoms and go on to do the things they want to do and be the kind of person they want to be.

What's Happening in Your Body

You may find it useful to understand, so far as is known at this time, what is going on in your body when you are deeply depressed or experiencing an extremely elated mood. Some people want to know these things. Others are most interested in feeling better and moving on with their lives. It is not necessary to learn how the brain works in order to recover. For those who are interested, the following information may be useful. Since this is not the focus of this book, other resource books will give a more in-depth description.

The *limbic* system is the part of the brain that is responsible for regulating emotions. It lies deep within the brain below the cerebrum, which is the part of the brain responsible for thought. The limbic system also controls things like body temperature, appetite, hormone levels, sleep, blood pressure, and behavior. Another brain structure, the hypothalamus, is interconnected with the limbic system and plays an important role in regulating hormones, sleep, appetite, and sex drive.

Two mechanisms within this system allow signals to be passed from cell to cell. The first mechanism is *electrical stimulation*. An electrical impulse is generated in one nerve cell, also known as a neuron, and travels down the length of the cell until it reaches a very small space, or gap between that cell and the next (neurons are not really connected to each other). This gap between the neurons is called a *synapse*. For information to be transmitted, the nerve impulse from the first cell must somehow get across the synapse to the next cell. But it can't jump across this space.

Here a chemical mechanism comes into play. As the electrical impulse reaches the end of the first cell, it initiates a chemical reaction. Small sacks (vesicles) containing neurotransmitters, chemicals that transfer informational signals from one part of the brain to another, fuse with the cell wall. The sacks then open and empty the chemicals they contain into the gap between the cells. These chemicals float over to the second cell, attaching to the cell membrane at specific places called receptor sites. Each receptor site will only accept a chemical that is the right molecular shape to fit that site. When enough of the receptor sites are filled on the second cell, an electrical impulse is generated which travels down this cell until it reaches the next synapse. There the process is repeated. Electrical impulses, passing from cell to cell, travel in this manner throughout the limbic system and the rest of the central nervous system as well.

Exactly what information is transmitted depends on which neurons are activated, and what part of the brain is stimulated by these neurons. For instance, a particular series of neural firings will stimulate the area of the brain that tells you that you're tired. If another series of neurons fire and stimulate a different part of the brain, you may feel that it is time to eat. Still another series will let you know that you're angry at your boss or delighted with your child's A in math. Each series of neurons that stimulates a different area in the brain is called a neural pathway.

Most of the time this complex balancing act works well. People are able to experience normal patterns of sleep and appetite, to feel alert and energetic, and to have normal sexual feelings. However, for most people experiencing depression, subtle but important chemical changes occur in the limbic system, resulting in a host of physical symptoms. It's bad enough to have to endure the mood changes of depression; when sleep disturbances, fatigue, and other physical symptoms come on the scene, you feel worse and coping becomes even more difficult.

What Affects Your Neurotransmitters

There are many things that affect the activity of the neurotransmitters in the brain—certainly many more than are known at this time—and they are interrelated in ways that cannot be well documented.

One of the most commonly held theories is that there are genes that cause a person to experience depression and manic depression as well as other psychiatric conditions. This is because families have seen these symptoms recur over and over, generation after generation—with some people in each generation experiencing either depression or manic depression. You may have siblings, cousins, or children who are experiencing symptoms similar to yours. Your parents, grandparents, and other relatives may also be or have been affected. Stories of your ancestors may give you further evidence of a genetic link. However, even if you feel that your genetic makeup is causing some or all of your symptoms, there are many things you can do to help yourself feel better.

I was told that I inherited my symptoms from my mother when I first saw a psychiatrist in 1976. And perhaps that is true. However, I became aware of my mother's response to stress at a very young age. Sometimes she would get depressed and sometimes her mood became very expansive. In an institution, her symptoms became much more exaggerated—perhaps due to the horrible conditions there. Could it be that rather than inheriting bipolar disorder, it is learned? I choose not to spend much time thinking about this because I am not sure it really matters. I choose to spend my energies on managing and relieving the symptoms and enjoying my life.

Separating genetic factors from environmental ones is difficult at best. If depression is observed in individuals belonging to three consecutive generations, does this absolutely mean that the disorder is transferred genetically? Could a child become depressed because the depressed parent is not able to nurture the child adequately? What about conditions such as poverty and other high-stress factors? Could the same factors exist in each generation, thereby contributing to, or causing depression? And where does learned behavior fit in? Could a child learn, for example, poor nutritional habits and carry on the tradition of depression in this way? No one know the answers to these questions.

Another possible cause of these disorders is that the "chemicals" in the body are out of balance. There are specific diseases that can affect the production of neurotransmitters, even before you know you have the illness. These include diseases of the immune systems like lupus, diabetes (people with diabetes appear to have twice the normal rate of depression), and various allergies. There are also infectious diseases like mononucleosis and infectious hepatitis, and diseases of the central nervous system like multiple sclerosis. Various kinds of cancers can cause mood problems. Overgrowth of yeast (*Candida albicans)* in the body, caused by eating too much sugar or taking antibiotics, can be a factor. Imbalances in the hormones secreted by the glands of the body can also cause mood instability. The most common of these is thyroid malfunction. Hypothyroidism refers to an underactive thyroid, which can cause symptoms of depression. Hyperthyroidism, or an overactive thyroid, can result in symptoms that mimic mania. *If you are experiencing mood instability, your first step should be to visit your physician for a complete physical examination to see if you have a medical problem that needs treatment.*

Some doctors, especially outside of the United States, are studying nutritional deficiencies and the effects of these deficiencies on the neurotransmitters as a cause or partial cause of mood instability. These practitioners, who may be called naturopaths or nutritionists, are successfully using in-depth testing to prescribe food supplements like vitamins, minerals, amino acids, herbs, and homeopathic remedies, along with a special diet and other lifestyle considerations, to treat mood instability. Their work is gaining worldwide recognition.

In addition to what we put in our mouths, there are other lifestyle factors that are thought to affect the activity of the neurotransmitters, all of which give you clues when you are making choices about how to relieve these symptoms. Exercise or lack of exercise clearly affects mood. Some doctors say that exercise, or any kind of movement at all, helps to maintain neurotransmitter balance. Light through the eyes is also thought to affect neurotransmitter activity. People who live in northern climates often notice that they have more difficulties with depression when the days are short or there is a series of cloudy days. This problem is called seasonal affective disorder. Air quality, exposure to noxious vapors, and chemical sensitivities may also play a role.

In recent years there has been a greater appreciation of the connection between what you are thinking or what is happening in your life and how you are feeling, both physically and mentally. This has become known as the mind-body connection. You may be able to appreciate this by taking a close look at your daily life. Is your spiritual life crying out for some attention? Are you or have you been abused? Have you been severely traumatized in your life? Are you living in poverty? Are you lonely? Are you thinking a lot of negative thoughts? Do you have low self-esteem? Do the things you are doing—both your work and your other activities—nourish and sustain you, or drain you? These factors are all thought to affect the activity of the neurotransmitters in your brain.

The use of alcohol can cause or worsen depression. The following prescription medications can occasionally cause depression: minor tranquilizers (such as Xanax, Klonopin, Ativan, and Valium), steroids, high-blood-pressure medications, and estrogen. Street drugs that can cause or worsen depression include marijuana, any of the "downers," methaphetamine, cocaine, and any of the opiates.

Choices about Relieving Your Symptoms

Because there are many reasons why you experience depression and manic depression, there are also many ways that you can relieve these symptoms. *Unless your symptoms are so severe that your life is in danger, or you put the lives of others in danger, the choice on how you will relieve these symptoms is yours.* In the past you may have been dependent on your health care provider, particularly a doctor or psychiatrist, to make the decisions on how you would relieve these symptoms. But now it is widely believed that you will respond best to any treatment or recovery strategy if you make decisions on how to work toward wellness for yourself—using your health care providers to make recommendations and provide assistance as needed. If your symptoms become too severe from time to time for you to make those decisions, you may want to have an advanced directive (see the chapter on developing a Wellness Recovery Action Plan) that gives control in these hard times to the person or people of your choice and tells them what you want them to do and what you do not want them to do.

When my mother was experiencing deep depressions and severe mania in the late 1940s and 1950s, the only treatment choices that were suggested were some early and not very effective medications, electroshock therapy (which was very traumatizing at the time), and institutionalization (which can hardly be categorized as treatment). I wonder if she had been working with a good counselor, if family members had received some counseling so they could be more supportive, if she had had some intensive peer support, if someone had come in to do the housework and stay with the children for a time, if she could have gotten away from home for a vacation or taken a job, that eight years of institutionalization would have been necessary. Maybe some instruction in meditation or yoga would have helped. Maybe some regular exercise or dietary changes would have improved her well-being.

You do have these options. As you work your way through this book, you will learn many ideas that others have discovered on how you can relieve these symptoms and work toward recovery. Their ideas may help you to think of other things you can do to help yourself that are not mentioned in this book.

In the years since my mother was treated for manic depression, the focus of mental health treatment and care has changed dramatically. The huge old psychiatric institutions are being replaced by user-friendly, community-based treatment centers. The most exciting development from my perspective is the shift away from more invasive and traumatizing (even sometimes punitive) treatment to simpler, noninvasive self-help, wellness, and recovery-oriented strategies. Today there are many medication choices instead of the few that were available in the not-so-distant past. If one chooses to follow the medication route, there are new medications coming on the market all the time, medications that are purported to be more effective at relieving symptoms with fewer side effects.

Programs and Services

Various kinds of mental health–oriented community services are available everywhere. To find out what programs and services are available in your area, you may need to do some research. Ask your physician or psychiatrist. Call your local mental health or health care agency to find out what programs they have that might be helpful to you and how you could be involved. Contact any mental health organizations in your area, like local chapters of the National Mental Health Association and National Depressive and Manic Depressive Association (see the back of this book for a complete listing of these organizations). Universities in your area may have research projects and programs that might be helpful to you. Go to a support group and ask attendees what services have been helpful to them. The following list will give you an idea of some efforts that have been initiated around the country.

Recovery centers: A recovery center is a place where you can go to learn specific skills and strategies that support your recovery or that may be useful to you in your life. For instance, at the Boston University Center for Psychiatric Rehabilitation, you can attend free classes in things like computer use, yoga, and nutrition. Or you can learn to develop a Wellness Recovery Action Plan. A managed care company in Arizona has a similar recovery center.

Educational programs: Educational programs, either as part of or separate from a mental health center or mental health organization, are becoming more and more widely available. These programs are usually held on a weekly basis and may be from one to three hours in length. They teach attendees recovery skills and strategies as well as other life skills. There is a network of over 300 trainers nationwide who teach Wellness Recovery Action Planning, along with other mental health recovery skills, in mental health centers and in the community. There are many states, including Vermont and California, where the state department of mental health is supporting these educational efforts. The national technical assistance center known as CONTAC (see Resource List in the back of this book) teaches people who have mental health issues how to become leaders. A Connecticut-based group travels across the country teaching advocacy skills.

Peer support centers: Spaces are set up in the community where people who have experienced troubling symptoms like depression and manic depression can gather to do things like socialize, provide mutual support, prepare and share meals, and have educational and support groups. For example, the state of New Hampshire has a peer support center in each region of the state. These centers are organized and staffed by people who have experienced these symptoms.

Mental health centers: Mental health centers across the country offer a wide variety of services like case management, medication monitoring, financial assistance and oversight, vocational training, support groups, meals, and recovery-oriented educational programs. Many have a treatment program that you can attend during the day, going home in the evening—sometimes instead of hospitalization.

Respite centers: Respite centers are an alternative to hospitalization. You can go to a respite center when your symptoms are severe and be supported by trained people who have had symptoms similar to the ones you are experiencing. These centers have proven to be helpful, cost effective, and nontraumatizing. There is a national effort to support the development of more of these centers.

Counseling: Counseling services are available through both the public and private sectors. You can contact the mental health center or ask your doctor for referral to a counselor. Or you can contact a counselor who has a good reputation. Sometimes a counselor will help you address daily issues that are upsetting to you. Or the focus may be on your way of dealing with stress in your life. There may be a spiritual focus, or a focus on changing negative thought patterns to positive ones. The American Psychological Association has reviewed studies on effectiveness for various depression therapies. Cognitive behavioral therapy, interpersonal therapy, and brief psychodynamic therapy have passed their rigorous test for being either effective or probably effective. In order to be effective for you personally, you must be comfortable with your counselor and with the approach they are taking. Your choice of a counselor, how often you see your counselor and how much time you spend with your counselor, may be affected by your insurance coverage.

Holistic Approaches

Many people are reporting success in relieving their symptoms by consulting with holistic health care practitioners like naturopathic physicians and nutritionists, and using specific therapies like food supplementation (using vitamins, minerals, herbs, amino acids, homeopathics remedies, etc.), acupuncture, acupressure, and massage. Doctors like Abram Hoffer, Syd Baumel, Sherry Rogers, and Priscilla Slagle are doing work reporting excellent results in many cases. Some people prefer this option to medical treatment because they achieve higher levels of wellness without the side effects of traditional medication therapy.

If you want to consider using a holistic approach, you can begin by reading some of the references listed in the resources section of this book. Discuss any medication-reduction plans with the doctor who prescribed it.

The Trauma Connection

Studies are now showing the strong relationship between the experience of any kind of psychiatric symptom, including depression and mania, and having had a life experience of trauma—like sexual, physical, or emotional abuse, neglect, war, natural disaster, or an accident. It has been noted that many of the symptoms that are commonly referred to as mental illness are the same as those symptoms experienced by trauma victims. If you feel this is true in your case, be sure that 1) you are in charge of any treatment you receive, 2) your health care providers and counselors validate the experience of trauma in your life, and 3) some part of your treatment is focused on connecting you with other supportive people so that you regain the trust lost in the trauma. While there are effective trauma treatment programs in many areas, there are other areas where it is difficult or impossible to get help. You may need to use one of the many excellent self-help books that are available as a guide to working through these issues on your own or along with other treatment you are receiving.

Personal Growth or "Spiritual Awakening"

Some people feel that the onset of their symptoms was triggered by a need to address some pressing life issues or take a different life path. Many have considered it to be a time when they had to address issues related to spirituality that had "come up" for them or that they had avoided in the past. There is documentation of cultures that honor the occurrence of these symptoms as a time when a person needs to "look into their soul."

In the 1950s, John Weir Perry did some exciting work with people who were having troubling symptoms. He set up a comfortable home where people could come and, while being well supported, explore the depths of their soul in any way they chose. They could draw, paint, sing, cry, talk, rant, work with clay—whatever felt right to them at the moment—without guidance or criticism. They were given food and kept safe while they were going through this process. In time, usually five to six weeks, they felt better and went back to resume their lives. Judith Miller, in her book *Direct Connections,* describes her own fascinating renewal and process of release that she achieved through deep meditative work.

There are many self-help books that can give you information and guide you through this process. They might be classified as "new age." No one can tell you the right book or approach for you to take on this journey. You have to discover that for yourself. You can do it by reviewing books at the library until you find one or several that seem helpful. You may also want to attend some workshops or join a support group with a personal growth or spiritual approach. Researchers at the University of Kansas School of Social Welfare, along with a committed group of people who experience symptoms, have developed a self-help workbook called *Pathways to Recovery* intended to help you choose your spiritual pathway to wellness and recovery.

The Medical Approach

Many people choose to use medications as the cornerstone of their treatment, usually along with a variety of other strategies. Unfortunately there is no "magic pill." There is no one medication that works for everyone—even for people who seem to have the same symptoms. Doctors have to make their best guess at what will be helpful for each person when prescribing medications. They take two to four weeks or more to work, so they are not a way to quickly feel better. There is always the chance of overdosing. Medications must be taken regularly to be safe and effective. Many of them need to be closely monitored with regular blood testing. They may have intolerable side effects—like weight gain, loss of sexual function, or dry mouth. They can't fix lifestyle issues like poor diet, lack of exercise, lack of light, abusive relationships or life crises.

Dr. John Preston, author of *Consumer's Guide to Psychiatric Drugs*, shares the following information about medical treatment. However, when you are considering taking a medication, it is important that you get as much information as possible about the medication. Your pharmacist is a good source of information. In addition, your library will have books like the *Physicians' Desk Reference* or the *Nurses' Desk Reference* that can answer your questions. There is also information on medications on the Internet. If your symptoms are so severe that you cannot gather this information, make plans in advance so a supporter—a family member or friend—will do this for you. (See Crisis Planning in the chapter called "Developing and Using a Wellness Recovery Action Plan.")

There are more than 20 antidepressant medications currently available in the United States; they are not all alike. They are grouped into three classes: 1) first generation antidepressants, developed in the 1950s through the 1970s; most of these are known as tricyclics, 2) monoamine oxidase inhibitors (MAOIs), and 3) second generation antidepressants, which have been developed more recently.

Tricyclic medications work by increasing the amount of either or both of the neurotransmitters serotonin or norephephrine in the synapse, either by blocking or preventing reuptake of the neurotransmitter. They relieve some of the symptoms of depression in about 50 percent of cases.

The function of monoamine oxidase is to break down the neurotransmitters. Monoamine oxidase inhibitors prevent this, so higher levels of neurotransmitters are retained in the synapse. People who overeat and oversleep when they are depressed usually get the most benefit from MAOIs. Because of the chemical reactions caused by MAOIs, there are very strict dietary restrictions and medications that cannot be used when taking an MAOI.

Second generation antidepressants share two characteristics that have made them preferable to tricyclics and MAOIs: fewer side effects and greater safety (tricyclics and MAOIs are very toxic drugs that if taken in large amounts, for example in an accidental or intentional overdose, can cause fatalities. Most second-generation antidepressants, if taken in a large overdose, are not as dangerous as the older medications). These newer drugs are classified into the following groups:

a. Selective serotonin drugs (often referred to as SSRIs):
   Prozac, Zoloft, Paxil, Celexa, and Serzone

b. Selective norepinephrine drugs: Vestra (at the time of this publication this drug, which has been used for years in Europe, is not yet available in the United States)

c. Mixed-action drugs:
   Effexor (affects norepinephrine and serotonin)
   Wellbutrin (norepinephrine and dopamine)
   Remeron (norepinephrine and serotonin)

Although the side effects of these newer generation drugs are considerably less problematic than those of earlier antidepressants, they do still exist. The most common include nausea and sexual dysfunction (especially the serotonin drugs and Effexor), and a tendency to increase anxiety in some individuals (during the first week or two of treatment). Additionally, three side effects can occur for some people (possibly 10 to 15 percent) taking the serotonin drugs: apathy, a blunting of emotions, and weight gain. These side effects, if they occur, generally do not become evident early on; they are considered late-emerging side effects and may develop after 9 to 12 months of treatment.

All antidepressants require at least two to four weeks of treatment before the first signs of improvement are noticed. This is a critical point because in the United States the *majority* of people taking antidepressants stop taking the medication before this period of time, and thus do not benefit at all from the medication. Why the high dropout rate? Most of the time it is *not* due to side effects. Rather, people become pessimistic, thinking, "maybe this drug helps others, but it won't help me." Feelings of hopelessness that are so much a part of depression are to blame. Thus it is crucial for those beginning treatment with antidepressants to be given support from family members and friends, and to use coping strategies during the critical first weeks prior to the first signs of improvement!

Another important issue is that once depressive symptoms have been relieved by the antidepressant (and this generally takes a couple of months or more), discontinuing the medication at this point can spell disaster. Even though the depression is completely gone, most people who discontinue the medication at this point in time will have a relapse (often within a few weeks). The standard approach for treatment with antidepressants is to continue treatment for at least six months beyond that point when the symptoms have disappeared, and *then* discontinue. At that time the risk of an acute relapse is small.

Antidepressants are not habit forming. You cannot become addicted to antidepressants. Many people have found them to be helpful in the overall treatment of depression. However, they don't address all problems associated with depression—they primarily target the physical symptoms like low energy and sleep disturbances. Dr. John Preston shares the following information on medications.

Medications for People Who Experience both Mania and Depression

Medication treatment of manic depression depends on the phase of the disorder (i.e., whether the person is experiencing depression or mania). When the current phase is depression, an antidepressant and a mood stabilizer are usually given together. Mood stabilizers when given alone rarely are effective in reducing depressive symptoms and if antidepressants are prescribed without a mood stabilizer, there is a significant risk that the medication will set off a rapid shift from depression to out-of-control mania.

Any of the previously mentioned antidepressants can be used, although often the choice is Wellbutrin (this drug appears to have a somewhat smaller likelihood of causing a shift into mania, and is often used to treat bipolar depression). The antidepressant targets depressive symptoms and the mood stabilizer plays two roles: it helps to prevent a rapid shift into mania and once the depression is gone, the continued use of a mood stabilizer helps to prevent future episodes. Mood stabilizers (discussed below) are often very effective in preventing recurrence.

If a person is experiencing symptoms of mania, a different approach is used. Mania is typically treated with mood stabilizers. These drugs are usually effective in reducing manic symptoms, and once the mania has been controlled, may be used to prevent recurrence of the symptoms.

The most commonly used mood stabilizer is *lithium*. This drug has been in use in the United States since 1970 and is considered to be an effective medication for many people suffering from bipolar disorder. Lithium is a medication that, unlike antidepressants, must be monitored very closely to make sure the blood level is appropriate and well controlled. If lithium blood levels are a bit too low, the medication does not work; if a little too high, there are serious side effects. Thus frequent blood tests are required, especially during the first two months of treatment. Lithium side effects often include weakness, tremor, fatigue, lethargy, weight gain, nausea, diarrhea, and sedation. Most of these side effects disappear within a month.

Other medications that are also effective in treating mania are the mood stabilizing anticonvulsants: Depakote, Tegretol, Lamotragine, Neurontin, and Topamax. Anticonvulsants are used for individuals who cannot tolerate lithium side effects. Additionally, Depakote is often used if a person does not respond well to lithium treatment and experiences *rapid cycling* (where there are frequent shifts between depressive and manic episodes) or *dysphoric mania* (sadness with agitation).

The anticonvulsants often have sedation and weight gain as side effects. Some of these medications also require blood monitoring, but not as frequently as are needed with lithium. It is unclear how lithium and the anticonvulsants work to treat bipolar disorder, although some data suggest that they help to normalize the internal chemistry of certain nerve cells.

Sometimes other classes of medications are used in treating mania. These include antipsychotic medications (which appear to have some ability to stabilize mood), including drugs such as: Zyprexa, Clozaril, Risperdal, Geodon, and Seroquel. Minor tranquilizers are also sometimes used (medications such as Klonopin or Ativan).

Currently in the United States only one-third of people who experience mania and depression, and who use medication, are treated with a single medication. Combining medications often proves to be more effective. Two-thirds of people with manic depression are treated with at least two of the afore mentioned medications in combination.

The goal of treatment is to reduce the current symptoms and prevent relapse.

Stigma and Shame

Experiencing a mood disorder is painful and can seriously disrupt your life. The stigma and shame with which these symptoms are often viewed in society make the situation worse. Instead of getting the support and compassion you need to get through these very hard times, you may be ostracized by others, treated badly, and prevented from doing the things you want to do. In addition, you may have seen others with symptoms similar to yours being portrayed harshly in the media. This increases the stigma. Jobs, housing, relationships, respect in the community—all can be lost if you reveal or others find out you experience extremes of mood.

However, this situation is changing. I have seen great change in my lifetime. When my mother experienced extreme swings of mood in the 1940s, she was blamed for her condition and sent away to spend eight years in a psychiatric institution. It was only through her strong will that she was able to go home and, with great difficulty, be accepted again by her family, get a job, and be accepted into the community.

Education and understanding seems to be the answer to this difficult situation. The Center for Mental Health Services is sponsoring an ongoing national campaign to educate people about these and other kinds of psychiatric symptoms as a way to reduce stigma and shame. Other national mental health organizations whose members are people who experience these symptoms, and their care providers, are developing initiatives to combat this serious problem. National and regional mental health conferences have been set up where health care providers and people who experience these distressing symptoms meet to discuss and plan implementation of strategies for educating the public and reducing stigma.

In addition, changes in the way these symptoms are treated is helping to reduce stigma and shame. Today even short-term hospital care for these conditions is infrequent. Community based mental health centers and short-term care facilities that are becoming more and more user-friendly and helpful are becoming the norm rather than the exception.

Care providers are coming to understand that they cannot help you without your involvement. Instead of the care provider being the expert on you, you are seen as the expert on yourself. You, the person who experiences the symptoms, need to set your own goals and priorities and make your own choices about how you will deal with these symptoms and live your life.

If you were seeking treatment for these symptoms in the not-so-distant past, you may have been subjected to unusual and harsh treatment that was synonymous with punishment. Straitjackets, restraints, seclusion, forced treatments, and long-term institutionalization that you did not want or that further traumatized you in the hardest of times are much less frequently used and are under public scrutiny. In many places such inhumane treatments are being outlawed. Visible and vocal watchdog and advocacy organizations are continuing their efforts to end this sad era of harsh and stigmatizing treatment forever. However, there is much work that still needs to be done. People continue to share "horror" stories of what happened to them when they reached out for help. You may want to become part of this strong movement as a way to enhance your own wellness,

Things to Keep in Mind

In your quest to learn about depression and/or manic depression, you may have learned some things about these symptoms and how to deal with them that were true, some that were only partially true, and some that may not be true or not be true for you. You will learn many things that are contradictory. This can make it difficult for you to do the things you need to do to help yourself feel better. If you are given information and you are not sure whether it is true, ask your doctor and other health care providers as well as several other people whose opinions you trust. Learn about it. Then decide for yourself what you believe and how you want to proceed. The following list contains some of the things that people are often told when they experience depression or manic depression along with an alternate view you may consider.

> **You may be told:** "You will never recover. You will never get well."
> **Another perspective:** People who experience these kinds of symptoms do get well. They go on to do the things they want to do in their lives. You may continue to have symptoms, but you will know how to manage them so they have less impact on your life.

> **You may be told:** "There is nothing you can do to help yourself."
> **Another perspective:** There are many things you can do to help yourself. This book contains many self-help tools and strategies, including Wellness Recovery Action Planning that you can use to help yourself. In addition, you will discover things that are helpful to you that are not even mentioned in this book.

> **You may be told:** "It is your fault you have these symptoms."
> **Another perspective:** It is not your fault you have these symptoms. There are many possible reasons why you could have developed these symptoms, including genetics, environmental factors, and bad things that have happened to you.

You may be told: "You can never have children."
Another perspective: Many people who have these symptoms are wonderful parents. You can decide for yourself whether you want to have children, and whether you have the financial, emotional, and personal resources needed to be a good parent.

You may be told: "You cannot get the education you want or follow the career path of your choice."
Another perspective: People who have these kinds of symptoms move on in their lives and do the things they want to do. There are people who experience these symptoms who have followed every conceivable career path. They have gotten the needed education, training, and experience. Many of them have excelled in their chosen fields.

You may be told: "You will have to take medication for the rest of your life."
Another perspective: Medication may be helpful to you now. No one knows the future. Your doctor should work with you on an ongoing basis, assessing your condition to determine if you need to continue to take a particular medication, if other medications or treatments might be more helpful to you, and to adjust the dose.

You may be told: "If you have medication side effects, you just need to 'put up' with them."
Another perspective: You should not have to "put up" with medication side effects that make your life even more difficult—things like loss of sex drive, weight gain, or uncontrollable twitching and lethargy. There are many medications available today. There might be another that would be more helpful to you. Or you might find some other way to relieve your symptoms.

You may be told: "In order to get better, you must accept your diagnosis."
Another perspective: Many people in the mental health recovery movement find diagnosis to be stigmatizing. They say it gets in the way of their life. A diagnosis is just a label. You may find that it is helpful to you. Many people do. Or you may choose to ignore it and just do the things you need to do to help yourself feel better and recover. The most important thing is to acknowledge how you feel and do what you need to do to help yourself feel the way you want to feel.

Good News

When I first reached out for help in dealing with depression and mania that seemed to be taking away my life, there were few choices. I had to reach out to the mental health system. They were to be the experts on my care. They quickly diagnosed me, prescribed a medication that they said I would have to take for the rest of my life, and told me to come back for regular blood tests. When my symptoms worsened, I spent months in psychiatric hospitals getting little help and support. The most help I got was from the other patients. My family was told I would never get well—and that since they didn't institutionalize people for long periods of time like they used to, they would have to figure out how to take care of me. Various agencies set up systems so I could get the lifelong benefits that people with a diagnosis like mine were thought to need.

That was twenty-five years ago. Now if you have these same symptoms, you have options. You can get a diagnosis if you want one or you can decide that you want to address the symptoms that are troubling to you—that are getting in the way of your life. There are different paths to wellness that you can follow that will help relieve your symptoms and let you move on with your life.

2

Taking Charge

I had always depended on everyone else to do my thinking for me when it came to addressing issues about these deep depressions and the awful mania. Now that I am thinking for myself and doing what feels right to me, I am feeling so much better. I feel like I have gotten my life back.

You may have been told that you have clinical depression, chronic depression, unipolar depression, dysthymia, cyclothymia, manic depression, bipolar disorder, or any of a number of other words or diagnoses that describe "ups" and "downs" in mood that are more extreme than "normal." Or you may have noticed these variations yourself. If these mood swings are not uncomfortable for you, if they don't interfere with your life and don't impact the lives of others you care about, there is no need to do anything about them. But when these moods are hard to manage, make your life difficult, keep you from doing the things you want to do with your life, and harm your relationships, you will probably want to do something to keep your moods more stable.

What have you been told by health care professionals that you "have" (you may have several or even many different diagnoses)? _____

_____

_____

What do you feel you "have"? _____

How have these moods affected you life? _____

_____

_____

_____

_____

_____

_____

_____

_____

_____

How would you like your life to be? _____

_____

_____

_____

_____

_____

_____

_____

_____

_____

_____

_____

Causes of Mood Instability

Not too many years ago, it was thought that these extreme variations in mood were
totally out of the control of the person experiencing them—that they were caused by a
genetic problem in the brain, and that the only possible response was to go to a

psychiatrist who would prescribe one or several psychiatric medications that the person would need to take for the rest of his or her life.

More recently, thoughts on this subject have become much more broad-based. Most people, including health care professionals, feel that there are 1) genetic and/or physiological causes for these mood extremes, 2) medical problems like hypothyroidism or hypoglycemia that may be causing or worsening the problem, and 3) environmental and lifestyle factors that significantly influence the onset of these symptoms and their severity. Research linking these symptoms with traumatic life events—experienced currently or from the past—is being given increased credibility. Experiences like child abuse, sexual abuse, neglect, alcoholism, war experiences, accidents, natural disasters, being a crime victim, poor nutrition, job stress, and not being able to pursue the interests or career of your choice, are all being validated and seen as contributing factors in the onset and continuing experience of extreme mood swings.

What do you feel is the cause of your mood swings? _____

_____

_____

_____

_____

_____

Why do you believe this? _____

_____

_____

_____

_____

_____

When I first went to a psychiatrist for help in dealing with severe, recurring mood swings, he asked me about my symptoms. That was all. Now I know that my first visit should have included (check those that you have had):

1. A complete medical checkup to see if there is a medical problem that may be causing or worsening my symptoms, including a complete battery of thyroid tests and glucose tolerance testing.

If you have not had a complete medical checkup to see if there is a medical problem that may be causing or worsening symptoms, you may want to arrange for such a checkup as soon as possible. See the book *Living Without Depression and Manic Depression*

(M. Copeland, Oakland, CA: New Harbinger Publications, 1994) and *The Worry Control Workbook* (M. Copeland, New York, NY: Barnes and Noble Books, 2000) for more information on getting a complete medical checkup.

_____ I need to arrange for a complete medical checkup. I will contact:

(who) _____

(when) _____ .

2. An evaluation of my current and past life circumstances to see if there are lifestyle or traumatic life events that may be causing or worsening my symptoms.

Your psychiatrist or physician may be able to provide such an assessment. However, they may be too busy to give these issues the time and attention they require; or you may feel that one or several other people, like your therapist or counselor, could give you a better evaluation. If you don't know who to contact for such an evaluation, ask your doctor, another health care professional, or a local mental health agency or organization for a referral.

_____ I need to arrange for a complete evaluation of current and past life circumstances to see if there are lifestyle or traumatic life events that may be causing or worsening my symptoms.

I will contact:

(who) _____

(when) _____ .

Treatment Planning

On my first visit to the psychiatrist, he gave me prescriptions for two medications and appointments for follow-up visits to check blood levels and to see if the medications needed adjustment. He said I would need to take these medications for the rest of my life. He let me know that hospitalization might be an option if symptoms worsened and he even mentioned that electroshock therapy was used in the most severe cases. At the time, this was a common experience for people who were diagnosed with, or experienced, mood instability.

Now there is a much wider range of treatment options for mood instability that include not only medications and other medical treatments, but also a variety of self-help skills and strategies, psychotherapies, counseling, cognitive therapies, acupuncture, naturopathy, chiropractic, and lifestyle change. A good psychiatrist or health care professional is aware of this range of options. Deciding the best treatment for you should be done collaboratively, with you as the key participant, making decisions for yourself with input from your psychiatrist and/or physician along with the other health care professionals and supporters of your choice. The good psychiatrist or physician doesn't make long-term projections about the course of treatment, lets you know that you'll embark upon the mutually agreed-upon treatment plan for now, and that you'll both continue to assess the situation as it progresses.

Always keep in mind that for your treatment to be successful, it has to feel right to you. If a plan is developed by others that you don't agree with or are not willing to cooperate with, it will not be effective. Before making any decisions on treatment, learn as much as you can about the suggested treatment. There are resources and organizations listed at the end of this book that can give you this information. If your symptoms are so severe you cannot do this, ask a family member or supporter to do it for you.

In some instances treatment for mood instability can be mandated by the court. Laws surrounding court-mandated treatment vary from state to state but are usually initiated when a person is judged to be a danger to themselves or others or to be a nuisance in the community. People who experience mood instability and other psychiatric symptoms have found that they can avoid court-mandated treatment by carefully managing their symptoms using the systems described later in this book and in two of my other books, *Living Without Depression and Manic Depression* and *Winning Against Relapse* (published by Peach Press in Brattleboro, VT).

Do you feel you have come up with a treatment plan with which you are comfortable and that adequately addresses your mood instability? ____ Yes ____ No

If so, what is it? _____

_____

_____

_____

_____

If not, and you feel you need such an assessment and treatment plan, what are you going to do to see that you get it? _____

_____

_____

_____

Concepts Essential to Self-Help

I have found, from talking to thousands of people who experience mood instability, that understanding of, believing in, and acting according to the following concepts are essential to achieving the highest levels of wellness and stability.

1. There is hope. You must have a vision of hope that includes *no limits*, so that even when someone says to you, "You can't do that because you've had or have those symptoms, dear!", you know it's not true. It is only when you feel and believe that you are fragile and out of control that you find it hard to move ahead. Those of us who

experience depression, manic depression, and other psychiatric symptoms can and do get well and stay well. If you are in a very low period and don't believe in yourself, this book will remind you over and over that there is hope, until you can feel it yourself.

2. It's up to you to take responsibility for your own wellness. There is no one else who can do this for you. When your perspective changes from reaching out to "be saved" to one in which you work to heal yourself and your relationships, the pace of your recovery increases dramatically. Taking personal responsibility can be very difficult when uncomfortable feelings and sensations are severe and persistent. In these cases, it is most helpful to have your health care professionals and supporters work with you to find and take even the smallest steps to work your way out of this frightening situation. Ask them to do this for you.

3. Education is a process that must accompany you on this journey. Search for sources of information that will help you figure out what will work best for you and which steps you need to take on your own behalf. Health care professionals can play a key role in this educational process—directing you to helpful resources, setting up educational workshops and seminars, working with you to understand information, and helping you to find a path that feels right to you. This educational process will be ongoing throughout your life.

4. You must advocate for yourself to get what it is you want, need, and deserve. You may have the mistaken belief that you have lost your rights as an individual and that you cannot ask for what you want. This often happens when you are depressed, having mood swings, or experiencing other psychiatric symptoms. As a result, decisions may be made about your treatment and your life without your approval, your rights may be violated, and these violations may be overlooked. Advocating for yourself will become much easier as you work to improve your self-esteem and to understand that you are often as intelligent as anyone else—and always as worthwhile and unique, with special gifts to offer the world—and that you deserve all the very best that life has to offer. It is also much easier if you are supported by health care professionals, family members, and supporters as you reach out to get your personal needs met and work toward your goals. Take whatever steps in self-advocacy you can manage, even if they are small. Be persistent. You will get better and better at this.

In order to effectively work toward your goals, you must know what your rights are and advocate for yourself to ensure that your rights are not violated. These rights include the right to:

- ask for and work toward getting what you want and need for yourself, and have those wants and needs respected by others

- make decisions based on your own feelings

- say no to requests or demands that you can't or don't want to meet

- change, grow, and change your mind

- make mistakes

- follow your own values and standards and determine your own priorities

- express your feelings

- make life and treatment choices for yourself, no matter how different they are from traditional treatment

- develop your own crisis and treatment plans

- gain access to all your records

- access information about medication side effects and make choices based on your findings

- refuse treatment

- have your own personal space and time

- be in a nonabusive environment

- be playful and have a good time

- choose your own relationships and spiritual practices

- be treated with dignity, respect, and compassion

- create the life of your choice, and

- be happy

5. Mutual relationships and support are necessary and support the wellness process. See Part II: Support is Essential.

Additional Things to Think About

Diagnosis

You can decide how you feel about your diagnosis. You may have been taught to think of a doctor's diagnosis as incontrovertible and infallible. Many people have come to understand that the diagnosis offered by their doctors is very arbitrary, usually not helpful, and often harmful. The diagnosis may even be stigmatizing, getting in the way of career goals, relationships, and even needed attention to medical problems. Many people would rather talk about how they feel, how these feelings are keeping them from doing the things they want to do with their lives, and how they can minimize or eliminate these feelings. Other people may find relief in having a diagnosis, which they feel provides a focus for deciding what to do.

How do you feel about your diagnosis? _____

_____

_____

Would you prefer to talk about how you feel rather than be diagnosed? ____ **Yes**
____ **No**

Why or why not? _____

_____

_____

Denial

If you refused to accept your diagnosis, you may have been told that you are in "denial." Actually, there is nothing to "deny." You may be unwilling to accept the diagnosis but very willing to accept how you are feeling. You may need to remind those who use this kind of language that these attitudes are not acceptable to you. You also need to remember that, whether or not you accept your diagnosis, you are responsible for your own behavior.

How do you feel about it if people have told you that you are in "denial"? _____

_____

_____

_____

_____

How does it feel to look at this denial in a different way? _____

_____

_____

Prognosis

You may have been told that you will never get better and that you will have these mood swings for the rest of your life. You may have been told that these feelings will probably get worse as you get older, and that there is nothing you can do about it except to take your medications and "do as you are told." Many of you have been told that you can't pursue your goals and dreams because of this "illness." It is important to understand that there is no one, not even the most well-trained doctor, who can make predictions about the course of your life. You have the right to ask your doctors, other health care professionals, family members, and anyone else to stop making these dire prognoses and just give you assistance and support as you deal with what you are currently experiencing.

Describe any "prognosis" you have received about the course of your illness: _____

_____

_____

How did you feel about it? _____

_____

_____

What would you like to hear from health care professionals, family members, and other supporters that would be helpful? _____

_____

_____

Compliance, Noncompliance

Many people who experience depression, manic depression, and other psychiatric symptoms feel that the words "compliance" and "noncompliance" (in referring to whether a person is following a course of treatment prescribed for them by someone else) are not okay. They feel that the use of these words implies that there is someone outside of them who is in control and to whom they must be responsible.

How do you feel about the words "compliance" and "noncompliance"? _____

_____

_____

How would you like people to talk to you about whether or not you are following the prescribed treatment? _____

_____

_____

Manipulation

You may have been told that your depression, manic depression, and other behaviors are manipulative, inappropriate ways of getting things you want and need for yourself or for getting attention. The implication is that this is "bad." When others say this to you, you may want to remind them that it is often very difficult to get what you need when you have these kinds of symptoms, and therefore you often try a variety of different ways to get your needs met. Sometimes they may not like the ways you choose to get your needs met, but it is always your choice.

Have you ever been accused of being manipulative? _____

_____

_____

How did you feel about this? _____

_____

_____

What can you do about it if it happens again? _____

_____

_____

Medications

While this book is about self-help strategies for dealing with depression, manic depression, and other psychiatric symptoms, medication is so commonly recommended that it deserves attention. Medication is often a valuable tool to be used along with other tools in achieving stability and wellness. It's no longer seen as the only solution, but one of many solutions to dealing with depression, manic depression, and other psychiatric symptoms. Medications alone cannot correct contributing factors like a bad diet, lack of exercise, healing from the effects of trauma, or a hectic, chaotic lifestyle.

Just a very few years ago, there were no medications available for treating mood instability, but now there is a wide array of medications available. These include antidepressants, antianxiety medications, mood stabilizers, and medications that will help you sleep. New medications are coming on the market all the time. These medications have helped people get well and stay well. They have helped people feel better, stay out of hospitals, do the things they want to do with their lives, and work on using other self-help strategies to improve their wellness and their lives.

However, these medications sometimes have side effects that can be serious and can keep your life from being the way you want it to be. They may include significant weight gain, loss of sexual function, dry mouth, tremor, poor concentration, and fatigue. You may have been told that you must "put up" with the side effects, even if they are clearly as unhealthy as weight gain or keeping you from doing the things you want to do with your life. There are many medication choices. A good health care professional will work with you to find a medication that is helpful without causing side effects that may be upsetting or even aggravating to your symptoms.

Are you putting up with some medication side effects that are intolerable and may even be worsening your condition? ____ Yes ____ No

If so, what do you plan to do about it? _____

_____

_____

If your health care professional recommends medication as part of your treatment, you need to learn as much about it as you can. There are books available on specific medications that are written so anyone can understand them (some of them are listed in the resource section at the end of this book). Information on the newest medications and current research on the long-term effects of medications that have been on the market for some time can be accessed by asking your pharmacist or through the Internet. In order for you to successfully use medications they must be very carefully managed. The following guidelines will help you do this effectively:

- learn all you can about recommended medications

- be aware of the possible side effects of the medication you are using, and if you experience them, report them to your physician

- take medications only on the recommendation of a trusted health care professional

- use medications only as prescribed

- work closely with a competent pharmacist who knows you and your symptoms

- develop and use systems like sectioned pill boxes to ensure that you take your medications regularly

- report any lapses in medication treatment to your doctor and decide with him or her how to proceed

- insist on regular blood testing

- pay close attention to lifestyle issues such as diet, exercise, light, rest, and stress when you are taking medications

- avoid using alcohol or illegal drugs

See *Living Without Depression and Manic Depression* for more information about medication management.

3

Experiencing Depression

I feel like I am in a grave and someone is continually throwing dirt in to cover me—there is a small bit of light, but I am smothering.

The experience of depression varies widely from person to person. Yet there are common threads that weave their way through this morose tapestry.

Study participants have shared how they feel when they are depressed. **Which of their feelings and symptoms do you relate to?**

- ☐ hopeless
- ☐ useless
- ☐ apathetic
- ☐ unresponsive
- ☐ desire only to sleep
- ☐ low energy level
- ☐ sad
- ☐ anxious
- ☐ short-tempered
- ☐ miserable, terrible, horrible, lousy
- ☐ void, empty, hollow
- ☐ guilty of everything
- ☐ scared

- ☐ worthless
- ☐ might as well be dead
- ☐ emotionless
- ☐ extremely fatigued
- ☐ no motivation
- ☐ slow
- ☐ down
- ☐ irritable
- ☐ black attitude
- ☐ lonely, alone, abandoned
- ☐ self-accusing
- ☐ cry easily
- ☐ helpless

☐ low self-esteem
☐ inability to concentrate
☐ ugly
☐ inability to function
☐ inability to experience pleasure
☐ angry
☐ want to be alone
☐ tense
☐ quiet
☐ heavily burdened
☐ sense of futility
☐ wanting to be unconscious
☐ guilty
☐ like a gray, dirty windowpane
☐ as if the world is cloud-covered
☐ heaviness, and it's a burden to move
☐ as if I'm in hell

☐ hoping to die
☐ like a failure
☐ fat
☐ frozen, dead inside
☐ unbearable
☐ inability to sleep
☐ disorganized
☐ silent
☐ paranoid
☐ hateful
☐ obsessed with past mistakes
☐ physically unhealthy
☐ hating my existence
☐ pain so deep it can't be fixed
☐ want to curl up and not exist
☐ deeply buried anger, and knowing it can never be resolved

Other descriptions of depression from study participants include:

"Pain—dark—totally empty—in a fuzzy fog—nothing penetrates."

"Nothing is any good nor is anybody, and I'm trouble—I don't want to do anything or see anybody."

"All will never be right, everyone is not what they appear, and I'm not what others want me to be."

"It feels heavy, slow, hard to move, to do ordinary tasks. I feel fearful and berate myself for past actions."

"The hopelessness of hell. I feel like a nonperson; life feels meaningless. I lose all feeling for my family. I can't make myself do anything. I am alive physically but not mentally."

"Sometimes I feel as though I have two kinds of depressions. One is responsive to adversity in my life, whereas the other one comes even if things are going well for me. Sometimes joyful things will relieve my depressions, whereas sometimes nothing will make depressions go away. The nonreactive depression seems to ruin my appetite and causes sleep problems."

"I feel like someone has clamped a brake on my brain and thrown a thick, gray blanket over it, and everything has ground to a halt. I can't see anything positive anywhere, but at the same time experience constant, overpowering panic."

"Wishing, thinking of bad things happening to me or my family—why do I hate myself so much? The depression curtain is trying to engulf me—I have to fight back! Full of anxiety—I want to run outside with nothing on. Waiting for things to happen—usually bad. Cannot make decisions. Think I am going to die the next day. I have given away too many things in this mood. I become real stingy with money, find fault with all persons and things, cannot close my eyes at night for fear."

"My kind of depression is endogenous, or internal, that is, it arises out of internal, biological mechanisms. Once started, the depression is self-sustaining and does not respond to changes in the environment. I call it depression with a capital D."

"I sometimes sit and stare at the wall for hours while crying. I tell people to stay away, and I vacillate between no appetite and binge eating. I become unkempt."

"I become sure each time that this time it won't go away—that the wonderful part of mania won't return. I am filled with fears and nightmares."

"I put on a mask and act like nothing is wrong."

"Too much daydreaming—all fears, real or not, converge on me. I become self-centered, sloppy in dress, unclean. I don't sleep at night. Too much burping. Tear at fingernails, rub big sores into my face, completely negative. Cannot see anything good or positive. Cannot make positive decisions. Have made costly mistakes at the onset of my depression. No sex drive—want to be left alone, want to divorce the human race. My mind wants to close me down."

One person in the study shared this in-depth experience of depression:

"These depressions feel very much like physical illness. In fact, some times I've been coming down with the flu and at first mistaken it for the beginning of a depression—the body/mind sensations are so similar. In endogenous depressions, my moods are lowered. My body is fatigued and exhausted. I have no energy, no drives of any kind, whether sex, appetite, or work. I experience no pleasure in the usual things I enjoy—everything seems to be a drag. My sleep is disturbed by insomnia or hypersomnia.

"My thoughts seem to revolve around an incessant surging of negative past memories. It's as though the positive experiences of my life aren't available for retrieval at this time. My perceptions of things in my present environment are colored negatively; even on sunny days I see gloom. I have negative expectations and have fears of the future. I can no longer look forward to tomorrow. The blackness ushers in suicidal ideation almost without my needing to give any conscious direction to my thoughts. I didn't choose to think these thoughts; they entered my mind uninvited and unwanted. It wasn't so much that I felt so miserable I wanted to end it all, as that the thoughts of suicide constantly forced their way into my consciousness. And, in fact, I had to work to survive these thoughts.

"For years before I knew my depressions had a name or a treatment, I sensed that they were something constitutional, something beyond my control. My mother, exasperated, used to cry at me: 'You don't have anything to be depressed about!' This was true—I didn't have anything to be depressed about. That should have been the clue! This was not a depression with a little d; this was depression with a capital D: a system malfunction, a lack of lower limits on my mood state. I needed to be treated, not rationally talked out of my perceptions. Those of us with depressions most need people who will try and understand us and not label us as lazy or weak-willed or inferior. When I'm in one of my depressions, I have a need to confide in someone that I am down. It helps to have a caring—and a careful—listener."

Describe your experience of depression: Getting in touch with how it feels can be the first step to overcoming these feelings. Use extra paper if you need it. _____

_____

_____

_____

_____

_____

_____

_____

Forty-four people in the study reported that their body physically hurts when they are depressed. This pain can be, and has been for me, absolutely excruciating and totally debilitating. **Which of these symptoms relate to how you have felt?**

☐ aching all over   ☐ headache
☐ stomach tight   ☐ stomachache
☐ nausea   ☐ backache
☐ chest aches   ☐ chest feels constricted
☐ chest feels empty   ☐ chest pain
☐ pain deep inside the heart   ☐ arrythmia
☐ constipation   ☐ diarrhea
☐ aching limbs   ☐ heaviness in limbs
☐ jaws clenched   ☐ eyes ache
☐ eyes feel heavy   ☐ gums ache
☐ low blood pressure   ☐ fainting spells
☐ muscle spasms   ☐ burning, searing pains

"My head feels like it will explode, and I hope it does so I will die."

"I feel like I'm being electrocuted."

"My heart hurts; it feels like it will stop beating."

"My head feels stuffy and I have no energy."

"My chest aches and I have difficulty breathing."

"Indescribable pain radiates from the center of my being."

"My entire body is wracked with pain. It feels like a thousand knives being driven into me at the same time."

"I have splitting headaches, almost blinding, in the back of the head."

"I have a dull ache in my chest and abdomen, gnawing like hunger that can't be satiated."

"My whole body feels heavy and paralyzed. I feel catatonic."

"As if I have a bad case of the flu, as if a chunk of lead is bearing down on my brow, as if I and my body and the hour and the world weigh tons."

Describe your experience of the physical pain of depression: _____

_____

_____

_____

_____

_____

4

Experiencing Mania

I feel like I am trying to hold back a 400-pound boulder on a 90-degree slope, like every atom in my body is speeding a million miles per hour, trying to escape through my skin.

Note: If you have depression only, rather than manic depression, you don't have to read this chapter.

With depression, all is bad and lost. However, the experience of mania is a double-edged sword. While everyone enjoys lifting out of the depression and cycling up, up, up to a place where everything seems possible and all the world is beautiful, at its extreme mania is infinitely dangerous and destructive.

These are feelings and symptoms of mania as described by study participants. **Which ones can you relate to?**

- [ ] energetic
- [ ] speedy
- [ ] pressured
- [ ] can't be still
- [ ] talking very fast
- [ ] financially irresponsible
- [ ] need little food
- [ ] insightful
- [ ] very happy
- [ ] optimistic
- [ ] authoritarian

- [ ] quick movements
- [ ] hyperactive
- [ ] need to do something
- [ ] pressurized speech
- [ ] compulsive buying
- [ ] need little sleep
- [ ] brilliant, wonderful
- [ ] "know-it-all"
- [ ] exalted
- [ ] euphoric
- [ ] domineering

- ☐ grandiose
- ☐ confident
- ☐ perceptive
- ☐ alert
- ☐ creative
- ☐ work very hard
- ☐ overenthusiastic
- ☐ inflated self-concept
- ☐ overtly friendly
- ☐ excessive, loud laughter and giggling
- ☐ full of fun
- ☐ childish
- ☐ socially unacceptable behavior
- ☐ easily infatuated
- ☐ argumentative
- ☐ aggressive
- ☐ haughty
- ☐ racing thoughts
- ☐ dangerous
- ☐ cruel
- ☐ poor judgment
- ☐ impulsive
- ☐ impatient
- ☐ inability to trust others
- ☐ inability to calm down
- ☐ suggestible
- ☐ happy and sad at the same time

- ☐ invincible
- ☐ super aware
- ☐ clear
- ☐ sharpened thinking
- ☐ more intelligent speech
- ☐ able to accomplish a great deal
- ☐ preoccupied with self
- ☐ outgoing
- ☐ life of the party
- ☐ rapid, unpredictable emotional changes
- ☐ live in a fantasy world
- ☐ poor social interactions
- ☐ bizarre behavior
- ☐ increased interest in sex
- ☐ verbally abusive
- ☐ obnoxious
- ☐ arrogant
- ☐ confused thoughts
- ☐ irresponsible
- ☐ wild dancing
- ☐ destructive to self, others
- ☐ boisterous
- ☐ hallucinations
- ☐ inability to concentrate
- ☐ "flight of ideas"
- ☐ feeling driven

"The flip side of depression is mania and hypomania. They can be kind of fun, especially hypomania; however, they're really a mixed blessing. For me, mania and hypomania last too briefly and are always followed by unpleasant depressions. In mania, I become hyperactive, hypersexual, overly talkative, overconfident, and extremely elated. I cannot remember being down, and I think I am the best person around! I think, speak, and act very rapidly and become impatient with how slow the rest of the world is going. I have been known at those times to start finishing other people's sentences for them—not an endearing quality, believe me! And I have experienced such intense mania that it frightened me."

"I wear makeup, my hair is done up. I'm smiling, laughing, good natured, busy. I make sure my bed is made, pick up after myself, dishes are done, etc."

"I feel that others are less alive and cannot see the correctness of my ideas. I do lots of sweating, am jerky, feel very edgy and uncomfortable."

"I feel like the filters have been removed from my senses."

"I want to be alone and do what I want to do when I want to do it, like an engine that has revved up beyond its highest speed and if left that way will destroy itself by burning out."

If you have experienced mania, **describe what it was like for you.** Use extra paper if you need it. _____

_____

_____

_____

My own personal experience of mania includes extreme pain. I feel unable to stay physically still or to quiet my brain. My body hurts all over. Every cell says I want to rest, but the body and mind cannot and will not cooperate.

Aspects of mania that feel painful or unbearable to people in the study include the following descriptions. **Which of the feelings and symptoms can you relate to?**

- [ ] become s-o-o-o tired but can't slow down enough to rest or sleep
- [ ] wanting to cry with every other person's hurt, feeling angry with others' anger
- [ ] unable to relax
- [ ] skin hurts, even to be touched
- [ ] physically ache all over
- [ ] ache for someone to hold me
- [ ] psychic pain
- [ ] feel like something is eating away at my brain
- [ ] feel like I'm being tortured

"I feel like my whole body is on fire. I can't sit still. I'm terrified."

"Like so many ideas whirling around, like BB's in a #10 can being shook."

"I feel like a high-speed engine that finally self-destructs in a million unrecognizable pieces."

"Sheer hell! Once I got lost in my home town, didn't recognize my father, thought strangers were old friends, saw and heard things that weren't there, forgot my name."

If mania is ever painful for you, **describe what you feel.** _____

_____

_____

_____

Aspects of Mania That People Enjoy

The paradox of mania is that there are aspects of it which people really enjoy, especially after they have been depressed for a long period of time. Often when people sense early warning signs of mania, they like the feeling so much that they don't want to do anything to stop that upward spiral.

Which of these pleasant aspects of mania, as cited by people in the study, are similar to what you have experienced?

☐ happiness
☐ super-sensitive senses
☐ feeling smart
☐ excessive energy
☐ unleashed abilities
☐ sociability
☐ self-confidence
☐ being alert mentally
☐ feeling free
☐ feeling like nothing can go wrong
☐ relief from depression
☐ being able to do difficult things with very little effort
☐ feeling like I am floating in a sea of glass

☐ full of good feelings
☐ feeling attractive
☐ euphoria
☐ productivity
☐ creative, free-flowing ideas
☐ feeling powerful
☐ feeling better than everyone else
☐ analytical
☐ intuitive
☐ lose all inhibitions
☐ weight loss
☐ feels like everybody loves me and I love everybody
☐ establishing friendships that get shelved during depression

Describe the aspects of mania that you enjoy: _____

_____

_____

_____

Negative Aspects of Mania

Looking at the positive aspects of mania, one might say, "What's wrong with that?" Plenty! Mania often gets people in serious trouble with family, friends, the community, and the law. Here are some descriptions from people in the study. **Which of the following negative aspects of mania do you experience?**

☐ detrimental effect on relationships

☐ embarrassment to self, family, and friends

☐ physical wear and tear on the body

☐ loss of support

☐ my not knowing how much is too much

☐ losing my thoughts

- ☐ poor judgment
- ☐ incoherence
- ☐ feeling of failing others
- ☐ disruptive behavior
- ☐ absence from school or work
- ☐ others to be scared
- ☐ lack of control
- ☐ me to become easily confused
- ☐ inappropriate lusting
- ☐ me to ignore responsibility
- ☐ lack of sleep
- ☐ professional damage
- ☐ kleptomania
- ☐ me to get into trouble
- ☐ my being called unreasonable
- ☐ friends and family to hate the rages and forcefulness
- ☐ having to correct things done wrong, picking up the pieces afterwards
- ☐ fear of what will happen: flights, accidents, injuries, hangovers, illness

- ☐ hospitalization
- ☐ paranoia
- ☐ carelessness with relationships
- ☐ anesthetized emotions
- ☐ offense to others
- ☐ financial crisis
- ☐ my not knowing what is real
- ☐ stigmatization
- ☐ feelings of anger, rage
- ☐ carelessness with driving
- ☐ me not to take good care of myself
- ☐ lost careers
- ☐ me to be avoided
- ☐ my being called weird
- ☐ being sick and not knowing it
- ☐ knowing I will come down and not be able to live up to expectations
- ☐ sexual impositions that destroy relationships and are dangerous

"I lost everything—my husband, family, daughter, home, car, possessions, jobs."

"Manic depression has cost me my career, my kids, and almost my independence. I was a nurse and my two teenage kids are in a foster home. That makes me angry."

"You can't function when you can't filter any stimulation out of your brain. You need help with everything you do, including dressing. Agony—at risk of dying due to delusion-induced accident, cardiac arrest."

"I tried to fly off my twentieth-floor porch, thinking I was superwoman."

"I sleep poorly and my head feels bad, like it is moving. I want to bang my head against the wall to relieve the excessive matter in my brain."

Describe the aspects of mania that are negative for you: _____

_____

_____

_____

Describe your personal reasons for wanting to prevent mania: _____

_____

_____

_____

_____

_____

5

Taking Responsibility for Your Own Wellness

It became very clear to me in compiling the data from the study that those people who personally take responsibility for their own wellness achieve the highest levels of stability, the highest levels of wellness, control over their own lives, and happiness.

Resources

Review the Resource List at the back of this book. Check at least five resources that seem most appropriate to you at this time. Some you may want to own, to make them available at any time for reference. These might include *Living Without Depression and Manic Depression, Thoughts and Feelings, The Relaxation and Stress Reduction Workbook. The Worry Control Workbook,* and *Winning Against Relapse.* You can borrow others for shorter-term use from your library. List the resources that you feel are a high priority for you to explore here:

1. Resource: _____

What I hope to learn from this resource: _____

_____

☐   *I plan to purchase it. Where?* _____

Why? _____

☐   *I will borrow it from the library.* _____
☐   *I will borrow it from a friend.* _____

Other possible places I will look for it: _____

2. Resource: _____

What I hope to learn from this resource: _____

☐   *I plan to purchase it. Where?* _____

Why? _____

☐   *I will borrow it from the library.* _____
☐   *I will borrow it from a friend.* _____

Other possible places I will look for it: _____

3. Resource: _____

What I hope to learn from this resource: _____

☐   *I plan to purchase it. Where?* _____

Why? _____

☐   *I will borrow it from the library.* _____
☐   *I will borrow it from a friend.* _____

Other possible places I will look for it: _____

4. Resource:

What I hope to learn from this resource:

☐   *I plan to purchase it. Where?* _____

Why? _____

☐   *I will borrow it from the library.* _____
☐   *I will borrow it from a friend.* _____

Other possible places I will look for it: _____

5. Resource: _____

What I hope to learn from this resource: _____

☐ *I plan to purchase it. Where?* _____

Why? _____

☐ *I will borrow it from the library.* _____
☐ *I will borrow it from a friend.* _____

Other possible places I will look for it: _____

Get these resources and read them. Learn and make those adjustments in your life that seem appropriate based on what you are learning. When you finish with these, continue to read and learn. Review the Resource List repeatedly for possible choices. Another good source of follow-up reading ideas is the bibliographies of the books you are reading.

Spend some time in the reference section of the library. Take a look at the *Physicians' Desk Reference (PDR)* and other books that describe medications. Learn how to use them. Then when your doctor suggests use of any medication, use these references to check it out (or you can ask your doctor to make you a copy of the information from his *PDR*). Then you can make appropriate decisions based on all the facts. Introduce people on your support team to this reference, so they can make decisions for you when you cannot make them for yourself.

Internet

These days you can find information on almost anything on the Internet. Many people are using it as an excellent source of helpful and useful information. There are numerous Web sites and other Internet resources listed in the Resources List at the back of this book. in addition, you can search for information on medications, diagnosis, organizations, resources, support—it's almost endless. However, a word of caution—just because it is on the Internet does not mean that it is true. If the information you receive doesn't sound right, check it out with a knowledgeable friend or health care provider.

Most libraries have computers you can use. If you don't know how to use it, ask a librarian for assistance.

Newsletters

The resource section at the back of this book has a list of organizations, many of which put out newsletters with valuable wellness information. Send the organizations a postcard requesting a complimentary copy of their newsletter. Subscribe to the ones that seem most appropriate to you. They can be an excellent source of inexpensive information, and are usually written by people who have experienced depression, manic depression, or other psychiatric symptoms, their family members and supporters, or health care professionals.

Workshops and Seminars

Watch newsletters and newspapers for workshops and seminars that will be useful to you in your search for stability and wellness. Then go. You will meet other great people with similar problems, and you will come away with useful ideas.

Mental Health Professionals

Your team of mental health professionals will have a wealth of information to share with you. If they don't, you have the wrong team of health professionals working with you. Pick their brains. Ask them questions. That is what they are there for.

Other People Who Experience Depression and/or Manic Depression

Through the study, I have found that other people who have mood disorders are the greatest resource available to any of us. Why reinvent the wheel if someone else has already solved the problem you're facing? The best way to meet these people is through support groups, which are in themselves a rich source of information. Locate support groups through the community calendar in the newspaper or by checking with local mental health organizations. (See chapter 13, "Support Groups," for information on how to set up a support group if there is none available in your area.)

How It Helps

Knowing all you can about mood disorders empowers you to make good decisions about your treatment, lifestyle, education, career, relationships, living space, parenting style, and leisure pursuits.

Being educated enables you to ask the right questions, leading you to discover the most appropriate treatments.

How have you learned what you know about mood disorders? _____

_____

_____

Do you feel that you take responsibility for your mood swings? If so, give yourself a pat on the back. You deserve it. How do you feel when you take responsibility for your ups and downs? _____

_____

_____

Why do you feel it's important to know all you can about mood disorders? _____

_____

_____

In what ways do you plan to take more responsibility for your mood swings? _____

_____

_____

Educating Others

The next chapter gives instructions for building a strong support system of friends, relatives, and health professionals. It's important to educate other people in your support system so they can make good decisions for you when you are not able to make them for yourself. The people in your support system should learn all they can about mood disorders by reading appropriate literature, visiting with mental health professionals, attending workshops and seminars, and listening to you.

Like anyone else who has a history of mood swings, you need to have several people who can make decisions for you when you are unable to make decisions for yourself. When in a deep depression or an agitated manic state, it may be impossible to concentrate well enough to make appropriate decisions about your own treatment. To avoid having such decisions made by people who don't know you or understand mood disorders, it is important to have several people whom you trust to make decisions when you're incapacitated. These people might include a spouse, parents, children, siblings, close friends, or trusted health professionals.

People I want to make decisions for me when I am unable to make decisions for myself:

1. _____   2. _____

3. _____   4. _____

Talk to these people about taking responsibility for you when you are unable to take responsibility for yourself. (And make certain that they're willing to assume this responsibility!) Educate them about your illness. Direct them to resources you have found useful. Ask them to attend informational meetings with you. Introduce them to your health care professionals. You may want to include them in a counseling session. Tell them what kinds of treatment are acceptable to you and what kinds are not. Be very clear and precise in making your wishes known: you might want to write them down and review them together.

Hospitals, doctors, and counselors have confidentiality rules that may keep people in your support system from getting the information they need to make appropriate decisions about your treatment. To avoid this situation, have a legal document available which allows health care professionals to consult with, and get permission for treatment from, designated members of your support system. Here's an example of a format you might use:

I give (name) _____ *the authority to consult with my mental health professionals about my treatment and to make decisions about my treatment in the event that I am unable to make these decisions for myself.*

Signed: _____   *Date:* _____

Witness: _____

Witness: _____

Make copies of this document and give them to your health care professionals and the designated members of your support system.

6

Possible Causes of
Mood Disorders

I don't believe there is one answer for everyone. Controlling the symptoms must be dealt with first, then each individual must explore his or her own problem. Different people respond differently to different approaches. There's bound to be something that will work—it just takes time to find it.

If you are suffering from a mood disorder, have a complete physical examination with a physician you trust. He or she must come well recommended, be able to communicate clearly, be willing to answer questions, respond to your concerns, and address the possibility of a medical basis for your symptoms. Your physician must also be open to exploring all possible causes and treatments, particularly those that are least invasive.

My own personal experience yields enough evidence to support this course. I was completely disabled for three years with rapid cycling, inability to concentrate, loss of memory, inability to lose weight, and periodically, extreme fatigue. I was hospitalized for extended periods four times. A local doctor found—through appropriate testing—that I had hypothyroidism. With hormone replacement treatment, the extreme, rapid-cycling mood swings were eliminated, I regained my ability to concentrate, my memory returned, I lost weight, and my energy level increased dramatically. This, or some other easily treated problem, may be causing some or all of your erratic moods.

Twenty-three people in the study have had conflicting diagnoses of their mood disorder. Only thirty-nine participants feel that all possible causes of their mood disorder have been explored. Forty-six people are not satisfied that all possible causes of their mood disorder have been explored.

Learn all you can about mood disorders. Then insist that you get the necessary testing. Don't let anyone talk you out of a given test unless the procedure itself has harmful side effects. If your doctor won't order a test that you feel is warranted, then find a different doctor. Your life is too important to miss any clue. You owe it to yourself to be thorough.

If cost is keeping you from getting the testing you need, explore other payment options with your doctor and your medical facility. Many doctors and medical facilities have funds available for people who are unable to pay for testing.

Why do I owe it to myself to see that I am tested for every possible condition that may be causing or exacerbating my mood swings?

_____

_____

_____

The following possible medical causes for mood swings were suggested by study participants. Which ones do you feel you need to explore?

☐ allergies—food and environmental

☐ endocrine system problems, including hypothyroidism—make sure you get a complete thyroid battery, which includes Total T4, Free T4, Total T3, and TSH (this test will cost over $150. If it doesn't, it's the wrong test)

☐ anticandida antibody test

☐ chemistry 20 screening test

☐ complete blood count with differential

☐ seasonal affective disorder

☐ PMS

☐ medication interactions

☐ acute or chronic stress reactions

Other possibilities you plan to explore that you have discovered through your research:

_____

_____

For more information on possible medical causes of depression and mania see *Living Without Depression and Manic Depression*.

Always ask your doctor for a copy of test results, even if you don't understand what they mean. The results should be in your own file, so that they'll be available to you if you see another doctor. Make sure that all your doctors have a copy of any test results.

Do you feel that all possible causes of your problem with mood disorders have been explored? _____ If not, what are you going to do about it? _____

_____

_____

A complete physical examination showed that I have the following health problems which may be causing or exacerbating my mood swings: _____

_____

_____

Based on these findings, I am going to take the following action: _____

_____

_____

As a result of the above action, I have made the following changes in my treatment: _____

_____

_____

What are the changes in the way you feel that might be attributable to new treatment strategies? _____

_____

_____

_____

7

The Way Out
of Depression

I have developed a program that includes reading anything current on depression, forcing myself into self-help to slowly reverse the depressive cycle, using self-practiced cognitive therapy, and forcing myself to return slowly to life's surroundings and functions. I must use all of these techniques; they work together. I have spent many years developing these techniques and I know how important they all are: it's like being a world-class chef who would never leave any ingredient out of his best recipe.

Early Warning Signs

As you become more aware of the subtleties of your depression through your research and by charting your moods, you will become familiar with your own early warning signs of depression. These may be quite subtle indeed: for instance, an early warning sign of depression for me is that I don't look both ways before I cross the street.

When you notice such signs, there are simple, noninvasive, safe, and inexpensive techniques you can use to slow or halt the downward spiral. By being aware of your early signs of depression and taking action early, you may be able to avoid plummeting to the depths of depression.

What are your early warning signs that you are on a downward spiral?

☐ withdrawal	☐ not wanting to do anything
☐ inactivity	☐ inability to function
☐ tire easily	☐ low energy level
☐ excessive sleep	☐ talk little
☐ slow speech	☐ insomnia
☐ premature awakening	☐ stay in bed for long periods
☐ poor appetite	☐ nausea
☐ irritability	☐ negative attitude
☐ poor ability to concentrate	☐ mind slows down
☐ confused	☐ low self-esteem
☐ cry easily	☐ lack of interest in everything
☐ despondent	☐ suicidal ideation
☐ self-destructive thoughts	☐ feel no one understands me
☐ inability to experience pleasure	☐ feel like giving up on life
☐ unable to do what I normally do	☐ boredom
☐ insecurity	☐ fear
☐ anxiety	☐ desire to be taken care of
☐ agitation	☐ ache all over
☐ sore shoulders and neck	☐ headache
☐ low back pain	☐ trembling
☐ low libido	☐ senses shut down
☐ extreme grief-type emotions	☐ paranoia
☐ overeating	☐ eat a lot of salty foods
☐ eat junk foods	☐ craving for carbohydrates
☐ inability to show affection	☐ easily frustrated
☐ void of emotions	☐ avoid people
☐ everything seems disorganized	☐ feel clumsy, drop things
☐ hair becomes wiry	☐ I start wearing a coat all the time
☐ my learning disabilities are more pronounced	☐ as my eyesight does not seem right, becoming sure I need new eyeglasses
☐ eczema	☐ swollen thyroid
☐ see white spots	☐ increased consumption of alcohol
☐ have trouble getting dressed	☐ skin problems
☐ feelings of regret for past decisions	

One study respondent wrote:

"A sign that depression is imminent is that to my ears everybody speaks to me in a critical tone of voice. 'You're so quiet tonight' is heard by me as 'Thank God you're quiet—you're usually such a loud mouth.' Everything my husband says seems to be in a fault-finding tone of voice. Strange, because he never criticizes or belittles me."

Other early indications of depression you have noted: _____

_____

_____

Learn what your early warning signs of depression are. Take appropriate action when you notice these signs.

Strategies for Alleviating or Eliminating Depression

On the next pages are checklists of ways in which the study respondents alleviate their depression. These strategies are divided into five categories: activities, support, attitude, management, and spirituality. Which strategies have you used successfully? Which ones do you feel you should use more often? Which methods have you never used that you would like to try? Remember—what works for someone else may not be the right thing for you. Cleaning is such an example. For some people it is depressing and discouraging. Others are uplifted by it.

Activities	Have tried successfully	Should use more often	Would like to try
Exercise			
Sports (such as basketball, soccer, volleyball)			
Long walks			
Yoga			
Dancing			
Reading			
Listening to music			
Long, hot baths			
Making love			
Gardening			
Long drives			
Needlework			
Working with wood			
Working with clay, pottery			
Drawing, painting			
Journal writing			
Writing poetry			

Writing letters			
Canoeing			
Horseback riding			
Shopping			
Relaxing in a meditative natural setting			
Day trips			
Playing a musical instrument			
Spending time with young children			
Cleaning			
Watching a funny movie			
Watching TV			
Watching videos, a movie, or a play			
Buying something I've been wanting			
Helping others			

What other activities have you used successfully to help alleviate your depression?

_____

_____

_____

_____

Support	Have tried successfully	Should use more often	Would like to try
Talking it out with an understanding person			
Getting emotional support from a person I trust			
Talking to a therapist or counselor			
Peer counseling			
Talking to people who validate my feelings			
Spending time with good friends			
Talking to staff at a crisis clinic or hotline			
Arranging not to be alone			
Reaching out to someone			

Being held by someone I love			
Going to a support group			
Spending time with and taking responsibility for a pet			

What other kinds of support have been helpful to you in alleviating your depression?

_____

_____

_____

_____

_____

_____

Attitude	Have tried successfully	Should use more often	Would like to try
Changing negative thought patterns to positive ones			
Waiting it out			
Staying active			
Remembering that depression ends			
Recalling good times			
Being good to myself			
Diverting my attention			
Being gentle with myself			
Refusing to feel guilty			
Focusing on living one day at a time			
Endorsing and affirming my efforts			
Laughter			

What other attitudes have you developed and used to help alleviate your depression?

_____

_____

_____

_____

_____

Management	Have tried successfully	Should use more often	Would like to try
Medication			
Full-spectrum light			
Spending time outside			
Keeping busy			
Eating a diet high in complex carbohydrates			
Eliminating foods that worsen my depression			
Rest			
Forcing myself to get up in the morning			
Forcing myself to go to work			
Doing whatever I need to do to meet my needs			
Maintaining a balance of rest and good times			

Study participants wrote:

"I use activity and exercise together. Using the body fully stimulates the brain."

What management strategies have you found for alleviating your depression? _____

_____

_____

_____

_____

_____

Spirituality	Have tried successfully	Should use more often	Would like to try
Prayer			
Getting in touch with my spirituality			
Meditation			
Keeping up with a 12-step program			

What other spiritual practices help to alleviate your depression? _____

_____

_____

_____

_____

Use Scheduling and Planning to Help Depression

A person who is experiencing depression may spend a whole day or many days literally doing nothing. This inactivity and lack of accomplishment can deepen your depression and lower your self-esteem. If you accomplish anything, you may belittle it as "insignificant."

People with whom I talk and work find that the following strategies can help break this cycle and help the depressed person feel better.

- make and stick to simple plans

- break tasks down into smaller components

- learn to give yourself credit for whatever you accomplished

Make and Stick to Simple Plans

In everyone's life, there are some things you have to do—such as washing the dishes or vacuuming; and other things you really enjoy—such as going for a walk or listening to good music. When planning the day's schedule, it is important to include some things you "have to do" (so you come out with a sense of accomplishment) and some things you "enjoy doing" (to increase your good feelings about being alive). Referring to the lists on the previous pages, make a list of things you must do on a daily basis and things that you really enjoy doing. These lists will be different for everyone. Before you start your list, take a look at these examples:

Things I have to do	**Things I enjoy doing**
Examples:	*Examples:*
wash the dishes	take a hot shower
vacuum	pet the dog
mow the lawn	pick some flowers
go to work	paint
make my bed	chat with a friend
balance my checkbook	play with a baby
shovel snow	go to a movie
organize my closet	watch TV

What do I have to do?   **What do I enjoy doing?**

_____   _____

_____   _____

_____   _____

_____   _____

_____   _____

_____   _____

_____   _____

Keep these lists in a handy place so you can refer to them when you need to. Build activities from each list into your daily plan. Avoid spending the whole day doing things that "must be done," as that is a recipe for failure.

As you develop your daily plan, assess your expectations of that activity by rating it on a scale of 0 to 5, with 0 being that you expect you could do it or could enjoy it, 3 being that you think you could do the activity and/or would enjoy the activity, and 5 being that you expect to be able to do the activity very well or that you would enjoy it immensely. For instance, if the activity is something you have to do, such as washing the dishes, and you think you will be able to do it, you could rate the activity H (for "have to do") 3, meaning that you expect to be able to do the task. If the activity were something you usually enjoy, such as going to a movie, but you don't think you'll be able to enjoy it now, you could rate it E (for "enjoy") 1, meaning that you don't think you'll have a good time. When you complete the activity, rate how well you did it or how much you actually enjoyed yourself. You will discover that your expectations and what actually happens can be very different!

Example of a Schedule for a Person Who Is Depressed but Able to Work
(Note that even on a workday, activities for enjoyment are included.)

Date: Nov. 20   *Mood:* low, depressed

Time	Planned Activity and Expectations	Actual Activity	How It Felt
7–8 a.m.	Get up; shower; make and eat hot cereal **H1**	Got up; took a shower; had tea and toast	Better than if I had stayed in bed **H3**
8–9 a.m.	Walk to work, picking up the mail on the way **H3**	(As planned)	Exercise lifts my spirits **H4**
9–10 a.m.	Open and sort mail; return two phone calls **H1**	Opened and sorted mail; made one phone call	At least it feels better to be doing something **H3**
10–11 a.m.	Attend office meeting **H0**	(As planned)	Hard for me to be with a group, but I did it **H2**
11–12 Noon	Write press release **H1**	(As planned)	Glad I got it done **H3**
12–1 p.m.	Have lunch with Jane in the park; take a 15-minute walk with her **E1**	Ate lunch with Jane at park	It felt good to share how I have been feeling **E4**
1–2 p.m.	Watch a management video **H1**	(As planned)	OK, but I fell asleep for part of the time **H0**
2–3 p.m.	Interview a candidate for a data entry position **H1**	(As planned)	Hard, but I did it **H3**
3–4 p.m.	Enter data in computer **H2**	(As planned)	Felt slow **H4**
4–5 p.m.	Walk home from work; stop at store for milk **H3**	Walked home, but did not stop at store	Tired **H3**
5–6 p.m.	Relax, meditate **E2**	(As planned)	Helped me feel better **H4**
6–7 p.m.	Cook frozen pizza and eat **H2**	Had a peanut butter sandwich instead	Wish I had cooked the pizza **H0**

7–8 p.m.	Do the dishes; straighten up the house **H0**	Did the dishes	Fine; the housework can wait **H3**
8–9 p.m.	Watch *Nature* on PBS **E2**	(As planned)	OK **E4**
9–10 p.m.	Call a member of my support team for a talk; read a light novel, go to bed **E2**	Talked to Claire for 15 minutes; read and went to bed	OK **E4**

Example of a Schedule for a Person Who Is Unable to Work

Date: November 20   *Mood:* low, depressed

Time	Planned Activity and Expectations	Actual Activity	How It Felt
7–8 a.m.	Get up, dress; sit in front of the light box and read a light novel **H1**	(As planned)	OK, but mornings are always hard **H4**
8–9 a.m.	Eat a bowl of cereal; make bed; put up load of wash **H1**	Skipped doing wash	OK **H3**
9–10 a.m.	Take the dog for a walk **H2**	(As planned)	Difficult, but I did it **H3**
10–11 a.m.	Sit on sun porch and read **E2**	(As planned)	OK; fell asleep for 15 minutes **E5**
11–12 Noon	Put wash in dryer; clean bathroom **H1**	Put wash in washer; scrubbed sink and tub	OK **H3**
12–1 p.m.	Lunch with Tom (he is bringing Chinese food) **E2**	(As planned)	He did all the talking; I felt weary **E3**
1–2 p.m.	Nap **E3**	(As planned)	Fine—I was ready for it **E5**
2–3 p.m.	Drive to the store for groceries **H0**	(As planned)	Did not like being in the store, but I got through it **H2**

3–4 p.m.	Put away groceries; meditate with audio tape **E1**	(As planned)	Hard time really relaxing **E2**
4–5 p.m.	Appointment with counselor **H3**	(As planned)	It really helps **H5**
5–6 p.m.	Watch sitcom on TV **E2**	(As planned)	OK **E5**
6–7 p.m.	Cook frozen pizza and eat **H1**	(As planned)	OK **H4**
7–8 p.m.	Peer counseling with Janet **E2**	(As planned)	Helps a lot **E5**
8–9 p.m.	Watch concert on PBS **E1**	(As planned)	OK **E4**
9–10 p.m.	Read light novel; go to bed **E2**	Fell asleep soon after I started reading	Wish I had been able to stay awake longer **E2**

Review these charts after you have completed them. When people are depressed, they often feel quite negative prior to undertaking an activity. Upon completion of the activity, you may realize that you actually had a better time, or did a better job, than anticipated. Being tuned in to this can encourage you to have more realistically optimistic expectations.

Make copies of this form to plan daily schedules for yourself when you are depressed

Date: *Mood:*

Time	Planned Activity and Expectations	Actual Activity	How It Felt
7–8 a.m.			
8–9 a.m.			
9–10 a.m.			
10–11 a.m.			
11–12 Noon			
12–1 p.m.			
1–2 p.m.			
2–3 p.m.			
3–4 p.m.			
4–5 p.m.			
5–6 p.m.			
6–7 p.m.			
7–8 p.m.			
8–9 p.m.			
9–10 p.m.			

How I felt on a day when I was depressed and did not follow a plan: _____

_____

_____

How I felt on a day when I was depressed and followed a plan: _____

_____

_____

Based on my experience, I intend to take the following action with regard to scheduling my days when I am depressed: _____

_____

_____

_____

_____

(time of day) _____ *is the best time for me to make plans when I am depressed.*

Breaking Tasks Down into Smaller Components

When you're depressed, even the smallest and most familiar task can feel overwhelming. By analyzing a task and breaking it down into smaller components, it can be made manageable. Talking through the task with a support team member, and writing down the steps necessary to accomplishing the task, will facilitate the process. Your sense of accomplishment from getting something done—even something very simple—can help lift your depression.

For example, when I'm depressed, doing the laundry seems absolutely impossible. If I break this task down into smaller components, and tackle one component at a time, I can often get it done.

1. Gather all dirty clothes in the laundry room.

2. Sort light colors from the dark. Empty pockets.

3. Set the dials to the right water temperature and agitation speed.

4. Add the detergent and turn on the machine.

5. When the soap is dissolved, add the light-colored clothes.

6. When the cycle is complete, move the clothes into the dryer. Set the timer on the dryer and turn it on.

7. Repeat this process with the dark clothes.

8. As the clothes dry, fold them or put them on hangers.

9. Put the clothes away.

What tasks do you have a hard time tackling when you're depressed? _____

_____

_____

_____

_____

_____

_____

_____

With the help of a friend, if necessary, break down one of the tasks you listed into smaller, incremental components. This will make the task manageable for you.

Step 1 _____

_____

Step 2 _____

_____

Step 3 _____

_____

Step 4 _____

_____

Step 5 _____

_____

Step 6 _____

_____

Step 7 _____

_____

Step 8 _____

_____

Learn to Give Yourself Credit

"I just can't get anything done!" "I never accomplish anything!" "I have never amounted to anything!" These are the kinds of negative thoughts that hamper people who experience mood swings. By paying close attention to what you do, you can learn to give yourself credit for even the smallest accomplishment. Each accomplishment, in turn, will add to your optimism and self-esteem.

Remember, there is no set rule for what anyone must accomplish in a given day (unless you are working on an assembly line!). Some days you may be able to get a lot done. Other days, you may not accomplish as much. Sometimes you may not get anything done at all.

A person in the study said, "When I am depressed, I can't get much of anything done. What I do get done, I don't feel very good about. But when I am well, I get a lot done and do it very well."

My doctor told me to give myself credit if all I do on a given day is plant one package of carrot seeds. If you are able to get out of bed in the morning, give yourself credit for that.

You also deserve credit for taking a shower, getting dressed, eating breakfast, walking to work, feeding the birds, petting the dog, encouraging your child, doing the exercises in this workbook, and so on.

Make a list of the things you have done so far today for which you can give yourself credit. This will help you focus on the positive instead of the negative. Include such things as *washed my face, made and ate toast and tea, made my bed, fed the cat, drove to work, walked to the corner to get a newspaper, filled the car with gas, answered the phone, watered the plants, listened to a friend, encouraged a friend, paid a bill, organized my desk, read a chapter in a book, played a game with a child.*

List of my accomplishments for today: _____

_____

_____

_____

_____

Other Suggestions on How to Alleviate Depression

"I start in on a new project, clear my mind, and re-program myself—sometimes this works."

"I don't push myself any more than necessary, and I tell those around me what is going on."

"The best way for me to deal with depression is like the old adage, 'Doc, it hurts when I do this.' The doctor replies, 'Then don't do that.' If I am depressed, I am experiencing a problem with my lifestyle. When I was first in recovery, if I went to a party where people were drinking or getting high, I would start to feel sorry for myself because I couldn't drink or get high. I had to quit going to parties where that happened. If my car broke down, I would get depressed, so I learned to work on my car myself. I went to school and studied to get the exact job I wanted. Twelve-step, traditional self-help has been a lifesaver for me, because I learned to recognize my spiritual [component]. I am not religious, but I am spiritual. Spirituality is my relationship to the universe. I am the wounded healer. I help others through my experience, strength, and hope. Two people with similar pain helping each other is a very spiritual matter."

"Don't withdraw from people or activities. Use principles of cognitive/behavioral therapy: change your negative, distorted thoughts to realistic ones (this takes knowledge of distortions and a strong will to fight for your mental health). A typical affirmation is, 'Symptoms of depression are distressing but not dangerous.' With practice, it is possible to function adequately even while enduring a fairly severe 'down.' Belief that the world is basically ordered (by God), as opposed to the chaos that many modern philosophers suggest, has helped me greatly. The meaninglessness of the existential view of life undermined my stability and, I believe, contributed, along with other things, to my depressions."

A technique I have found useful in alleviating depression, and that I know has worked for others, is to block out the day, planning it very carefully, considering every aspect in terms of how it will affect my mood. When very depressed, you may need to ask a support person to help you with this process.

Here is a sample plan for a day that follows some of my early warning signs of depression.

6:45–7:00	Meditation
7:00–7:15	Stretching exercises
7:15–7:30	Write in my journal
7:30–8:00	Warm bath, dress
8:00–8:30	Prepare and eat a breakfast of hot cereal with yogurt, and herb tea
8:30–9:30	Leisurely walk
9:30–10:00	Relax, meditate
10:00–11:00	Meet with counselor
11:00–12:00	Find a good book in the library
12:00–1:00	Lunch with a good friend

1:00–2:00	Relaxation exercises and nap
2:00–3:00	Peer counseling
3:00–4:00	Take the dog for a walk
4:00–5:00	Read something light and humorous
5:00–7:00	Prepare brown rice and vegetable stir-fry for supper, eat it with family
7:00–9:00	Watch a good but light video
9:00–10:00	Read or listen to music
10:00–10:15	Meditation
10:15	Go to bed

Use extra paper to make several detailed plans for a perfect healing day for yourself when you are feeling low. Then, when that day comes, put one of them into action. Refer to the lists above for ideas about activities that make you feel good. Have plans for several days on hand so you can choose the one that feels best. Having these available protects you from needing to make decisions at a time when decision-making is very hard.

Seeking Help for Dealing with Depression

People in the study cited different criteria for when they should seek help for depression. The general feeling seems to be "The sooner the better." Many feel that it's best to seek help at the first warning signs of depression. One respondent said that she seeks help "when all my usual attempts to help myself aren't working." When do you seek help for depression?

☐ as soon as I notice early warning signs of depression

☐ when the depression stays with me for more than a day

☐ when the depression is out of proportion to circumstances

☐ when I need help in prioritizing and sorting out feelings

☐ when I become unable to care for myself

☐ when it lasts a week or more

☐ when suicidal thoughts start

☐ when my thoughts become jumbled

☐ when I start thinking about divorce

☐ when I feel emotionally unstable

☐ when I have extreme feelings of despair

☐ when I feel out of control

☐ when I can't move anymore

☐ when the pain is unbearable

☐ when I can finally cry

☐ when I can't get out of bed

☐ when I notice that I'm spending too much time on the couch

☐ when my sex drive disappears

☐ when I am unable to sleep

☐ when I lose my appetite

☐ when I overeat to feel better

☐ when I am hallucinating

☐ when the depression continues too long

☐ when I want to die

☐ when it overwhelms me

☐ when I become irrational

☐ when I lose interest in things

☐ before I can't function anymore

☐ when I can't get motivated

☐ when it is starting to hurt

☐ when I can't work

☐ when I can't relax

☐ when I isolate myself

☐ when I see no colors

☐ when I can't snap out of it

☐ when I sleep poorly

What are some other criteria you use to determine the right moment to seek help?

_____

_____

_____

Explain your reasons: _____

_____

_____

_____

These are the kinds of help people prefer. **What is your preference?**

☐ counseling—who? _____

☐ psychiatric—who? _____

☐ medication—what? _____

☐ self-help program _____

☐ peer support program _____

☐ group therapy—with whom? _____

☐ 12-step program—which one? _____

☐ close friends—who?   1) _____ 2) _____

                         3) _____ 4) _____

What do you want from your close friends?

☐ support

☐ someone to do errands

☐ reassurance

☐ lots of love, hugs, touching

☐ affirmation that I am a good person

☐ someone to take me out or do things with me

☐ one-on-one talking

Other things you want from close friends: _____

_____

_____

_____

_____

Other kinds of help you prefer: _____

_____

_____

_____

_____

This is how people in the study feel if others suggest that they get professional help. Check the reactions that apply to you.

☐ I don't like it, but deep down I know I need it.

☐ With those I trust, I want them to tell me; with those I don't trust, I hate it.

☐ If they are real friends, I know they know what is best for me.

☐ I've learned to listen and take their advice.

☐ They don't have to—I do it on my own.

☐ I usually know it first, but appreciate another's caring.

☐ I'm grateful they're watching my symptoms, because I am likely to miss them.

☐ If they see the changes more clearly and earlier than I do, I realize that I need to see the doctor.

☐ I feel down and more depressed.

☐ I appreciate it.

☐ I consider it.

☐ It's fine unless they get too insistent.

☐ I ignore it.

☐ I feel sad.

☐ I feel resentful.

☐ I go into denial.

☐ It depends on who it is.

☐ I feel like all my personal struggles to keep myself alive are being negated—like I am not doing my part.

☐ I agree.

☐ I seek help.

☐ It makes me afraid.

☐ It makes me angry.

☐ It makes me feel helpless.

☐ I feel misunderstood.

☐ I don't like it.

☐ I don't listen.

☐ It depends on what they offer.

How do you think you should feel or respond? _____

_____

_____

How would you like to be encouraged to get help?

☐ with respect

☐ firmly

☐ I don't want people to push too hard

☐ simply and honestly

☐ quickly

☐ gently

☐ with compassion

- ☐ by not turning against me
- ☐ lovingly
- ☐ by offering time to talk and listen
- ☐ by reaching out to me because I cannot reach out to them
- ☐ by making suggestions, but letting me make the final decision
- ☐ by sharing their concerns with family members
- ☐ by asking me outright if I am having a depression
- ☐ the same as if I had a physical problem
- ☐ with concrete ideas of what I can do
- ☐ by reminding me to stick to the techniques I have found that help me alleviate depression
- ☐ by telling me directly in a kind, not condescending or patronizing manner about the behaviors that concern them
- ☐ by letting me decide how dangerous the situation is (I want to make the decision)
- ☐ by telling me to call my doctor—that I am getting sick
- ☐ by making the call to my psychiatrist when I can't
- ☐ by explaining the symptoms and what they think is wrong

In what other ways would you like to be encouraged to get help? _____

_____

_____

How People Want to Be Treated When They're Depressed

How do you like to be treated when you're depressed? These are some of the answers of the study participants:

- ☐ with love
- ☐ kindly, gently
- ☐ with compassion
- ☐ with respect
- ☐ I want to be listened to
- ☐ with patience
- ☐ with tolerance
- ☐ firmly
- ☐ I want someone to keep me safe

☐ I want someone to pray for me

☐ I want reassurance

☐ I want touching

☐ with understanding

☐ with caring

☐ as a normal person

☐ with encouragement

☐ with acceptance

☐ I want to be comforted

☐ with an effort to keep me involved

☐ with honesty

☐ I want someone to stay with me

☐ I want people to let me work it out

☐ with nurturing

☐ in an uplifting manner

☐ with help to take care of my responsibilities

☐ I want others to take over if necessary

☐ I want people to remind me that it has happened before

☐ I want someone to encourage good grooming, help me with clean clothes and house-keeping

☐ I want people to include me, but just at the level I can participate

☐ quietly, without panic; I want people to come over and visit briefly, but also to give me space

☐ I want people to be sympathetic to the pain I go through and understand that it is not just me, it is an illness

☐ I want people to be nearby but not watching over me, not to try and cheer me up, just to listen: not to try to have any answers

☐ just be there—without talk about how wonderful life is

☐ I want people to show extra attention through invitations, especially involving food—there's nothing like good homey food

☐ I want people to remind me not to be so hard on myself

☐ I want to be allowed more time to complete tasks

☐ by people reducing the demands on me

☐ with concrete ideas about what to do

☐ I want people to be direct and ask if I need to talk

☐ I want people to take me out to eat or for some activity

"To know enough about the illness to not be trite, to sense that my depression is automatically imposed from within my brain, that I can no more stop it or dilute it than an epileptic can willfully interrupt a seizure or a heart patient can curb a coronary. There is a naturalness to it which is especially hard for onlookers to understand."

How would you like to be treated when you are depressed? _____

_____

_____

What People Don't Want from Others During Depressive Episodes

These are some of the answers given by people in the study. *I don't want people to*

☐ blame me for what I cannot help

☐ humiliate me

☐ desert me

☐ put undue demands on me

☐ tell me to get my act together

☐ tell me to "pull yourself up by the boot straps"

☐ pressure me to go out (although being invited is better than not being invited)

☐ make fun of me

☐ avoid me

☐ give me sympathy

☐ tell me to cheer up

"I find that people are angry with me because I have difficulty caring for myself. They label me as 'lazy' and wanting to be a patient and playing the sick role. I've been told that I am not busy enough and that I need pets to solve my problems. Many times I am trying very hard to put my life back together and people don't recognize that. Telling me to 'get my act together' or to 'buck up' makes it even more difficult to cope. I feel more hopeless than ever before. That is one of the worst things someone can do for me."

What other ways do you not want to be treated? _____

_____

_____

_____

_____

_____

You have just explored your experience of depression in an in-depth manner. Based on what you have discovered through this exercise, **what changes are you going to make in the way you cope with depression?** _____

_____

_____

_____

_____

_____

_____

Photocopy the next page—or rewrite it to suit you own needs; then post it on your refrigerator.

What to Do When You Are Getting Depressed

These are some simple ways to help yourself alleviate symptoms while you're waiting for other help, or trying to keep things on an even keel. They may not solve the underlying problem, but they will provide some relief.

- Get help while you still can: the longer you wait, the harder it gets.

- Use cognitive therapy techniques to get you out of negative thought patterns (read self-help books: refer to Resource List).

- Plan your day with some activities you have to do and some activities you enjoy. Rate your expectations of these activities, and then reassess how you felt after their completion.

- Break down difficult tasks into smaller incremental parts.

- Give yourself credit for even the smallest things you get done.

- Remember that depression passes. Focus on living one day at a time.

- Get emotional support from a family member, friend, or mental health professional. Get involved in a fun activity with someone you enjoy. Cuddle with your mate. Spend some time with your pet.

- Talk to an understanding, nonjudgmental person for as long as you need to talk (or several people might take turns talking with you). It needs to be okay to talk about anything and to be emotional.

- Listen to or help someone else.

- Use whatever spiritual resources you are comfortable calling on.

- Get some exercise, whatever you can muster—walk, run, bike, swim, etc.

- Get out in the sunlight as much as possible. If you must be inside, sit or work near a window.

- Use full-spectrum lighting indoors (read the chapter in this book on full-spectrum lighting). Avoid areas lit with conventional fluorescent lights.

- Eliminate sugar, caffeine, and junk food from your diet. Eat three healthy meals a day.

- Buy yourself something you have been wanting and would enjoy.

- Read a funny or light book or watch a funny video. Listen to music that you enjoy.

- Get dressed, putting on something that makes you feel good.

8

Coming Down from Mania

"I never can understand how people can say that mania is good or fun. I suffer with it just thinking about it. It reminds me of what I've gone through."

Note: If you have depression only, you don't have to read this chapter.

Early Warning Signs

In order to prevent a mania, it is essential to be aware of your early warning signs and to take action. The following behaviors and symptoms were noted by people in the study as signals of impending mania. Which behaviors and symptoms are early warning signs for you?

- ☐ insomnia
- ☐ surges of energy
- ☐ flight of ideas
- ☐ writing pressure
- ☐ irritability
- ☐ spending too much money
- ☐ unnecessary phone calls
- ☐ wanting to keep moving

- ☐ sleeping much less
- ☐ others seem slow
- ☐ speech pressure
- ☐ making lots of plans
- ☐ inappropriate anger
- ☐ money loses its value
- ☐ difficulty staying still
- ☐ restlessness

☐ increased appetite
☐ euphoria
☐ feeling superior
☐ increased creativity
☐ overambition
☐ taking on too much responsibility
☐ nervous and wound up
☐ anxious
☐ overly self-involved
☐ negativism
☐ feeling unreal
☐ more sensitive than usual
☐ out of touch with reality
☐ inappropriate behavior
☐ poor judgment
☐ oblivious
☐ increased alcohol consumption
☐ dangerous driving
☐ increased community involvement
☐ tingly feeling
☐ friends notice behavior change

☐ compulsive eating
☐ feeling great
☐ feeling very important
☐ obsessions
☐ unusual bursts of enthusiasm
☐ very productive
☐ doing several things at once
☐ inability to concentrate
☐ outbursts of temper
☐ disorganization
☐ ability to foresee things happening
☐ noises louder than usual
☐ bizarre ideas, thoughts
☐ laugh to self uncontrollably
☐ thrill seeking
☐ more sexually active
☐ danger to self and others
☐ spotless, energetic housekeeping
☐ itching
☐ flushed and hot
☐ increased sociability

"It begins with waking for a couple of days at 3 A.M. and lining up several days' work or shopping to be done in one day."

"Life feels as clear as fresh air and I am in the middle of my life, ready to act."

"I do so much work that I am exhausted and catch colds or flu easily. I feel much more alive—but it is a ragged and warped vivacity. I begin thinking I can do many things superbly."

"My doctor told me that insomnia is the very first sign of mania. He said that, when insomnia starts, it forces the sympathetic nervous system into 'overdrive' and, in turn, the rapid racing thoughts begin, along with poor judgment. My therapist told me it is very difficult to detect early signs, because usually the first thing to go is good judgment. She said that's why seeing a therapist weekly will help a lot, because they can pick up on signals I may not be aware of."

What are other early warning signs of mania for you? _____

_____

_____

_____

_____

Strategies for Alleviating or Eliminating Mania

Following is a checklist of ways that people in the study use to alleviate mania. These strategies are divided into five categories: activities, support, attitude, management, and spirituality. Many of these strategies are similar to those used for alleviating depression. **Which ones have you used successfully? Which ones do you feel you should use more often? Which methods have you never used that you would like to try?** Remember— what works for someone else may not be the right thing for you.

Activities	Have tried successfully	Should use more often	Would like to try
Exercise			
Long walks			
Yoga			
Reading			
Listening to music			
Long, hot baths			
Gardening			
Needlework			
Working with wood			
Working with clay, pottery			
Drawing, painting			
Journal writing			
Writing poetry			
Writing letters			
Canoeing			
Horseback riding			
Relaxing in a meditative natural setting			
Playing a musical instrument			
Cleaning			
Watching TV			
Watching videos, a movie, or a play			

Helping others			
Turning energy into creativity			

What other activities have you used successfully to help alleviate mania? _____

_____

_____

_____

_____

_____

_____

Support	Have tried successfully	Should use more often	Would like to try
Talking it out with an understanding person			
Getting emotional support from a person I trust			
Talking to a therapist or counselor			
Spending time with good friends			
Talking to staff at a crisis clinic or hotline			
Arranging not to be alone			
Reaching out to someone who understands			
Going to a support group			
Peer counseling			

What other kinds of support have been helpful to you in alleviating mania? _____

_____

_____

_____

_____

Attitude	Have tried successfully	Should use more often	Would like to try
Changing negative thought patterns to positive ones			
Remembering that mania ends			
Focusing on living one day at a time			
Understanding what is happening			
Staying neutral			
Stopping regularly to ask myself, "How am I feeling right now?"; bringing my mind into touch with my body			

What other attitudes have you developed and used to level out mania? _____

_____

_____

_____

_____

_____

_____

_____

Management	Have tried successfully	Should use more often	Would like to try
Consulting with doctor			
Sleeping			
Eating a diet high in complex carbohydrates			
Avoiding caffeine and sugar			
Maintaining a balance of rest and activity			
Avoiding stimulating places and activities			
Using relaxation tapes and exercises daily			

Writing down a list of things to do and sticking to it			
Being in a quiet room with no outside stimuli			
Using self-control as much as possible			
Biofeedback			
Staying away from alcohol and illegal drugs			
Staying home			
Avoiding overextending myself			
Stimulating the left brain (by paying attention to detail)			
Surrendering all credit cards, checks, etc., to a responsible person			
"Tying" self down emotionally to familiar surroundings			
Staying away from groups of people			
Reducing environmental stress			

"If my mania gets to be too much to handle, I should have the right to use hospitalization without feeling guilty. I like to try and use the most conservative treatment possible."

What other ways have you found to manage mania? _____

_____

_____

_____

_____

_____

Spirituality	Have tried successfully	Should use more often	Would like to try
Prayer			
Getting in touch with my spirituality			
Extensive meditation			

What other spiritual practices help you alleviate mania? _____

_____

_____

_____

_____

_____

_____

_____

Use Planning and Scheduling to Help Alleviate Mania

When experiencing a mania, a person may have so many ideas and so much energy that fragmentation and a lack of ability to focus can lead to a sense of not getting anything done, or not doing anything well.

The goal in mania is to stay grounded and focused enough to get something done, rather than being very scattered and initiating lots of projects that remain unfinished. A daily plan can help you meet this goal.

Refer to the lists of things you have to do and things you like to do in the chapter called "The Way Out of Depression." When planning your schedule for relieving mania, include activities from both lists.

As described in that chapter, rate your expectations of an activity on a scale of 0 to 5. A 0 indicates your expectation that you could do or enjoy a given activity; a 3 indicates that you think you could do an activity and/or would enjoy it; a 5 indicates that you expect to be able to do the activity very well or that you would enjoy it immensely. An "H" in your rating categorizes the activity as a have-to-do; an "E" is the label for an activity you normally enjoy. You might give an H5 to washing the dishes when you stuck to the activity and did a very good job. Lunch with a friend might rate E2 if for some reason your friend seemed distant and preoccupied. When you complete the activity, rate how well you did it or how much you actually enjoyed yourself. This exercise should reinforce the fact that your expectations and what actually happens can be very different.

Example of a Schedule for a Person Who Is Experiencing Mania

Date: Nov. 20   *Mood*: High, manic

Time	Planned Activity and Expectations	Actual Activity	How It Felt
7–8 a.m.	Get up, shower, dress, walk the dog *H3*	(As planned)	Fine, everything feels fine *H5*
8–9 a.m.	Cook and eat breakfast, wash the dishes, start the wash *H4*	Also made bed and cleaned bathroom	Kind of speedy *H4*
9–10 a.m.	Meditate for 1/2 hour; walk to post office and drug store *H4*	(As planned)	Fine *H5*
10–11 a.m.	Peer counseling with Sue *E4*	(As planned)	She is very understanding *E5*
11–12 Noon	Clean hall closet *H1*	(As planned)	Feels good to get things organized *H5*
12–1 p.m.	Buy a grinder for lunch, eat it in the park, go for a walk *E4*	(As planned)	Played on the swings for a while *E5*
1–2 p.m.	Relax for 1/2 hour with audio tape; read for 1/2 hour *E2*	(As planned)	Hard to relax, but it helps *E4*
2–3 p.m.	Write a list and shop for groceries *H2*	(As planned)	Hard to stick with list, bought a few things I didn't need *H2*
3–4 p.m.	Put away groceries, clean the kitchen *H2*	Also swept the porch and sidewalk	Cycling up at this time of day *H3*
4–5 p.m.	Counseling appointment *E3*	(As planned)	Hard to sit still *E1*
5–6 p.m.	Write in journal, write letters to friends *E5*	Wrote 4 pages in journal along with 2 letters	I want to write and write and write *E5*
6–7 p.m.	Fix dinner of vegetable stir fry and rice, eat dinner *E4*	Also watched PBS News	Ate too fast, want to slow down *E2*

Time	Planned Activity and Expectations	Actual Activity	How It Felt
7–8 p.m.	Walk *E3*	(As planned)	Feels good to be outdoors *E5*
8–9 p.m.	Work with clay *E4*	(As planned)	Feels really good *E5*
9–10 p.m.	Relax with audio tape *E3*	(As planned)	Helped me get to sleep *E3*

Make copies of the form below to plan daily schedules for yourself when you feel like you have signs of mania.

Time	Planned Activity and Expectations	Actual Activity	How It Felt
7–8 a.m.			
8–9 a.m.			
9–10 a.m.			
10–11 a.m.			
11–12 Noon			
12–1 p.m.			
1–2 p.m.			
2–3 p.m.			
3–4 p.m.			
4–5 p.m.			
5–6 p.m.			
6–7 p.m.			
7–8 p.m.			
8–9 p.m.			
9–10 p.m.			

How I felt on a day when I had signs of mania and did not follow a plan: _____

_____

_____

_____

How I felt on a day when I had signs of mania and followed a plan: _____

_____

_____

_____

Based on my experience, I intend to take the following action with regard to scheduling my days closely when I have signs of mania:

_____

_____

_____

_____

(time of day) _____ *is the best time for me to make plans when I am feeling manic.*

Breaking Tasks Down into Smaller Components

Breaking tasks down into smaller components can be helpful when you're experiencing mania. In mania you may be able to get a lot done, but you are moving so fast that the quality of your work may suffer. (I was nicknamed "Smash, Rip, and Ruin" by some friends when I was experiencing mania!) By analyzing tasks, and by having a clear picture of how to accomplish what you want, you can stabilize both your performance and your mood.

Make a list of tasks that are hard for you to accomplish satisfactorily when you're experiencing mania: _____

_____

_____

Take one of the tasks you listed, and break it down into smaller incremental components. This will make it easier for you to do a good job, even if you are experiencing mania.

Step 1 _____

_____

Step 2 _____

_____

Step 3 _____

_____

Step 4 _____

_____

Step 5 _____

_____

Step 6 _____

_____

Step 7 _____

_____

Step 8 _____

_____

People in the study added these thoughts:

"I shop with credit cards and leave all tickets on items for easier exchange and refunds, but sometimes outsmart myself by removing tickets so I can keep items."

"I use exercise coupled with warm, soothing beverages and baths—conscious relaxation."

"I seemed to be more easily influenced—especially by music. I learned to use music to gain control of my moods. When my moods or emotions are more in control, my thoughts change and become manageable, too."

"My husband uses my energy to hire for our home's benefit. He rented a jack hammer to tear up a sidewalk. 'Let me try,' I said, so he did. Four hours later he gave me a list of safe things to do. 'No problem,' I said, and three days later my energy was gone—and I felt much better."

Seeking Help for Dealing with Mania

Most people who responded to the study felt that getting help early was important in avoiding mania. **When do you seek help for mania?**

☐ when I have difficulty sleeping

☐ the moment I'm aware of "going up"

☐ when I start getting too busy

☐ when I'm very restless

☐ when I start to feel high

☐ when I'm psychotic

☐ at the instant of the switch

☐ when I'm out of control

☐ when I can't sit still

☐ when I'm acting differently

☐ when I'm hallucinating

☐ before I am out of reality

☐ when I feel too aggressive

☐ when it becomes stressful

☐ when I am using poor judgment

☐ when I'm unable to make plans

☐ when my therapist confronts me

☐ when I become grandiose and paranoid

☐ when I am a danger to myself or others

☐ when my spending is out of control

☐ when I feel the pressure of thoughts

☐ when the mania continues for more than two days

☐ when I start getting into trouble with other people

☐ when I become extremely tired and my body aches but I still can't slow down

☐ when the best I can do for myself is not enough to get me through

☐ when I feel like I have to act on a huge decision with real urgency

☐ when I start overdoing and feel irritable to the point of being enraged

☐ when I feel as though something is eating away at my brain and I will go berserk

☐ before I have lost three or four nights of sleep, spent all my money, and seduced half the world

What kind of help do you seek when you feel you need assistance in dealing with mania?

☐ psychiatric care   ☐ psychotherapy
☐ hospitalization   ☐ self-help groups
☐ crisis hotline   ☐ assurance, a hug
☐ self-help books   ☐ medication
☐ counseling   ☐ friends
☐ crisis clinic staff   ☐ 12-step program
☐ family

"I seek out someone who is understanding, has similar problems, knows how to be calm, and will not alienate me."

"My family is well educated and knows my views on the illness. They have my permission to get me the help I need when I am not capable of making decisions for myself."

"I let my roommate and parents have open communication with each other and my doctor. There have been times when I didn't notice the change coming on and they did. They were able to alert my doctor and watch me more closely, and some potential situations were stopped before they got out of hand. I had to swallow a lot of pride and let others step in when needed; but over time, we've reached a compromise of restrictions (no overprotectiveness) and extreme trust."

Inducing Mania

Some people who took part in the study have tried to induce mania, usually because of long-term chronic depression. However, overwhelmingly, the people in the study agreed that this is a *very dangerous thing to do and should be avoided under any circumstances.*

How People Want to Be Treated When They Are Experiencing Mania

How do you like to be treated when you're experiencing mania? These are some of the preferences described by people in the study. Check the descriptions that match your own feelings. *I want people to*

☐ get help for me as soon as possible to save me from having too many pieces to pick up after it is over

☐ understand that I am doing my best to cope

☐ treat me the same as when I'm feeling okay

☐ give me space, leave me alone

☐ treat me gently, calmly

☐ be tough, with an eye on reality

☐ treat me with respect

☐ treat me as a person who needs help

☐ treat me with support

☐ let me enjoy myself

☐ give me guidance

☐ support my self-care efforts

☐ make me aware

☐ treat me with compassion

☐ treat me firmly

☐ treat me with patience

☐ take me seriously

☐ treat me with love

☐ listen

☐ encourage me

☐ slow me down

☐ be available

☐ encourage me to avoid stress

☐ go with the mood, yet control my irrational behavior

☐ realize that I have a medical problem and it is not just me

☐ be calm, to smell the edge of sadness emanating from mania, to refuse to be sucked in by my garish, warped enthusiasm

In what other ways would you like to be treated when you're experiencing mania?

_____

_____

_____

_____

_____

What People Don't Want from Others When They Are Experiencing Mania

Some friends and family members always know the right things to do and say; others only make things worse! Participants in the study cited many behaviors and attitudes on the part of others that just make things worse. **Which ones can you relate to**?

- [ ] reinforcement of bizarre behavior
- [ ] taking advantage of me
- [ ] abandonment
- [ ] being treated coldly
- [ ] being treated with cruelty
- [ ] being stigmatized
- [ ] believing everything I say
- [ ] avoidance
- [ ] reacting with fear
- [ ] blaming me
- [ ] ridicule
- [ ] anger
- [ ] reserve
- [ ] indignation
- [ ] being ignored
- [ ] terseness
- [ ] hatred
- [ ] being rebuffed
- [ ] being teased
- [ ] reacting with disgust
- [ ] being patronizing
- [ ] acting exasperated
- [ ] reacting with confusion
- [ ] impatience
- [ ] expecting all I promise to be accomplished
- [ ] acting like they sense something is wrong with me
- [ ] giving me more things to do
- [ ] raising their expectations of me

"People worry more about me when I am 'high.' In many instances, my depressions are ignored. People want to subdue my behavior and expect me to stay in the background and not deal with my problems. I don't like being treated this way."

Describe what else you don't want from others when you're experiencing mania: _____

_____

_____

_____

_____

Handling Inappropriate Treatment

How should you handle treatment by others when you're experiencing mania? Here's what people in the study group said:

- ☐ ignore it
- ☐ try to educate others
- ☐ withdraw
- ☐ count to ten
- ☐ thoughtfully
- ☐ keep trying
- ☐ find understanding friends
- ☐ quietly
- ☐ give in more
- ☐ listen to music
- ☐ find the right help for myself
- ☐ address the issue and talk it out
- ☐ avoid people
- ☐ be patient
- ☐ go to the doctor
- ☐ think through their side of the situation
- ☐ apologize
- ☐ forgive
- ☐ maintain my dignity
- ☐ meditate
- ☐ assertively
- ☐ try to be in control as much as I can
- ☐ wait until I am more level and then handle it if the situation still seems unfair
- ☐ with judgment—but that is what is lacking when I am experiencing mania
- ☐ I like to be able to say, "I am out of control and need your help"
- ☐ later educate them and make my preferences known
- ☐ tell them to look at the positive aspects of my behavior
- ☐ tell them what I think about the way they treat me
- ☐ talk specifically about it in *I* and *them* statements when I am feeling in better control

Describe how you would like to change your response to people when they treat you inappropriately during the times when you are experiencing mania: _____

_____

_____

_____

Responding to "Slow Down"

When people are experiencing mania, others often tell them to "slow down," "relax," or "take it easy." People in the study responded in a variety of ways to such statements. **Which answers reflect the way you feel when people tell you to "slow down"?**

☐ okay

☐ I don't listen

☐ I don't like it

☐ I try to comply

☐ I become irritated

☐ I feel insulted

☐ I tell them that whatever I am doing is important

☐ I tell them I will when things ease up

☐ I feel agitated

☐ I feel confused

☐ I try to take control, and feel frustrated when I can't

☐ I feel resentment

☐ I ignore them

☐ I tell them to hurry up

☐ I feel puzzled

☐ I agree

☐ I feel embarrassed

☐ I feel that they have discovered I am sick

☐ I try to listen but am unable to

☐ I feel hurt

☐ I become more vigilant about myself

☐ it feels too good to care what others say

☐ I feel that they are laggards and spiritless

☐ I feel like they don't understand that I can't slow down

☐ I've learned about my own behavior from the observations of others

☐ I feel like they are in slow motion and should try to hurry up

☐ I feel they are wrong—there is nothing wrong with me

☐ they can't realize you have this power to ration things out quickly and accurately

☐ I feel that they are being wet blankets and don't want me to have fun

☐ I accept it from my spouse; from others I do not like it

In what other ways do you respond when people tell you to slow down? _____

_____

_____

_____

_____

Dealing with Embarrassment and Guilt

Many people have a difficult time dealing with the embarrassment and guilt that often follow mania. People in the study responded in the ways described below.

Mark which of these reactions reflects how you have handled the embarrassment or guilt when you've realized you've behaved in a bizarre manner. Think about which of these reactions seem most appropriate and/or in your own best interest.

When I feel embarrassed and guilty after a manic episode, I

☐ apologize

☐ don't blame myself, I blame the illness

☐ try to erase it from my mind

☐ get up and go on, swallow it, cope, etc.

☐ give matter-of-fact explanations

☐ laugh and let it blow over

☐ forgive myself

☐ try not to make it more than it was

☐ withdraw

☐ make amends

☐ turn it inwards

☐ send homemade "I'm sorry" cards

☐ cry

☐ feel like I hate myself, that I'm dirty

☐ try to pass it off

☐ try to avoid repeating that type of action

☐ avoid feeling guilty

☐ try to keep my dignity

- ☐ take the punishment
- ☐ make swift corrections of the situation
- ☐ attend Al-Anon meetings
- ☐ sometimes put distance and time between me and the person involved—I withdraw
- ☐ discuss it and face my feelings with a therapist or another understanding person
- ☐ realize that all the important people involved are health professionals or friends who understand the situation

"[I react with] lots of blushing, quivering, stammering, shying away and avoiding people."

"I have made mistakes the same as everyone else. I talk and apologize about them the same as others."

"Depression can be made worse and longer lasting by the things I've done during a mania. Sometimes I've offended people and then become afraid to rekindle a friendship with them. Sometimes people are also afraid to approach me again. I've lost some good friends because of this. For a number of years my life became stagnant because of my fear of interacting with people. The fear led to mistrust and resentment."

In order to ease the guilt and embarrassment for themselves, people in the study have used the following techniques. **Which ones have you used?**

- ☐ exercise to try and release energy
- ☐ counseling
- ☐ "come out" as manic depressive
- ☐ apply as much humor as possible
- ☐ have a strong support system
- ☐ have someone with me wherever I go
- ☐ ride it out
- ☐ cognitive therapy
- ☐ close down emotionally
- ☐ humor and openness
- ☐ leave room for unexpected stresses
- ☐ prevention through self-monitoring and use of self-help techniques
- ☐ avoid stressful activity
- ☐ progress to control highs
- ☐ make amends
- ☐ forgive myself
- ☐ join a support group
- ☐ maintain an easy lifestyle
- ☐ hide it

☐ keep my dignity

☐ go with the flow

☐ avoid overextending myself

☐ catch mania before it gets out of hand

☐ personal training and extensive self-practice

☐ jump back into life and start back up again

☐ be honest with those close enough to care or who want to care

☐ try not to think about it a lot

☐ discuss it and face the feelings with a psychiatrist, therapist, or friend

☐ educate others about these issues

☐ try to realize I have never done anything too bizarre and take comfort in that knowledge

☐ I decided it wasn't worth the effort to make most people understand

"Guilt can paralyze us from relating to others and this relating is vital if you have a mood disorder."

What other ways of easing guilt and embarrassment have you found to be useful following a period of mania? _____

_____

_____

_____

_____

How can you best handle your guilt and embarrassment in the future? _____

_____

_____

_____

_____

Increased Libido in Mania

Many people in the study have experienced increased libido when experiencing mania. These are some of the strategies they've used to manage it.

☐ masturbation

☐ having frequent sex with mate

☐ abstinence in some situations

☐ more active sex life

☐ going with the flow

☐ enjoying it

☐ no problem, spouse loves it

☐ fantasizing

☐ recognizing the feelings, but not reacting

☐ asking assistance from trusted friends

☐ staying away from situations that might be overtly tempting or compromising

How I plan to deal with the increased libido of mania in the future: _____

_____

_____

_____

_____

Dealing with Psychosis

People in the study reported that they frequently experienced psychosis (being out of touch with reality) when they were experiencing mania. Below are some of the ways in which they respond. Check the reactions that correspond with your own experience.

When I experience psychosis in mania, I

☐ let it happen

☐ call my therapist or counselor

☐ enjoy it but don't tell anyone

☐ tell people I trust

☐ reduce sensory input

☐ try to sleep and relax

☐ sort out delusion from reality

☐ remain calm and don't get frightened

☐ travel only with friends or family, not alone

☐ contact my doctor

☐ adjust my medication

In what other ways have you reacted to psychosis in mania? _____

_____

_____

_____

_____

My plan for dealing with psychosis in the future is: _____

_____

_____

_____

_____

Increased Clarity

Increased clarity is a symptom of mania experienced by many people who participated in the survey. They handle or use this clarity in a variety of ways. **Which of these ways have you used successfully?** *When my clarity increases as a symptom of mania, I*

- ☐ write a lot
- ☐ catch up on projects
- ☐ enjoy it
- ☐ go with it as long as it lasts
- ☐ use it to see the bigger picture more clearly
- ☐ express myself more
- ☐ get a lot done
- ☐ try to make changes
- ☐ take advantage of it
- ☐ realize that my thoughts are so quick, I am not making rational decisions
- ☐ set priorities more easily and come up with solutions or compromises
- ☐ recognize it as a delusion

"I decrease stimuli, regulate my time so I have less time to work on things, increase routine, remind myself that I am high and it is not dangerous."

"At first I doubt if my 'new' perceptions are reliable. Soon I am convinced they are truer and crisper than everyone else's."

"I ride it like a wave, because I know the time is limited. I try to pace myself so I don't overextend. I put together a stigma-busting workshop at a conference, which I thought was very creative and enlightened; but I am not sure whether anyone else did."

What other ideas do you have about ways in which to use this increased clarity? _____

_____

_____

_____

_____

Increase in Intensity of Mania Relative to the Time of Day

Many people experience an increase in the intensity of mania as the day goes on. People in the study use the strategies below for dealing with this increase in intensity. Check the strategies that are relevant to your own experience. *If my mania increases in intensity as the day wears on, I*

☐ lower my stressful activities   ☐ work hard

☐ read a good book or write letters   ☐ draw

☐ focus on self-care activities   ☐ write in my journal

☐ listen to music   ☐ do relaxation exercises

☐ try to mentally ride it out   ☐ talk it out with a supportive person

What other strategies have you used? _____

_____

_____

_____

_____

Very few people in the study said that their mania was more intense in the morning; but when this is the case, they deal with it by

☐ trying to accomplish what I need to get done during this time

☐ trying to do things to tire me out

If you experience more intense mania in the morning, what other ways do you have of managing it? _____

_____

_____

_____

_____

At what time of day is your mania most intense? _____

How are you going to deal with that in the future? _____

_____

_____

_____

Increased Intensity of Mania at Different Times of the Month

Thirteen people in the study noticed that their mania is more intense at different times of the month. Women tend to notice that their mania is more intense just before ovulation and menstruation. **When is mania most intense for you?** _____

Women in the study have developed various coping strategies to deal with the problem of these energy surges. If this has been a problem for you, **which coping strategies have you used?**

☐ trying not to make important decisions at that time

☐ reminding myself that this will pass

☐ taking PMS medication

☐ letting someone else handle my business at that time

☐ scheduling activities heavily then

☐ exercising five or six times a week

☐ charting menstrual cycle to maintain awareness and better utilize upsurge of energy in a constructive way

☐ enjoying it, because I am more relaxed at this time (pre-ovulation)

Other: _____

_____

How do you plan to deal with this problem in the future? _____

_____

_____

_____

_____

_____

_____

Seasonal Patterns and Mania

Twenty-eight people noted a seasonal pattern to their mania. Most of them found that they are more likely to experience mania in the spring, with summer ranking second and fall ranking third. Only a few people said they had experienced mania in the winter. **If you have noticed a seasonal pattern to your mania, what is it?** _____

Which of these ways of dealing with these patterns has helped you?

☐ be aware
☐ go out a lot
☐ regular medication checks
☐ monitor carefully at these times
☐ rely on family to help me through
☐ try to keep it under control
☐ have health care appointments more often

☐ enjoy it
☐ expect the unexpected
☐ save projects to do at this time
☐ channel energy into projects
☐ relax as much as possible
☐ go with the flow

☐ in the spring I sleep on the west instead of the east side of house to keep morning light from setting it off

How do you plan to deal with the seasonal aspects of mania in the future? _____

_____

_____

_____

_____

_____

You have just explored your experience of mania in an in-depth manner. Based on what you have discovered through this exercise, **what changes are you going to make in the way you handle mania?** _____

_____

_____

_____

_____

_____

_____

What to Do When You Are Experiencing Symptoms of Mania

Photocopy this section—or rewrite it to suit your own needs; then post it on your refrigerator.

- Use your support system. Let your supporters know how you are feeling. Talk with them for as long as you need to, expressing all emotions that come up.

- Stay at home or in familiar surroundings. Steer clear of stimulating environments such as bars or dances.

- Reduce the stress in your environment. Keep away from stressful people.

- Make a list of things to do for the day and stick to it.

- Regulate your activities to avoid overstimulation. Restrict yourself to activities that are quiet and soothing, such as a long, slow walk; a long, warm bath; a relaxing swim; sitting for a while in a steam room or hot tub; listening to quiet music; reading a soothing book; watching a nature show on TV.

- Keep a list of things you can do to use up excess energy, such as washing the floor, weeding the garden, painting, cleaning out closets; but make sure that these activities are not overstimulating.

- Practice relaxation techniques several times during the day.

- Avoid sugar, caffeine, and alcohol. Eat regular meals. Do not skip meals. Do not eat too much of any one thing.

- Do not make any major decisions. Put off decisions until you feel calmer.

- Do not commit yourself to extra activities outside your usual routine (unless they're things that you've chosen for the express purpose of burning up excessive energy).

- Avoid spending money. Give your credit cards and money to a trusted support person.

- Regularly stop what you're doing, bring your focus onto yourself, and ask yourself how you are doing. Keep your mind focused on what you are doing. Don't allow your thoughts to ramble or become obsessive.

- If all of your relaxation techniques are not working to put you to sleep, and you are not sleeping, get help from a doctor right away. Loss of sleep exacerbates mania.

- Get help before things get out of hand. Do not hesitate to call a doctor or your counselor if needed.

9

Using a Chart to Keep Your Moods Controlled

Develop a chart listing your own early warning signs that your mood needs attention. While many of these signs are experienced almost universally by people who have ups and downs of mood, others may be unique to you. That's why it's essential to create a chart that's tailored to you individually.

Check the chart at the same time each day to help you determine how you're feeling. The chart will enable you to respond early, before the situation gets out of hand and is harder to bring back under control.

Even small changes are important and need to be recognized. It's particularly important to use the chart regularly in those seasons when you have had problems before, or in times of acute stress, such as when you are beginning a new job, beginning a new relationship, embarking on parenthood, or suffering a loss or illness.

After you design your chart, make a good supply of copies to have available. I make my charts up with space for checking off moods and behaviors for one week. That way I can get an overview of how I'm doing. If your chart is as long as mine, you may want to use legal-size paper, so you can get it all on one side for easy review.

Save charts after you have used them. This record will allow you and your health care team to analyze patterns in your mood swings.

Get input on developing your chart from your health care professionals and other members of your support system. They may be able to bring to your attention danger signs that you may have overlooked or ignored. The chart will also assist them in under-standing and making appropriate recommendations about your treatment. When the chart is complete, give everyone on your support team a copy. This will give them a handy reference for checking in on how you're feeling.

This is the chart that I use. Remember—you have to tailor it to your own needs, based on your knowledge about your own patterns of thought and behavior.

Warning Signs
Daily Checklist

I will be honest with myself in this assessment. When I note signs of mania or depression, I will let my support system know and will take the necessary corrective action.

Month and Year _____

Early Warning Signs of Depression:	Mon.	Tues.	Wed.	Thurs.	Fri.	Sat.	Sun.
Excessive appetite							
Lethargy							
Extreme fatigue							
Difficulty exercising							
Unwillingness to ask for things							
Down on self							
Down on future							
Low self-confidence							
Procrastination							
Avoid crowds							
Irritable, impatient							
Negative attitude							
Insecurity							
Hard time getting up							
Sleep problems							
Poor judgment							
Obsessive thoughts							
Repetitive words, actions							
Unable to concentrate							
Misperceptions							
Destructive risk-taking							
Suicidal thoughts							
Paranoia							
Unable to experience pleasure							

Early Warning Signs of Mania:	Mon.	Tues.	Wed.	Thurs.	Fri.	Sat.	Sun.
Insomnia							
Argumentative							
All-knowing							
Controlling							
Overcommitting							
High energy							
Racing thoughts							
Very talkative							
Obsessive thoughts							
Sexually overactive							
Thrill-seeking							
Irresponsible risk-taking							
Poor judgment							
Change in appetite							
Self-medicating							
Drug or alcohol abuse							

What to Do Every Day (*Check off activities or behaviors that you manage to fit into each day*)	Mon.	Tues.	Wed.	Thurs.	Fri.	Sat.	Sun.
Eat well (high carbohydrate, low fat, no sugar)							
Exercise							
Take good care of self							
Be with positive people							
Get plenty of light							
Spend at least one hour outside							
Talk with support system							
Have fun							

Medications (*Record the medications* *you use each day*)	Mon.	Tues.	Wed.	Thurs.	Fri.	Sat.	Sun.

Use the early warning signs from the previous two chapters, "The Way Out of Depression" and "Coming Down from Mania," as well as input from people in your support system, to help you in developing your personal chart of early warning signs. Make copies of your chart for ongoing use (here's a sample of a format you can use).

Early Warning Signs

Month and Year _____

Early Warning Signs of Depression:	Mon.	Tues.	Wed.	Thurs.	Fri.	Sat.	Sun.

Early Warning Signs of Mania:	Mon.	Tues.	Wed.	Thurs.	Fri.	Sat.	Sun.

What to Do Every Day (*Check off activities or behaviors that you manage to fit into each day*)	Mon.	Tues.	Wed.	Thurs.	Fri.	Sat.	Sun.

Medications (*Record the medications* *you use each day*)	Mon.	Tues.	Wed.	Thurs.	Fri.	Sat.	Sun.

Comments: _____

_____

_____

_____

Necessary Action: _____

_____

_____

_____

10

Developing and Using a Wellness Recovery Action Plan

Since I have been using WRAP my symptoms are much less frequent, they are not nearly as severe, and I can quickly relieve them and get on with doing the things I like to do.

Several years ago I was teaching the various skills and strategies that have been found useful in relieving symptoms of depression, manic depression, and other "psychiatric symptoms" to a group in northern Vermont. At the end of the program they felt that they needed a better system for using these tools. Working together, we came up with the Wellness Recovery Action Plan (WRAP). This plan is now being used extensively all over the country. Anecdotal reporting from people who are using this system indicates that it's working by letting people feel that they can be proactive in helping themselves feel better more often and improving the quality of their lives. People are finding that by identifying and working with uncomfortable feelings when they're first noticed, they can help themselves feel better sooner and avoid more upsetting feelings and incidents.

The Wellness Recovery Action Plan is a structured system for monitoring uncomfortable and distressing feelings like depression, and, through planned responses, reducing, modifying, or eliminating those feelings. WRAP also includes plans for getting the support you need when the way you feel has made it impossible for you to continue to make decisions, take care of yourself, and keep yourself safe. Every aspect of this plan was developed by people who feel they might need to use it at some time.

To implement this plan for yourself you will need a three-ring binder, a set of five tabs or dividers, and lined three-ring paper. This is a five-part system developed by you, *the person who experiences the depression or other symptoms.* While you may be assisted in developing the plan by people you choose, it cannot be developed for you by another person. Self-management is a very personal task.

Developing a Wellness Toolbox

The first step in developing a WRAP is to identify and list those things you do now, or feel you *can* do, to stay well or help yourself feel better when you're not feeling well. It is an inventory of good ideas, a journal of things you have tried or want to try. This is your Wellness Toolbox. You will refer to this list for ideas when you are developing your plan. Some ideas include:

- eating three healthy meals a day

- drinking plenty of water

- getting to bed by ten o'clock every night

- doing something you enjoy, like playing a musical instrument, watching a favorite TV show, knitting, or reading a good book

- exercising

- doing a relaxation exercise

- writing in your journal

- talking to a friend on the telephone

- taking medications

- taking vitamins and other food supplements

You can get more ideas for your Wellness Toolbox from other chapters in this book and from other resource books. You can also ask your friends and family members for suggestions on things you might add to your list, including things that they have used for themselves and things that they have noticed have been helpful to you. Add to your Wellness Toolbox list whenever you have a new idea or learn something helpful.

There is space allowed after each section of this Wellness Recovery Action Plan for you to write your responses. You can list your wellness tools here and copy them to the front of your three-ring binder as though they were your "preface." Or, you might wish to write them directly onto your three-ring binder paper for easy reference as you develop the rest of your WRAP.

Wellness Toolbox

_____

_____

_____

_____

_____

_____

_____

_____

_____

Daily Maintenance List

The first section of your WRAP is called "Daily Maintenance List." Write that on the first tab and insert it in the binder, followed by several sheets of filler paper. The purpose of this section is to 1) describe yourself when you are well (so you can refer to this list when you have been having such a hard time that you cannot remember what it's like to feel well), 2) list those things you must do every day to keep yourself well, and 3) list those things you need to consider doing each day.

On the first page, describe yourself when you're feeling all right so you can refer back to how you really want to feel. If you can't remember how you feel when you are well, describe how you would like to feel. Make it easy. Do it in list form. Some descriptive words that others have used include: "bright," "talkative," "outgoing," "energetic," "humorous," "reasonable," "argumentative," "compulsive."

What I'm Like When I'm Feeling Well

_____

_____

_____

_____

_____

_____

_____

On the next page, describe those things you need to be sure to do every day to maintain your wellness. Writing them down and reminding yourself daily to do these things is an important step toward wellness. When you're starting to feel "out of sorts," you can often trace it back to not doing something on this list. You can refer to your Wellness Toolbox list for ideas. Make sure you don't put so many things on this list that you couldn't possibly do them. This is the part of my WRAP that is most important to me and that I use most frequently.

Following are some ideas for a Daily Maintenance List:

- eat three healthy meals each day and three healthy snacks that include servings of whole grain foods, vegetables, and smaller portions of protein

- drink at least six eight-ounce glasses of water

- avoid caffeine, sugar, junk foods, alcohol

- exercise for at least one half hour

- get exposure to outdoor light for at least one half hour

- take medications and vitamin supplements

- have twenty minutes of relaxation or meditation time

- write in my journal for at least fifteen minutes

- spend at least one half hour enjoying a fun, affirming, and/or creative activity

- check in with my partner for at least ten minutes

- check in with myself about how I'm doing physically, emotionally, spiritually

- go to work, if a week day

Daily Maintenance List

_____

_____

_____

_____

_____

_____

_____

_____

On the next page, make a reminder list for yourself of things you *might* need to do each day. Having this check-in list reduces the risk of stress from forgetting or avoiding tasks and helps assure that you will continue to stay well. Write "Do I need to (or would it be good to):" at the top of this page and then list things like:

- set up an appointment with one of my health care professionals

- spend time with a good friend or be in touch with my family

- do peer counseling

- do some housework

- buy groceries

- do the laundry

- have some personal time

- plan something fun for the evening or weekend

- write some letters

- go to a support group

Reminder List of Things I Might Need to Do Every Day

_____

_____

_____

_____

_____

_____

_____

_____

These elements make up the first section of your WRAP binder. When any part of your plan stops working for you, you can tear out the pages and write some new ones.

You will be surprised at how much better you'll feel after just taking these positive steps in your own behalf.

Triggers

To start with, write "Triggers" on the next tab and insert it into your WRAP binder, along with several sheets of paper.

Triggers are external events or circumstances that may produce feelings that are very uncomfortable. You may even feel like you're getting ill. A trigger may be fairly universal, or it may be something personal to you. It is normal to have reactions to events in our lives, but if we don't notice and respond to our feelings, they may actually cause a worsening of our symptoms. Being aware of triggers and developing plans to deal with triggering events when they come up will increase your ability to cope and help you avoid the development of severe symptoms.

When listing your triggers, write those that are likely to occur, such as those listed in the example. It's not important to project horrible things that might happen, like a war, a natural disaster, or a huge loss. If such things occur, you might use the actions you describe in the triggers action plan more often and increase the length of time you use them.

On the first page after the tab, write down those things that, if they happened, might cause an increase in your symptoms. They may have triggered or increased symptoms in the past. Some examples of common triggers include:

- the anniversary dates of losses or trauma

- traumatic news events

- too much to do, feeling overwhelmed

- family friction

- a relationship ending

- spending too much time alone

- being judged, criticized, teased or put down

- financial problems or getting a big bill

- physical illness

- sexual harassment

- hateful outbursts by others

- aggressive-sounding noises (sustained)

- being around someone who has treated you badly

Triggers

_____

_____

_____

_____

_____

_____

_____

_____

_____

_____

On the next page, referring to your Wellness Toolbox, develop a plan of what you can do to keep your reactions from becoming more serious symptoms when your triggers come up. Include those tools that have worked for you in the past and ideas you have learned from others. Your plan might include:

- make sure I do everything on my daily maintenance program

- call a support person and asking them to listen while I talk through the situation

- do a half-hour relaxation exercise

- write in my journal for at least one half hour

- ride my stationary bicycle for forty-five minutes

- play the piano or work on a fun activity for one hour

Triggers Action Plan

_____

_____

_____

_____

_____

_____

_____

_____

If you find yourself triggered and you do these things and they are helpful, that's great. If they are only somewhat helpful, you may want to revise your action plan. If they are not helpful, take out those pages and develop a new plan.

Early Warning Signs

Write "Early Warning Signs" on the next tab and insert it and several more sheets of paper in your binder.

Early warning signs are internal and may be unrelated to stressful situations or external events. They may come in response to triggers as well, but in any event you must learn to recognize them. In spite of your best efforts at reducing symptoms, you may begin to experience early warning signs, subtle signs of change that indicate you may need to take some further action. Reviewing the early warning signs list regularly helps you to become more aware of them, allowing you to take action before they worsen.

On the first page in this section make a list of early warning signs you have noticed in the past. They might include things like:

- anxiety
- nervousness
- forgetfulness
- inability to experience pleasure
- lack of motivation
- feeling slowed down or speeded up
- being uncaring
- avoiding others or isolating
- being obsessed with something that doesn't really matter
- the beginning of irrational thought patterns
- feeling unconnected to my body
- increased irritability
- increased negativity
- not keeping appointments

You can ask your friends, family members, and other supporters for early warning signs that they've noticed, if you want to.

Early Warning Signs

_____

_____

_____

_____

_____

_____

_____

_____

_____

_____

_____

On the next pages, develop an action plan for responding to your early warning signs, again referring to your Wellness Toolbox for ideas. Some of the things you list may be the same as those you wrote on your triggers action plan. If you notice these early symptoms, take action while you still can.

Following is a sample plan for dealing with early warning signs:

- do the things on my daily maintenance plan whether I feel like it or not

- tell a supporter/counselor how I am feeling and ask for their advice; ask them to help me figure out how to take the action they suggest

- peer counsel at least once a day

- do at least one focusing exercise a day

- do at least three ten-minute relaxation exercises each day

- write in my journal for at least fifteen minutes each day

- spend at least one hour involved in an activity I enjoy each day until early warning signs diminish

- ask others to take over my household responsibilities for a day

I also might:

- check in with my physician or other health care professional

- spend some time with my pet(s)

- read a good book

- dance, sing, listen to good music, play a musical instrument

- exercise

- go fishing

- go fly a kite

Early Warning Signs Action Plan

_____

_____

_____

_____

_____

_____

_____

_____

_____

_____

Again, if you use this plan and it doesn't help you feel better, revise your plan, or write a new one.

When Things Are Breaking Down

Write "When Things are Breaking Down," or something that means that to you, on the next tab and insert it into your binder with some paper.

In spite of your best efforts, your symptoms may progress to the point where they are very uncomfortable, serious, and even dangerous, but you are still able to take some action on your own behalf. This is a very important time. It is necessary to take immediate action to prevent a crisis or having your symptoms get out of control. I define it as that time when you can still do for yourself the things that you need to do to help yourself feel better and keep yourself safe.

On the first page of this section, make a list of symptoms that would indicate to you that "things are breaking down or getting much worse." Remember that symptoms and signs vary from person to person. What may mean "things are getting much worse" to one person may mean a "crisis" to another. Some of the signs or symptoms might include:

- feeling very oversensitive and fragile

- irrational responses to events and the actions of others

- feeling very needy

- being unable to sleep

- sleeping all the time

- avoiding eating

- wanting to be totally alone

- substance abuse

- taking out anger on others

- chain smoking

- eating too much or not enough

Signs That Things Are Breaking Down

_____

_____

_____

_____

_____

_____

_____

_____

_____

On the next page in your binder, write an action plan that you think will help reduce your symptoms when they have progressed to this point. The plan now needs to be very directive with fewer choices and very clear instructions. Some ideas for an action plan include:

- call my doctor or other health care professional, ask for and follow their instructions

- call and talk as long as I need to my supporters

- arrange for someone to stay with me around the clock until my symptoms subside

- make arrangements so I can get help right away if my symptoms worsen

- make sure I am doing everything on my Daily Maintenance List

- arrange and take at least three days off from any responsibilities

- have at least two peer counseling sessions

- do three deep breathing relaxation exercises

- do two focusing exercises

- write in my journal for at least one half hour

Ask myself if I need:

- a physical examination, doctors appointment, or a consultation with another health care provider, or

- to have medications checked

When Things Are Breaking Down Action Plan

_____

_____

_____

_____

_____

_____

_____

_____

_____

As with the other plans, if this plan doesn't work, or doesn't work as well as you wish it had, develop a different plan or revise the one you used.

Crisis Planning

On the next tab write "Crisis Plan." Copy the form at the end of this chapter on binder paper and insert in your notebook.

In spite of our best planning and assertive action on our own behalf, we may find ourselves in a crisis situation, a situation where others will need to take over responsibility for our care. This is a difficult situation, one that no one likes to face. You may feel like you're totally out of control. Writing a clear crisis plan when you're well, to instruct others about how to care for you when you're not well, keeps you in control even when it seems like things are totally out of control. It will keep your family members and friends from wasting time trying to figure out what to do to help you. With a crisis plan, they will know what to do, saving everyone frustration and insuring that your needs will be met and that you will get better as quickly as possible.

A crisis plan needs to be developed when you are feeling well. However, you cannot do it quickly. Decisions like this take time, often requiring collaboration with health care professionals, family members, and other supporters. Over the next few pages, I will share with you information and ideas that others have included on their crisis plans. It may help you in developing your own.

This part of the plan differs from the others because this part will be used by other people, while you alone will implement the other four sections of the WRAP. You need to write this section so that it is easy to understand. While you may have developed other parts of the plan rather quickly, this part may take some time and some collaboration with others. Don't rush the process. Work at it for a while, leaving it and returning to it over the course of several days, until you have developed a crisis plan that you feel will work for you. Once you have completed your crisis plan, give copies of it to the other people you consider your supporters.

You may want to make another copy of the form to write a draft of your plan, writing you final version to be included in your binder and to make copies for your supporters when you feel comfortable with what you have developed.

In the first part of your crisis plan, write what you are like when you're feeling well, for use by people who might be trying to help you but don't know you well. You can copy it from the beginning of section 1 of your WRAP.

In the second part, describe those symptoms that would indicate to others that they need to take over responsibility for your care and make decisions on your behalf. This is hard for everyone. No one likes to think that someone else will have to take over responsibility for their care. And yet, through a careful, well-developed description of symptoms that would indicate to others that you need them to take over, you can retain fundamental control of your situation.

Allow yourself plenty of time to complete this section. Ask your friends, family members, and other supporters for input. However, always remember that the final determination is up to you. Be very clear in describing the symptoms. Don't try to summarize. Use as many words as it takes to describe each symptom.

Your symptoms might include:

- being unable to recognize family members and friends

- incorrectly identifying family and friends

- uncontrollable pacing, unable to stay still

- neglecting personal hygiene (for days)

- not cooking or doing any housework (for days)

- destructive to property (throwing things, etc.)

- not understanding what people are saying

- thinking I am someone I am not

- thinking I have the ability to do something I don't

- self-destructive behavior

- abusive or violent behavior

- substance abuse

- not getting out of bed at all

- refusing to eat or drink

The third section of the crisis plan lists those people who you'd like to take over when the symptoms you have listed come up. They can be family members, friends, or health care professionals. When you first develop this plan it may be mostly health care professionals. But as you work on developing your support system, try to rely more heavily on family members and friends in your crisis plan. You want to shift this focus because health care professionals are not consistently available. Using natural supports is less expensive, less invasive, and more natural.

It's best to have at least five people on your list of supporters. If you have only one or two, they might not be available when you really need them (like when they go on vacation or are sick). If you don't have that many supporters now, you may need to work on developing new and closer relationships with people by doing things like going to support groups, community activities, and volunteering.

You may want to name some people for certain tasks, like taking care of the children or paying the bills, and others for tasks like staying with you and taking you to health care appointments.

There may be health care professionals or family members who have made decisions that were not according to your wishes in the past. They could inadvertently get involved in your care again. So write on your plan, "I *do not* want the following people involved in any way in my care or treatment." Then list those people and why you don't want them involved. They may be people who have treated you badly in the past, have made poor decisions, or who get too upset when you're having a hard time.

Many people like to include a section that describes how they want possible disputes between their supporters settled. For instance, you may want to say that a majority of your supporters need to agree, or that a particular person or two people make the determination in case of a disagreement.

In part four of your crisis plan, name your physician, pharmacist, and any other health care providers, along with their phone numbers. Then list: 1) the medications you are currently using, the dosage, and why you are using them, 2) those medications you would prefer to take if additional medications became necessary, like those that have worked well for you in the past, and why you would choose those, 3) those medications that would be acceptable to you (as opposed to preferable) if medications became necessary, why you would choose those, and whether there are any side effects that will have to be managed, and 4) those medications that must be avoided, and why they should be avoided (for instance, if you're allergic to them).

In part five of your crisis plan, describe particular treatments that you would prefer in a crisis situation and also those that you would want to avoid. State your reasons for preferring or avoiding a treatment. The reason may be as simple as "this treatment has [or has not] worked in the past," or you may have some stronger reservations about a treatment. Treatments might include drug therapy, radiation, massage, physical therapy, and acupuncture.

In part six, describe a plan for your care that would allow you to stay at home, in your community, or part of your time at home and part of your time in the community, getting the care and attention you need in this hard time. Many people who would prefer to stay at home rather than be hospitalized set up these kinds of plans. You may need to ask your family members, friends, and community services what options are available for you.

Think about your family and friends. Would they be able to take turns providing you with care? Could transportation be arranged to health care appointments, or could they take you to health care appointments? Is there a program in your community that could provide you with care part of the time, with family members and friends taking care of you the rest of the time?

In part seven of your crisis plan, describe the treatment facilities you would like to use if family members and friends cannot provide you with care or if your condition requires hospital care. Your options may be limited by the facilities available in your area and your insurance coverage. If you're not sure which facilities you would like to use, talk to family members and friends about it and call the facilities to request information that may help you in making a decision. Also include a list of treatment facilities you would like to avoid—places where you have received poor treatment in the past.

In part eight, describe what your supporters can do for you that will help you feel better. This part of the plan is very important and deserves careful attention. In this section, describe what you want your supporters to do for you when you are in crisis—what would help you feel better or more comfortable. This section takes a lot of thought. You may want to ask your supporters and other health care professionals for ideas.

Some ideas of things others could do for you to help you feel better include:

- listen to me without giving me advice, judging me, or criticizing me
- hold me
- let me pace
- encourage me to move and/or help me move
- lead me through a relaxation or stress-reduction technique
- peer counsel with me
- provide me with materials so I can draw or paint
- give me the space to express my feelings
- don't talk to me (or do talk to me)
- encourage me, reassure me
- feed me good food
- make sure I take my vitamins and other medications
- play me comic videos
- play me good music (list the kind)
- just let me rest

Include a list of specific tasks you would like others to do for you, who you would like to do each task, and any specific instructions they might need. These tasks might include:

- buying groceries
- watering the plants
- feeding the pets
- taking care of the children
- paying the bills
- taking out the rubbish

- doing the laundry

You may also want to include a list of things that you do not want others to do for you, things they might do because they think it would be helpful but that might even be harmful or worsen the situation. They might include:

- forcing you to do anything, such as walking

- scolding you

- becoming impatient with you

- taking away your cigarettes or coffee

- talking continuously

Part nine, the last part of this plan, gives your supporters information on how to know when you have recovered enough to take care of yourself, so that they no longer need to use this plan. Some examples include:

- when I am eating at least two meals a day

- when I am awake for six hours a day

- when I can stand up for five minutes

- when I am taking care of my personal hygiene needs

- when I can carry on a good conversation

- when I can easily walk around the house

You have now completed your crisis plan. Update it when you learn new information or change your mind about things. Give your supporters new copies of your crisis plan each time you revise it.

You can help assure that your crisis plan will be followed by signing it in the presence of two witnesses. It will further increase its potential for use if you appoint and name a durable power of attorney—a person who could legally make decisions for you if you were not able to make them for yourself. Since the legality of these documents varies from state to state, you cannot be absolutely sure the plan will be followed. However, following these steps is your best assurance that your wishes will be honored.

You have now completed your Wellness Recovery Action Plan. At first you will need to spend fifteen or twenty minutes each day reviewing your plan so you can take the actions that will be helpful to you. Most people report that morning, either before or after breakfast, is the best time to review the information in the binder. As you become familiar with your triggers, symptoms, and plans, you will find that the review process takes less time and that you will know how to respond without even referring to the book.

Begin with the first page in section 1, Daily Maintenance Plan. Review the list of how you behave and seem if you are all right. If you are feeling good, do the things on your list of things you need to do every day to keep yourself well. Also refer to the page of things you *may* need to do to see if anything rings a bell with you. If it does, make a note to yourself to include it in your day.

If you are not feeling all right, review the other sections to see where the symptoms you are experiencing fit in. Then follow the action plan you have designed. For instance, if you feel very anxious because you got a big bill in the mail or had an argument with your spouse, follow the plan in the triggers section. If you noticed some early warning signs (subtle signs that your symptoms might be worsening), such as forgetting things or avoiding answering the phone, follow the plan you designed for the early warning signs section. If you notice symptoms that indicate things are breaking down, like having a continuously pounding headache or having more intense pain, follow the plan you developed for when things are breaking down.

If you are in a crisis situation, the plan will help you to realize that fact so you can let your supporters know that you need them to take over. However, in certain crisis situations, you may not be aware or willing to admit that you are in crisis. This is why having a strong team of supporters is so important. They will observe the symptoms you have reported and take over responsibility for your care, whether or not you're willing to admit you are in a crisis at that time. Distributing your crisis plan to your supporters and discussing it with them is absolutely essential to your safety and well-being.

I use my WRAP to address my fibromyalgia (a chronic pain condition), episodes of deep depression, and occasional experiences of extreme mood swings. My level of wellness and the quality of my life have improved dramatically as a result of dealing with my life in this structured way. I also find I am taking a lot more time to do the things I really enjoy. My life feels richer. It has definitely been worth the time and attention this plan requires.

Personal Crisis Plan

To be used if the circumstances described in Part 2 of this document occur

Name: _____   Date: _____

Part 1: What I'm Like When I'm Feeling Well

_____

_____

_____

_____

_____

Part 2: Symptoms

If I have several of the following signs and/or symptoms, my supporters, named on the next page, need to take over responsibility for my care and make decisions on my behalf based on the information in this plan.

_____

_____

_____

_____

_____

_____

_____

_____

_____

_____

_____

Part 3: Supporters

If this plan needs to be activated. I want the following people to take over for me.

Name   Connection/Role   Phone Number

_____

Specific Tasks for This Person

_____

_____

Name   Connection/Role   Phone Number

_____

Specific Tasks for This Person

_____

_____

Name   Connection/Role   Phone Number

_____

Specific Tasks for This Person

_____

_____

Name   Connection/Role   Phone Number

_____

Specific Tasks for This Person

_____

_____

I *do not* want the following people involved in any way in my care or treatment:

Name   I don't want them involved because: (optional)

_____

Name   I don't want them involved because: (optional)

_____

Settling Disputes Between Supporters

If my supporters disagree on a course of action to be followed, I would like the dispute to be settled in the following way:

_____

_____

Part 4: Medications

Physician _____   Psychiatrist _____

Other Heath Care Providers _____

_____

_____

Insurance _____   Numbers _____

Pharmacy _____   Pharmacist _____

Allergies _____

_____

Medication or health care preparations I am using   Dosage

_____

Purpose

_____

Medication or health care preparations I am using   Dosage

_____

Purpose

_____

Medication or health care preparations I am using   Dosage

_____

Purpose

_____

Medication or health care preparations I am using   Dosage

_____

Purpose

_____

Medication or health care preparations to use if necessary   Dosage

_____

Purpose

_____

Medication or health care preparations to use if necessary   Dosage

_____

Purpose

_____

** Medication or health care preparations to avoid   Why?

_____

Purpose

_____

** Take special note

Part 5: Treatments

Treatment

_____

When and how to use this treatment

_____

Treatment

_____

When and how to use this treatment

_____

Treatment

_____

When and how to use this treatment

_____

Treatment

_____

Treatments to avoid   Why?

_____

_____

_____

_____

_____

_____

Part 6: Home/Community Care/Respite Center

If possible, follow the following care plan

_____

_____

_____

_____

_____

Part 7: Hospital or Other Treatment Facilities

If I need hospitalization or treatment in a treatment facility, I prefer the following facilities in order of preference:

Name   Contact Person   Phone Number

_____

I like this facility because

_____

Name   Contact Person   Phone Number

_____

I like this facility because

_____

Name   Contact Person   Phone Number

_____

I like this facility because

_____

Avoid using the following hospital or treatment facilities

Name   Reason to avoid using

_____

Part 8: Help from Others

Please do the following things that would help reduce my symptoms, make me more comfortable, and keep me safe.

_____

_____

_____

_____

_____

_____

I need (name the person) _____ to (task) _____

_____

I need (name the person) _____ to (task) _____

_____

I need (name the person) _____ to (task) _____

_____

I need (name the person) _____ to (task) _____

_____

Do not do the following. I won't help and it may even make things worse.

_____

_____

_____

_____

Part 9: Inactivating the Plan

The following signs, lack of symptoms, or actions indicate that my supporters no longer need to use this plan.

_____

_____

_____

I developed this plan on (date) _____ with the help of _____

Any plan with a more recent date supersedes this one.

Signed _____ Date _____

Witness _____ Date _____

Witness _____ Date _____

Attorney _____ Date _____

Durable Power of Attorney _____

Substitute for Durable Power of Attorney _____

Also have this document signed and stamped by a notary public.

Any Personal Crisis Plan developed on a date after the dates listed above takes precedence over this document.

PART II

Support Is Essential

11

Building a Strong Support System

I know of others who have done research similar to yours. I believe they found from respondents that the most common reason for recovery is that someone believed in them. This is most often the catalyst in recovery.

Everyone needs at least five good friends or supporters they can call on when they need someone to talk to—people who can count on you when they need a friend as well. Family members and partners are also candidates for your support network. Choose people whom you love and trust. They should be people who can

- *Empathize with you*, be able to say, "I understand what you are going through," and "I can see that this is a really difficult time for you."

- *Affirm your individuality and your strengths*; treat you with love, humor, and honesty; validate and encourage you and your dreams.

- *Play with you*—sing, dance, join you in whatever fun activity you both enjoy!

- *Be open-minded*, let you describe how you are, what you feel, and what you want.

- *Accept your ups and downs* without being judgmental, who can help you as well as ask for your help.

- *Work with you* as you decide on your next best step, and support you as you carry through.

List five people on whom you can count in these ways. (These may or may not include the four supporters you named in Chapter 4.)

1. _____

2. _____

3. _____

4. _____

5. _____

This is a very hard exercise for many people. When they realize that they have no one, or only one or two people, it makes them feel very bad and increases their feelings of loneliness and isolation. If this is your reaction, don't give up. There is a lot you can do to change the situation. Changing this situation is very important to your wellness.

☐ *I wish I had more friends and a stronger support system.*

Many people in the study expressed feelings of loneliness and isolation. They feel deserted by family and friends; often these feelings are based in reality. The resulting social isolation often worsens their mood disorder.

These are some of the reasons that people in the study gave for the fact that they have a hard time making and keeping friends. **Which ones apply to you?**

☐ low self-esteem

☐ tend to be very needy and draining

☐ unreliable

☐ unpredictable

☐ have a hard time reaching out

☐ become overly dependent on one or a few people, wearing them down

☐ inappropriate behavior that embarrasses and turns off others

☐ lack of social skills

The kind of support people in the study said they wanted from their support system varies. **What do you want from your support system?**

☐ mutual support   ☐ companionship

☐ someone to talk to   ☐ someone who will listen

☐ understanding   ☐ caring

☐ counsel   ☐ empathy

☐ acceptance   ☐ sharing

☐ advocacy   ☐ monitoring

☐ diversion   ☐ activities

☐ time   ☐ correspondence

☐ phone calls

Other ways you would like a friend to be, and things you would like a friend to do:

_____

_____

_____

You may find that no one person can do all these things. Some supporters do some things well and other will do other things well.

Keys to Building and Keeping a Strong Support System

Use all the techniques described in this book to keep your moods as stable as possible. Enhance your wellness every way you know how.

I use the following techniques to keep my moods as stable as possible: _____

_____

_____

_____

Work with a counselor on development of appropriate social skills.

☐ *I am going to work with my counselor on developing appropriate social skills so that I can build a stronger support system.*

Use peer counseling techniques to work on the development of appropriate social skills and to build close relationships with other people (see the chapter entitled "How About Counseling?").

I am going to peer counsel with _____ *to work on the development of my social skills.*

Become an active member of a support group for people with mood disorders (see chapter 13, "Support Groups"). Check your newspaper, call your mental health center, or ask your counselor for information on support groups. This is the key vehicle by which people in the study found friends and established new family-type groups to replace those that had been lost. Some people even found appropriate partners in these groups.

☐ *I already belong to a support group.*

☐ *I'm going to join a support group for people with mood disorders.*

☐ *There is no support group in my area so I'm going to start one.*

You can do this by finding a place to gather and putting a notice in the newspaper. A community mental health center or your counselor could assist you in doing this (see "Support Groups").

Participate in community activities and special interest groups. Use your local newspaper to keep current with what is going on and then participate in those activities that interest you.

Community activities and special interest groups that I would like to check out include: _____

_____

_____

Do volunteer work. There are many agencies that could use your help. Inquire at churches, schools, hospitals, youth agencies, soup kitchens, the Red Cross, and so on. Some communities have organizations that organize volunteers: these are an excellent resource when you are looking for just the right place to become a volunteer.

I am going to explore volunteering in the following places: _____

_____

_____

This is what people in the study had to say about volunteer work:

"When you give of yourself to others, your own problems have a way of solving themselves."

"I volunteer in a local high school filling out financial aid forms—I do a good job for the students, and it makes me feel worthwhile. My experiences have given inspiration to others who are temporarily down. I get and give tremendous support from and to loyal friends and family, and I have never given up on life."

"I feel much better when I'm doing something for others or that I enjoy. I like to do things for others and not always let them know it was me."

Be mutually supportive. This means being there for others when they need you, as well as expecting them to be there for you when you need them.

☐   *I am going to pay more attention to the needs of my friends.*

Keep in touch with friends and acquaintances. Many of us lose contact with people we enjoy simply because we don't keep in touch. When you meet someone you like, invite him or her out for tea, lunch, or to share an activity. When you're parting, make a plan for the next time you'll get together. Renew acquaintances with old friends by inviting them for tea or lunch, or to share an activity with you. I have several close friends with whom I have a set time every week when we get together for an hour.

I am going to renew contact with the following friends and acquaintances: _____

_____

_____

I am going to schedule regular times to get together with: _____

_____

_____

_____

It's important that you have several friends so you don't put an undue strain on any one of them. Paying attention to their needs is important for you as well as for them. I can't emphasize this too much.

Now, try it again! **List five supportive or potentially supportive friends**.

1. _____

2. _____

3. _____

4. _____

5. _____

12

Finding Appropriate Health Care Professionals

My doctor listens to me and my ideas and perceptions of the illness, gives me sugges-tions, involves me in all levels of my treatment, and treats my mood swings like any other recurring illness.

Finding appropriate health care professionals who are willing to work with you on reliev-ing and/or eliminating mood problems and other upsetting symptoms is often a difficult task, especially when your symptoms are severe. However, locating such people is very important. This is a time when family members and friends who are well educated about mood disorders can be helpful. Ask your supporters for assistance if the task of finding good care is more than you feel you can handle.

Through the self-education process, and individual interviews where appropriate, you will be able to determine which health care professionals can best assist you in work-ing toward wellness and stability.

Those in the study almost unanimously recommend that people with mood swings and other psychiatric symptoms explore a variety of approaches, including safe and noninvasive holistic or alternative therapies. In addition to my endocrinologist, psychia-trist, and therapist, at various times in the course of my treatment I have worked with a homeopathic physician, an acupuncturist, a chiropractor, a body worker, a movement therapist, a nutritionist, and a career counselor. Each of these people has played an important and essential role in my treatment, as well as enhancing my wellness.

Study participants gave the following reasons for exploring a variety of treatment strategies. **Which reasons reflect your feelings?**

☐ It is the only hope.

☐ The more we can learn, the more we can do to control our condition.

☐ Any reduction of severity or incidence of mood swings helps.

☐ I feel more comfortable with alternative treatment.

☐ No one has all the answers to mental health.

☐ Medical approaches are very limited, biased, and exclusionary—the surface has merely been scratched.

☐ Treatments are so new in this field that much is yet to be accomplished.

☐ There is no one answer for everyone; controlling the symptoms must be dealt with first, then individuals must explore their own problems.

☐ Anything that can be gently effective is preferable.

☐ The action of searching for alternative approaches is a signal of hope and a willingness to try.

☐ Traditional treatments are not working.

☐ One has to do so much for oneself; the physicians cannot do it all.

☐ Different people respond differently to different approaches.

☐ There's bound to be something that will work—it just takes time to find it.

☐ We must do whatever we can to feel healthy, safe, and normal.

☐ A careful, inquisitive person can benefit in many ways.

☐ Any information that is helpful should be gathered to form a personal program.

☐ Always be open to suggestions that may help, always be willing to at least try, because you never know what may help until you try.

☐ Don't give up trying—you are important; you have a right to seek happiness, and you have a life to live.

Other reasons why you might explore alternative or holistic health care strategies: _____

_____

_____

_____

You have to decide which treatment is right for you, what works best for you, and the treatment strategies with which you are most comfortable.

Cost can be a limiting factor in determining your health care team. Coverage by Medicaid, Medicare, health management organizations, and other insurance is generally limited.

What kind of treatment does your health insurance cover? What are the limitations of your coverage? _____

_____

_____

_____

☐ I plan to advocate for appropriate health insurance coverage.

Health care professionals I want to include on my support team:

☐ medical doctors
☐ psychiatrists
☐ psychopharmacologists
☐ endocrinologists
☐ allergists
☐ pharmacists
☐ therapists or counselors
☐ social workers
☐ osteopaths
☐ chiropractors
☐ body workers
☐ art therapists
☐ nutritionists
☐ occupational therapists
☐ homeopathic physicians
☐ massage therapists
☐ naturopaths

Others whom you want to include on your health care team:

_____

_____

Whom I plan to consult in setting up a team of health care professionals:

☐ other people who have mood disorders and other psychiatric symptoms
☐ your general practitioner or a highly respected medical doctor
☐ respected mental health professionals
☐ mental health clinic
☐ hospital staff members
☐ mental health organization
☐ support group
☐ Better Business Bureau
☐ university health center
☐ clergy

Others who might give recommendations on finding appropriate mental health professionals: _____

_____

_____

_____

Study participants recommend that you

- shop around

- network

- interview until you find professionals with whom you're comfortable

- keep changing if necessary until you find those who are knowledgeable and interested

Other strategies you are going to use to find appropriate mental health professionals for yourself: _____

_____

_____

_____

_____

What attributes do you want from the health professionals on your team? (Remember, these qualities may differ according to the services you desire.) *I want to work with health professionals who*

☐ monitor my condition and prescribe accordingly

☐ are willing to use minimal medication dosages

☐ use appropriate testing procedures

☐ are willing to use a team approach

☐ are willing to explore and try new approaches

☐ listen well

☐ are caring

☐ are accepting

☐ are compassionate

☐ are supportive

☐ are perceptive

☐ consider individual needs

☐ are willing to be flexible

☐ are easy to communicate with

☐ are optimistic

☐ promote mutual understanding

☐ are empathetic

☐ are friendly

☐ are gentle and warm

☐ are trustworthy

☐ emphasize self-care

☐ share their religious background

☐ are respectful

☐ are compatible

☐ have a sense of humor

☐ know the dangers of mood disorders and other psychiatric symptoms

☐ promote individual growth

☐ can be firm and protective when necessary

☐ have expert knowledge of issues like mine

☐ encourage me to make my own decisions about treatment

☐ are willing to keep trying until appropriate, successful treatments are found

☐ have ample time to provide adequate services

☐ encourage development of positive self-esteem

☐ are knowledgeable about medications, side effects, and the latest medical advances

☐ are willing to educate me and members of my support system about these issues

☐ specialize in working with people with depression, mania, and other psychiatric symptoms

☐ are usually available and have appropriate people to cover at other times

☐ have personally experienced mood disorders

☐ are able to admit the possibility of being wrong or not knowing what to do

☐ understand and adjust to my personal financial constraints

☐ know me and can quickly access my situation

☐ only resort to hospitalization when a danger exists to myself or others

☐ encourage personal responsibility

☐ are fluent and easily understood in my language

Other attributes you want from health care professionals: _____

_____

_____

_____

The following are quotes from study participants sharing their view of ideal health care professionals:

"I want health care professionals who are willing to try other medications if one doesn't work and who want me to feel as well as possible with few side effects."

"I want someone who is current on drug treatment, compassionate, open-minded, and willing to defer to and work with others."

"I want a health care team with more emphasis on alternative/supplemental kinds of treatment (vitamins, exercise, etc.), creating options and education. Using the whole person approach is indicated because of the effects which appear in every aspect of the person's life. The limits of traditional psychiatry must be recognized."

"My health care professionals must acknowledge that what I am feeling is real."

". . . [someone who] identifies the cyclical nature of mood swings, gives credit to internal struggles, looks for established warning signs, knows that medications are not the whole answer, and strives to allow me as much independence as possible."

". . . [someone who] talks about your feelings before, during, and after they occur, helping you figure out what triggers them."

". . . someone who would hear my thoughts and treat me as a peer who was currently having difficulties, and would not suggest fixing it all with just medications."

"I need someone with whom I can check in twice a week, have a regular session every two weeks, and talk about suicidal feelings without feeling threatened."

"The professional must be willing to make sure that the diagnosis is accurate."

"I am a woman and I feel I must work with females, as I have a fear of male superiority brought on by abuse in my family."

"I want people on my health care team who are receptive to the idea of self-help, are honest, encouraging, very knowledgeable medically, and caring."

"The team approach works best for me, as it encourages doctors to try new approaches. It keeps me more informed about the medications. They listen to me when I say I have a problem taking medications due to my allergies and responses to medications. I am part of the team, not a victim of treatment."

"[My doctor] treats me like any other person with any disease—no discrimination, stigmatization, condescension, or paternalism. I am a respected, integral part of the planning of my treatment and management of my symptoms."

". . . must impart a sense of reasonable confidence in you—a realistic person who monitors your drug levels and who helps you when you deliberately go off your medications—who doesn't give you a hard time when you get into trouble and call for help . . . getting and giving you help and being matter of fact—not punishing—is very important."

"I prefer that before medications are given, more is found out about the individual. A couple of days of observation and rest should preface any drug therapy; the patient must be given choices to regain control. This active participation helps raise self-esteem and gives the person a sense of regaining control over their problem."

"My psychiatrist is retiring, and it's time to look for a new one. I had a good friendship with this fellow and hope to find some of his qualities in my new choice. He (or she) must be seasoned (I can live with a little rust), aggressive with medication (high miles per gallon), take an interest in my life's interests (tinted windows), does not dabble in psychological therapy (skip the vinyl roof), considers patient education as part of the services (full instrument control panel), and does not indulge in mind games (a lemon?). As you can see, finding a psychiatrist is like shopping for a car."

"By the grace of God, I found a wonderful psychiatrist who began working with me in a very intense manner. He allowed me to cry, to scream, to pound pillows, to, in a word, emote. I wrote poetry, I drew pictures, I acted out dramas, and I expressed my feelings in such a way that I was able to heal the deep wounds of my past. He is different from any other doctor I have been to, in that he is not afraid of feelings. He conducts his sessions in a room with mats on the floor and pillows everywhere. He is 100 percent ethical and pays 100 percent attention to his patients while they are there. I worked with him for a year and a half. I saw him every week for two hours each session. He believed in me and gave me the confidence in myself to ride out the mania and the depressions until I was through the tough times. His work includes Gestalt, Reichian, Jungian, and psychodramatic techniques. He is a genius at his work and he has freed me from the very heavy stigma of these symptoms. I have been completely off all drugs for almost two years and I have had no depression or mania for that period of time. I have complete confidence in my recovery and I believe that it is possible for other so-called manic depressives to recover. I say so-called because I have very strong doubts that the illness is totally biochemical and requires lifelong drug therapy. I believe there are physiological components to illnesses like manic depression, but there are heavy-duty psychological aspects, too, and when the psychogenics are dealt with, the biology rights itself. That's certainly been the case with me."

Below are some unwanted attributes of health care professionals cited by people in the study. Which ones relate to how you feel?

- ☐ relies only on drug treatment
- ☐ not available when needed
- ☐ has more patients than can be handled well
- ☐ condescending
- ☐ overcharges
- ☐ authoritarian
- ☐ patronizing
- ☐ overmedicates
- ☐ too busy to do a good job
- ☐ afraid to try new treatment methods
- ☐ judgmental
- ☐ egotistical
- ☐ rigid
- ☐ acts bored

What other qualities in health care professionals do you want to avoid? _____

_____

_____

_____

People who feel that the care they receive is not good or is inappropriate say:

"My psychiatrist doesn't have time for anything besides prescription writing."

"My doctor is good about explaining the effects of drugs but not good in relating to my situation."

". . . does not understand enough about lab tests and is a poor counselor for me."

"I have to ask for information about the illness."

Describe your ideal treatment scenario: _____

_____

_____

_____

_____

Why is this the ideal treatment scenario for you? _____

_____

_____

_____

_____

13

Support Groups

Other people with mood disorders know and understand exactly what I am feeling and exactly what I have to go through each day to maintain myself, and how frustrating the illness is. Listening to the various experiences with therapy and drug treatments helps in the exchange of information. Support during swings and advice on how others handle various situations is a tremendous coping device, probably the best.

Why Belong to a Support Group?

Fifty-two people who took part in the study belong to support groups. Twenty-three people who are not in support groups said they would like to be. My ongoing research continues to convince me that support groups are a very effective way to build support systems and learn to control symptoms.

Support groups are helpful to people in many ways. It is healing to be with people who have similar problems—people who understand. It helps you feel that you are not alone. Communication is easy. A group can help you appreciate how fortunate you are, that things are not as bleak as they seem; that there is hope; that others with similar problems are doing well.

A support group can also provide information and education on what you are experiencing, and is a great place to get tips from others on how they handle problems associated with mood swings. In my own experience, I've found support groups to be wonderful places to meet new, understanding friends. Several of my closest friends are people who I met through such groups. People in the study reported the same thing: many formed lasting friendships and even lifetime partnerships out of relationships begun in a support group.

You need a place where you can go and not feel that you have to hide your problem. A group can provide role models for solving the very same problems you are confronting every day. A support group helps counter social isolation.

Study participants offered the following comments about support groups:

"We share our ups and downs at meetings and elsewhere. We get to know the 'signs'—weight loss, talkativeness, spending sprees, no sleep; or if someone doesn't answer the phone, cancels appointments. We've exchanged house keys. We have a telephone lifeline system. When someone is having a hard time, it is also a great reminder to the rest of us."

"I think the importance of getting involved in support groups has not been emphasized enough. I have been involved as a member/leader in 'Breakthrough' (patient self-help), the state mental health association, and the local Depressive and Manic Depressive Association chapter. It has certainly helped me to help others with manic depression and share my experiences. Furthermore, I think it helps to remove the stigma."

What Happens at Support Group Meetings

People reported that the number of members in their support groups vary from 2 to 400 (I would assume that where there are this many they break up into smaller groups), with most having between 10 and 20 members.

Study participants described a wide variety of formats and activities for their support groups, including

- Sharing of people's problems and experiences—mutual counseling, advice, and support

- Pertinent educational speakers and programs

- Referral to appropriate services and resources

- Sharing of activities, such as crafts, games, field trips, cooking, and watching videos

- Lobbying for services

One group holds large informational meetings each month to discuss different topics related to mood disorders, and has smaller groups that get together more often to provide mutual support.

Some groups have a policy of not dwelling on "sad tales or negativity," and instead focus on how to cope. I do not encourage any limits on the topics that can be discussed; although lashing out at, or being judgmental of, someone else in the group should be avoided. People need a place where they can freely and safely discuss and express their feelings. The rest of the group is available to validate these feelings, even if they can't understand or accept them. This is one of the most healing aspects of a support group.

Some groups limit the amount of time that each person can spend talking to the group about what is on his or her mind; otherwise everyone in the group might not get an opportunity to share. It is possible to get a lot said in ten minutes; this is often the upward time limit for a person to share.

I have found the following rules to be helpful in allowing support groups to run smoothly:

1. There should be no criticism or judging of other people in the group.

2. Sharing is optional and should not be either encouraged or discouraged.

3. Group members can talk about anything they want to share (except criticizing or judging other people in the group).

4. Group members should not interrupt when another person is talking or give feedback unless it is requested.

5. Attendance is optional.

List other rules you think support groups should have: _____

_____

_____

_____

_____

_____

If you are in a support group, what do you get from it? _____

_____

_____

_____

_____

If there are changes you would like to see in your support group, what are they? _____

_____

_____

_____

_____

How could you help make these changes happen?

_____

_____

_____

_____

_____

If you are not in a support group and would like to be in one, describe what you would like the group to be like?

_____

_____

_____

_____

_____

_____

What would you want to get out of going to this support group? _____

_____

_____

_____

_____

_____

How to Start or Locate a Support Group

Locating an Existing Support Group

☐   *I would like to be in a support group.*

There are two categories of support groups: open and closed. An open support group is one that anyone can attend. A closed support group is one that may have started as an open group and then, when attendance stabilized, stopped accepting new members.

Check out the following sources to help you locate those support groups that are both open and appropriate to your needs and circumstances:

- Call the local mental health help line (listed in the front of your phone book under "Guide to Services, Health and Mental Health," or under "Mental Health Services" in the yellow pages).

- Contact mental health organizations and services in your community.

- Call local mental health facilities (inpatient hospital units will often have affiliated outpatient support groups).

- Check the community calendar listings of support groups in local daily and weekly newspapers and the radio and local public television stations.

- Ask your health care providers.

- Ask other people who have mood disorders and similar issues.

Here are some questions to ask when considering different support groups:

- When does the group meet? Will this fit into my work, activity, and family schedule?

- Will transportation be a problem? If so, is the location convenient to public transportation?

- Would car pooling with other group members be a possibility?

- Is there someone in my family or in the group itself who would help with transportation?

If there are several groups to choose from, attend different meetings to see which one feels most comfortable and best meets your needs. It's important to attend a group meeting several times before making a decision whether or not to continue participating in that group.

The first time you attend a group is not easy. It takes courage to go to a new group for the first time, especially if you are feeling low and your self-confidence is down. Remember that open groups are always glad to find new members. The other group members will understand your hesitation in coming the first time, and will be welcoming. You don't have to share your feelings or experiences until you feel comfortable doing so.

Give yourself a big pat on the back for attending the first time, even if your participation was limited. Subsequent meetings will be much easier.

Group meetings vary from session to session. After you go to a meeting, answer the following questions:

I attended the _____ *group* _____ *times.*

How did you feel at the meetings? _____

_____

_____

_____

_____

What did you hope to get out of going to these meetings? _____

_____

_____

_____

_____

Did they meet your needs or expectations? (Explain.) _____

_____

_____

_____

_____

_____

_____

This group feels right for me because _____

_____

_____

_____

_____

This group seems wrong for me because _____

_____

_____

_____

_____

Repeat this process until you find the group that best meets your needs. If you can't find an existing group that feels right, you may have to start your own.

Starting a Support Group from Scratch

Starting a support group is not as difficult as it might seem. However, you may want to enlist some help in getting the group started. Ask friends who have similar problems, members of your support system, health care providers, and members of mental health organizations for assistance.

I am going to ask the following people to help me get the group started: _____

_____

_____

Avoid holding the meeting in your home. It could be held in a school, church, library, or other public meeting place. A phone call is usually all that is required to make such an arrangement. Choose a time that you think will be convenient for most people.

Place a simple notice in the community calendar of local daily and weekly newspapers, and on the radio and public television stations. (There should be no cost for these notices.) Include the *place*, *time*, and *purpose* of the group, and, if you want, your phone number for further information.

Here's a sample text for an announcement for your local paper:

A support group for people is being started this (*day of the week and date*) at ____ o'clock at (*location*). Meetings will be free of charge and are open to the public. For more information call (*your phone number*).

Support groups effectively counter the feelings of isolation experienced by people with depression or mania and other psychiatric symptoms. The meetings provide a safe place where people can share their experiences and learn about community resources in an atmosphere of understanding, support, and acceptance.

For a community calendar listing, send your newspaper a brief note as follows:

Support Group for people who experience mood instability (depression and/or mania)

FREE   ALL WELCOME

(*Date*)

(*Time*)

(*Place*)

For more information call: (*Phone number*)

You can sometimes arrange for community calendar announcements to appear for several days before each meeting on an ongoing basis. Check with your local media.

The sample poster on the next page can be filled in and copied for posting in public places such as grocery stores, libraries, town offices, and health care facilities.

Support Group

for people who experience mood instability, depression, mania, and/or other psychiatric symptoms

FREE   ALL WELCOME

Education

Information

Understanding

Support

Date:

Time:

Place:

For more information, call:

Many people in the study who started support groups found it to be a very worthwhile and rewarding experience.

☐ *I am going to start a support group.*

This is how I am going to do it: _____

_____

_____

_____

_____

_____

At your first meeting, you'll be able to work with other group members in defining the group more precisely to meet everyone's needs. Some of the issues that the group may need to consider are raised below.

Finances. Most groups are arranged so that they do not incur expenses or require dues. In some circumstances, a group may need to raise money to pay for a meeting place, educational resources, printing, promotion, and speakers. You can raise money by requiring dues, taking up a collection at meetings, securing donations from individuals and organizations, applying for grants, or holding raffles and food sales. A treasurer can be elected from the group to be responsible for any monies. If you are going to raise money, it is best to hold it in a bank account, with two signatures necessary for withdrawal (that of the treasurer and one other person).

Our group will need to raise $ _____ to pay for _____

_____

_____

_____

Our group is going to raise money by _____

_____

_____

_____

Time and frequency of meetings. Some groups meet several times a week; others meet weekly or every other week. Meetings can be held at any time of the day that works well for the participants. Most groups hold their meetings in the evening.

Our group has agreed to meet (how often) _____ *on* (day) _____ *at* (time) _____

Facilitation. You have several options for how your group is run. Members of the group can take turns facilitating meetings, or one person who feels comfortable with this task can do all of the facilitating. Most of the groups described by people in the study are facilitated by people in the group.

Our group will be facilitated by: _____

Format. Many support groups restrict their activities to informal discussions allowing members to share their feelings, experiences, and progress. Another possible format is to have a sharing time for the first hour or so, and then have a more structured discussion. The topic for discussion can be planned in advance, or can be based on issues that came up during the sharing time. Speakers, workshops, and videos on various related issues can also be included in your program. Your group might want to try out a couple of different formats to see which works best for the individuals involved.

Here are some ideas for topics for structured meetings:

- Dietary considerations
- Getting a good night's sleep
- Employment
- Public services
- Medications
- Family support
- Cognitive therapy
- Warning signs charts
- Relaxation techniques

- Exercise
- Housing and transportation issues
- Getting the support you need
- Health care facilities and services
- Relationships
- Preventing suicide
- Early warning signs
- Stress reduction
- Wellness Recovery Action Plans

Other topics I'd like to see discussed at meetings: _____

_____

_____

_____

_____

Some groups include a social hour in their format, with refreshments before or after meetings. Other groups plan separate social gatherings which might include meals and activities.

Our group will use or try out the following formats for our meetings: _____

_____

_____

_____

_____

_____

Depending on the size of your group, it may be helpful to choose a program director or a program committee to be responsible for setting up special events, speakers, and workshops.

What an Ideal Support Group Might Look Like

Study participants gave the following descriptions of what, for them, would be an ideal support group:

"It should be run by the people who experience symptoms. Caring and sharing is the essence of the program, with reduction of stigma, along with education for the client, family, professionals, and the public at large. They all need to understand this illness."

"Support group implies the concept of 'self-help.' Sponsorship is helpful, particularly financial sponsorship; but when funders become involved, their own agenda may overtake the goals of the group itself."

"Meetings at least monthly with members as leaders, an educational topic, rap sessions."

"Regularly scheduled meetings that have guest speakers but also—and mostly—time for small group sharing."

"It should be caring, accepting, a place to go for haven from the storm."

Describe what would be an ideal support group for you: _____

_____

_____

_____

_____

_____

How do you plan to make this happen for yourself? _____

_____

_____

_____

_____

_____

14

Family Support

My sister can get through to me when no one else can. She's not afraid to touch me if necessary. She also sees symptoms quicker than anyone else, sometimes including myself.

Positive Influence on Family Life

Some people said that their illness actually strengthened their family relationships. Through the illness, they developed more mutual understanding, became closer, and learned to communicate better. One person said that her family hasn't given up on her and that they use each bout as a learning experience with love.

Those people who said that their families are supportive of them listed the following ways in which that support is expressed. **Which of these apply to you and your relationship with your family?**

- [ ] communication
- [ ] encouragement
- [ ] concern
- [ ] availability
- [ ] family members educated themselves about the problem
- [ ] monitoring
- [ ] financial support
- [ ] calling, writing, visiting

- ☐ understanding
- ☐ listening
- ☐ love
- ☐ tolerance
- ☐ attention
- ☐ education, advice, and counsel
- ☐ protection
- ☐ living space
- ☐ activities

> "Each episode is dealt with individually; mania is usually confronted while depression is watched to see how I will handle it."

> "When I am very ill, they do a lot. As I get better, they withdraw to give me and them time to pull ourselves together."

> "My 24-year-old daughter has an unashamed, unembarrassed feeling for me."

Describe the other positive aspects of your relationship with your family and ways in which they have been supportive of you during your mood swings: _____

_____

_____

_____

_____

_____

Negative Interactions With Family Members

Some people in the study reported that their mood swings have had a great deal of negative impact on their family life, often creating complete havoc. Following is a list of these negative impacts and resulting emotions. **Which ones apply to you and your family?**

- ☐ was or became a dysfunctional family
- ☐ disruption
- ☐ estrangement
- ☐ denial
- ☐ financially draining
- ☐ embarrassment
- ☐ they think it's all in my head
- ☐ tension, stress
- ☐ anxiety
- ☐ lack of trust
- ☐ emotionally draining
- ☐ confusion

☐ loss of hope

☐ lack of understanding

☐ turmoil

☐ loss

☐ anger

☐ physically draining

☐ worry

☐ they're tired of me

☐ they feel helpless

☐ caused depression in other family members

☐ patronizing attitudes

☐ everyone is affected by the stigma

☐ exclusion

☐ fear

☐ overprotection

☐ unpleasantness

☐ grief

☐ divorce

☐ I'm devalued by family members

"My family says it is 'like walking on eggshells,' never knowing what mood I will be in or when it will change. My family told this to the doctor. They also said that when I come to the house they would all stop talking until they could tell what mood I was in."

"A distance developed between us early in childhood; because of lack of understanding and support, it caused a great distance between myself and the rest of my family. I feel that my family is disgusted with my mood swings, yet they mention their concerns over the amount of medication. They do not understand the medications and make generalized statements like 'all these medications and they still don't seem to be working.' They do not understand that the episodes can and do occur even while I'm on medications."

"They think controlling me is a way of supporting me. I would have to do everything just my parents' way to have their support."

"They felt that I was trying to disgrace them, that my acts were a reflection on them, undermining their prestige."

"Some of my children and some of their spouses are supportive. Others, I feel, don't admit to my condition being caused by a physical thing—rather it's something I choose not to control. I realize in writing this—in doing the parts of the study—how angry I am with these children. One daughter who semi-understands said, 'Mom, you don't know what normal is: you've been swinging from high to low all your life. We kids don't know you any other way.' She still thinks anything can be overcome."

Describe any negative effect your mood swings have had on your family, and ways in which they have not been supportive: _____

_____

_____

_____

_____

_____

Involvement of Family Members

Forty-five people in the study said that the amount of support they receive from their family has changed over the years. Most of this change has been positive. They report:

"It has gotten better."

"There is greater understanding."

"They are more understanding and more accepting."

"They give me more support than in the past because of family counseling."

"My wife has always loved me and as I get better, she is encouraging."

"They realize it is not their fault."

"When I am trying to help myself, they're appreciative and support me even more."

"As bad as it is now, it used to be much worse. A few [family] members show that they are interested in knowing more about the illness and its treatment, and how the medications work. Fighting that used to occur has let up and overall there is a more generalized understanding, but only with a few family members."

"I am more able to cooperate and am more aware of [my family's] efforts and caring."

Describe any improvements in your relationship with your family relative to this illness. _____

_____

_____

_____

_____

What do you feel is responsible for these improvements? _____

_____

_____

_____

Is there anything you need to do to ensure that these improvements are maintained? If so, what? _____

_____

Forty-two people in the study have family members who have attended family meetings to discuss their situation. Family meetings can include either one or both parents, a spouse or significant other, grandparents, children (either minor or adult), brothers, sisters, aunts, uncles, cousins, and even close friends. The doctor, therapist, and other health professionals may also participate.

The meeting may be arranged and facilitated by the person with the mood disorder, by a family member, therapist, social worker, doctor, or other health care professional.

These are the issues often discussed at family meetings. Which of these issues would you like to have discussed at a family meeting that involved you?

☐ suicide
☐ medications
☐ relationships
☐ feelings
☐ depression
☐ getting outside help
☐ building trust
☐ housing
☐ ways to get along better
☐ mania
☐ support
☐ forgiveness
☐ understanding mood disorders and other psychiatric symptoms

☐ medical intervention
☐ family dynamics
☐ general mental health
☐ ways to protect you
☐ mutual concerns
☐ acceptance
☐ doing more things together
☐ childhood issues
☐ coping with stress
☐ communication
☐ stigmatization
☐ monitoring
☐ financial issues

What other issues would you like to cover? _____

_____

_____

_____

Out of the 42 people in the study who have tried family meetings, 31 found them to be helpful. They said:

"It gave me the feeling they were working with me—just knowing they loved me was so important."

"It helped me come to a better understanding with my family about my illness."

"It helped me to feel not so alone and isolated."

"It is very reassuring to know that people who truly love you do have a full understanding of what you are battling every day in your life."

"It gave me insight into the other person's point of view."

Eleven people felt that family meetings were not worthwhile. The reasons they cited included:

"Nothing was accomplished."

"My family felt blamed, intimidated, were defensive and uninterested."

"Everyone only sees their side, not mine; they hate me for being this way."

Which of the following models of ideal family meetings suggested by study participants would you prefer?

☐ Family, patient, and doctor discuss the situation together.

☐ Meeting with a therapist, uninterrupted for 1 to 1½ hours; the illness is explained and there is ample time for discussion and comments.

☐ Benevolently confrontational; people are free to say anything that they care to say without being hurtful; the other person is allowed to respond; the meeting is open and positive, with give-and-take.

☐ The people involved should be encouraged to talk to each other (and not just to the therapist).

☐ The patient and family discuss what happens, the symptoms, feelings, when not to intervene, and the risks involved.

☐ Everyone speaks their mind and gives their opinion.

☐ The family express their concerns and ask lots of questions; the doctor is supportive of me, and the family says, "What can we, as a family, do to ease your pain or help you?"

☐ I could freely tell them what a constant struggle I go through; they would *listen* and learn about mood disorders.

☐ Help and lift, not judge, condemn, or disown.

☐ Education: here's what to expect; here's how to help. Everyone has enough interest and courage to let the others speak openly and to speak openly themselves—the only way to really find out what is going on and resolve questions and misunderstandings.

Describe a possible meeting with your family. What issues would you like to discuss? Who would you like to be there? What kind of atmosphere would be most comfortable and helpful for you? _____

_____

_____

_____

_____

_____

_____

_____

_____

_____

Fifty-nine people in the study have other family members who experience extreme mood swings. Eighteen of these respondents have been able to work with other family members to find solutions to their problems.

Do you have family members with mood swings? If so, which of the following approaches or strategies that other people have used have worked successfully for you?

☐ discussion of problems

☐ encouraging each other

☐ mutual understanding and support

☐ monitoring

☐ unconditional love

☐ defusing situations by providing quiet, "alone" time

☐ advocating of appropriate treatment for each other

☐ mutual assistance in recognizing symptoms

☐ educating each other

☐ mutual counseling

☐ building each other up

☐ increased communication

What other ways, approaches, or strategies have worked for you and family members with mood swings? _____

_____

_____

_____

_____

What are some things that you'd like to try with other family members who have similar issues? _____

_____

_____

_____

_____

Below is a wish list for family relationships compiled by people in the study. Which items describe how you would like your relationship with your family to be?

☐ as it is
☐ accepting
☐ like any normal family
☐ trusting
☐ smooth
☐ humorous
☐ attentive
☐ understanding
☐ respectful
☐ honest
☐ patient
☐ calm
☐ having fun together
☐ more time together

☐ free and open
☐ loving
☐ closer
☐ I'd like to be appreciated for who I am
☐ happy
☐ cooperative
☐ less volatile
☐ having good communication
☐ supportive
☐ having everyone be knowledgeable
☐ caring
☐ less controlling
☐ helpfulness

Another respondent wrote:

"We have a very casual lifestyle that goes a long way toward keeping the stress levels down to an easily manageable level."

What other attributes would you add? _____

_____

_____

_____

_____

The support of my husband, grown children, and their partners, continues to be essential to my own level of wellness. They monitored my episodes without overreacting to normal highs and lows. They made decisions for me when I could not make them for myself. They took me to my appointments when I couldn't get myself there. They stayed with me, or found friends to stay with me, when they knew it wasn't safe for me to stay alone. When they realized that I wasn't cooking for myself or eating, they made sure that I had plenty of good food, often shopping for the food, coming to my house, preparing a meal, and eating it with me. When I needed a more appropriate living space, they all pitched in and helped in the search and the moving. Most important, I could always find one of them who would take the time to listen to my frustrations and my dreams. When I felt as if I would never be normal again, they comforted and reassured me. Their belief in me, and love for me, sustained me through my darkest hours.

PART III

Developing a Lifestyle
That Enhances Wellness

15

Taking a Look at
Your Lifestyle

I believe the first major depression I had at age 19 was linked to stress I experienced at college. It was the first year and first time away from home and I was 1,000+ miles from home. Poor coping skills, lack of friends, and certain negative aspects of the school contributed to my unhappiness.

Fifty-seven of the study participants believe their mood swings had started as the result of a particular life circumstance, stress, or experience. They reported high stress or increased levels of stress in general as triggering or exacerbating mood swings.

The way you live your life, take care of yourself, and feel about yourself affects mood instability and depression. These factors may be the whole problem, or may simply make matters worse. All the effort you direct toward relieving stress in your life, making positive changes in your lifestyle, and changing your negative thought patterns to positive ones will enhance your overall well-being and help stabilize your moods.

My own personal journey to get my life back began when I realized that my life was in my control. While I was honest with myself in knowing that I might always have a problem with mood instability, I began to see that there were many positive steps I could take on my own behalf, that many facets of my life were under my control, and that anything I could do to enhance my life would be a positive step toward stability and wellness.

It was at this point that I began to read everything I could find that was related to mood disorders and/or wellness, to attend related workshops and seminars, and to talk with people about their coping strategies. This book is one outcome of that search for clues as to how people cope with ups and downs of mood.

I have made many changes in my life in the past ten years. I have been in counseling almost continually. Through this process, I have changed my perception of myself as a dependent, needy, sick, incompetent, and limited individual to understanding that I am, in fact, competent, can take care of myself, and am a skilled writer, teacher, and counselor.

I left a very destructive and abusive marriage and am now in a loving marriage with a supportive partner. My relationships with my adult children and my wide circle of friends continue to improve. I have established myself in a living space that is cozy, comfortable, easy to care for—warm in the winter and cool in the summer—with easy access to transportation and services. I have explored a wide variety of traditional and alternative health care practices, and continue to use those that have had a positive effect for me. I use cognitive and relaxation techniques to help me sleep and calm my spirit. I am healthier and happier than I have ever been.

Using available public services and resources, I have fully developed a career for myself which takes into account my interests and abilities, my need for a flexible schedule, and my need to take good care of myself.

One study participant wrote:

"At age 24 I was so very depressed emotionally. I lost weight and stopped menstruating, although I was able to function in my work. This [depression came about] because I was rejected by a man. At age 28, I had a similar, less serious depression. At age 55, I had a very good position. The hospital where I worked closed, I saw nothing ahead, and became extremely depressed.

I believe my mood swings are a genetic predisposition affected greatly by environment and my cognitive and behavioral reactions to that environment. This is a complex, constantly changing interaction. It is impossible to distinguish the components with absolute certainty, at least in my case."

Take Stock of Your Life

This is a list of the stressful events that survey participants feel triggered or worsened their mood swings. **Do any of these circumstances apply to your present situation or personal history**?

☐ marital problems
☐ divorce
☐ alcoholism in the family
☐ sexual abuse
☐ child abuse
☐ separation from loved ones
☐ death of a loved one or loved ones
☐ overwork
☐ job stress
☐ job termination
☐ a workaholic attitude
☐ postpartum depression
☐ hormonal surges
☐ recall of past emotional hurts
☐ poor career or lifestyle choices
☐ low self-esteem
☐ working with toxic chemicals
☐ severe exhaustion
☐ midlife crisis
☐ sexual anxiety
☐ menopause
☐ trying to endure too much alone

☐ lack of assertiveness   ☐ excessively high expectations
☐ perfectionism   ☐ poor social skills
☐ problems relating to peers   ☐ trying to meet the expectations of others
☐ substance abuse   ☐ neglect during childhood
☐ loss of custody of child or children   ☐ physical disability
☐ physical disfigurement   ☐ self-neglect
☐ lack of exercise   ☐ poor diet
☐ eating disorders   ☐ obesity
☐ smoking   ☐ chronic health problems
☐ health problems of family members   ☐ excess responsibility
☐ co-dependency issues   ☐ lack of self-confidence
☐ lack of a support network   ☐ financial problems
☐ control issues   ☐ inappropriate living space
☐ lack of emotional support from parents

What have been other sources of tension, stress, and pressure in your life?

_____

_____

_____

_____

Review the events you have noted. Which ones do you think are causing you the most stress, or having the greatest impact on your life? The next exercise will give you the chance to examine these events and their repercussions in more detail.

As you read about the coping strategies in this section of the workbook, think about which ones might be relevant to the events or situations you've noted. For now, simply fill in the blanks under Problematic Situation with a brief description of the top six problems from your list. Put a paper clip on this page to make it easy for you to find your place again.

As you get ideas from your reading, jot down notes in the places provided. You'll review the effects of the situation on your life and feelings; you'll consider which coping strategies might help; you'll record plans for implementing these strategies; and, finally, after you've tried some of the strategies, you'll record how they worked. Don't expect to complete this exercise until you've finished reading the entire workbook.

Problematic Situation

_____

_____

The effect of this situation on your life and the way you feel: _____

_____

_____

_____

_____

Strategies that might help: _____

_____

_____

_____

Plans for implementing these strategies: _____

_____

_____

_____

How these strategies have worked: _____

_____

_____

_____

_____

Problematic Situation

_____

_____

The effect of this situation on your life and the way you feel: _____

_____

_____

_____

_____

Strategies that might help: _____

_____

_____

_____

Plans for implementing these strategies: _____

_____

_____

_____

How these strategies have worked: _____

_____

_____

_____

_____

Problematic Situation

_____

_____

The effect of this situation on your life and the way you feel: _____

_____

_____

_____

_____

Strategies that might help: _____

_____

_____

_____

Plans for implementing these strategies: _____

_____

_____

_____

How these strategies have worked: _____

_____

_____

_____

Problematic Situation

_____

_____

The effect of this situation on your life and the way you feel: _____

_____

_____

_____

_____

Strategies that might help: _____

_____

_____

_____

_____

Plans for implementing these strategies: _____

_____

_____

_____

_____

How these strategies have worked: _____

_____

_____

_____

_____

Problematic Situation

_____

_____

The effect of this situation on your life and the way you feel: _____

_____

_____

_____

_____

Strategies that might help: _____

_____

_____

_____

_____

Plans for implementing these strategies: _____

_____

_____

_____

_____

How these strategies have worked: _____

_____

_____

_____

_____

16

How About Counseling?

In therapy we identified issues and worked to resolve them. It enhanced my understanding of my mood and behaviors.

Almost all of the 120 people in the survey have been involved in counseling for help in dealing with their mood swings and in working through related issues. Here are some of the reasons given by people in the study for going into counseling. **Which reasons apply to you?**

☐ depression

☐ need to understand the diagnosis

☐ to enhance recovery

☐ paranoia

☐ guilt

☐ fear

☐ an acute situation following an episode

☐ family problems

☐ stress

☐ inability to work

☐ desire to understand how to deal with stress

☐ desire to learn how to get along with people

☐ mania

☐ an interim period following hospitalization

☐ suicidal thoughts and/or attempts

☐ anxiety

☐ worry

☐ feeling like my life is out of control

☐ marital problems

☐ problems in another relationship

☐ job stress

☐ severe personal losses

☐ desire to work on achieving goals

☐ childhood issues

☐ sexual abuse

☐ alcoholic family members

☐ incest

☐ partner abuse

☐ co-dependency

☐ desire to change negative thought patterns to positive ones

☐ desire to change inappropriate behavior patterns

☐ desire to pick up more quickly on signs of oncoming mood swings

☐ desire to avoid more invasive treatment modalities

☐ other treatment modalities not working

Other reasons you might have for going into therapy: _____

_____

_____

_____

_____

What are your goals for therapy, even if you're not in therapy now? _____

_____

_____

_____

The Therapist

These are some of the attributes people want in a therapist:

- Extensive knowledge about dealing with mood swings and other psychiatric symptoms

- Availability, with someone else on call as needed

- Willingness to try alternative therapies

- Knowledge and judgment needed to prescribe drugs appropriately

- Skill at giving support, counsel, advice, and understanding

- Skill in communicating an attitude of caring and interest

- Affordable rates and/or willingness to work with insurance plans and Medicaid

Several people in the study said that they prefer working with a counselor of the same gender as themselves and of at least the same age or older.

What would your ideal therapist be like? _____

_____

_____

Study participants found appropriate therapists by

- Getting recommendations from other people who have mood swings

- Getting recommendations from mental health organizations

- Getting referrals from their physician or psychiatrist

Before making a plan with a counselor to begin a series of sessions, ask if you can visit free for one time to see if you both feel comfortable working together. (Many therapists find that they must charge, even for an initial consultation—make sure that you settle this beforehand.) You may have to visit with several counselors before you find the one who best meets your needs.

Kinds of Therapy

Look in any list of classified ads for counseling, and you will find different kinds of therapists. Perhaps you've already made a study of the many kinds of therapy available; if you haven't, the range can certainly seem bewildering. I'll make some basic distinctions here, based on my own experience and that of people in the study, to help you make the wisest possible choices when choosing what type of therapy you want to pursue.

Therapeutic approaches can be divided into three basic categories:

- Psychodynamic

- Humanistic

- Problem-Solving

Psychodynamic Therapies. Freudian analysis is the most famous among the psychodynamic therapeutic approaches; it is also fading enormously in popularity as clients and therapists turn to more immediate and practical problem-solving techniques. In psychodynamic therapy, the emphasis is on gaining insight into the roots of problems (rather than finding ways to solve them). These therapists are almost always geared to the long term. The analyst or psychiatrist will explain symptoms in terms of emotional damage sustained during your early stages of development. You'll spend a lot of time hashing and rehashing the past, and may analyze dreams in terms of their personal symbolism. The focus is on the unconscious. It's quite possible to go through years of this type of therapy without ever discussing solutions to present symptoms at all!

As you might guess, psychodynamic therapies have not been shown to be effective treatment for depression, mania, or the management of their symptoms.

Humanistic Therapies. Some of the therapeutic approaches that fall into this category are Gestalt, existential, client-centered, and interpersonal therapy. All of these focus on your emotional growth and expressiveness, and strive toward evolving healthy patterns of communication. Many people find these kinds of therapies to be very useful.

Problem-Solving Therapies. Problem-solving therapeutic approaches—such as cognitive-behavioral therapy—are often effective nonmedical intervention for the management of mood swings. These therapies tend to be short-term and are aimed at practical solutions to problems in the here and now. Your unconscious or subconscious motivations don't enter the picture at all, although gaining some insight into your thinking process may be important. The basic tenet of cognitive-behavioral psychology is that if you change the way you think, you can change the way you feel.

Therapy Is Just One Tool

Bear in mind that your therapy will be just one tool in your wellness kit. There are many other tools you can use, such as light, diet, exercise, and perhaps medication, which will all play their parts as well. You have the right to pursue exactly the kind of treatment that will give you the most help in managing your symptoms.

Unless you live in a very isolated community, it's a buyer's market out there. Be as savvy and aggressive in looking for a therapist as you would be shopping for a car. You have a duty to yourself to be a proactive consumer and to choose carefully. Listen to your gut feelings: a therapeutic relationship has all the inherent complexities of any other relationship, and perhaps a few more. Find someone you can trust. Find someone who inspires you with hope.

People in the study reported varying degrees of success in therapy, ranging from good and very effective to completely worthless. Therapy was not looked upon by most respondents as a cure, but mainly as a way of improving their ability to cope with mood ups and downs.

Here's a sampling of what people had to say about their experience with different kinds of therapy:

"It was excellent, but it couldn't motivate me during the lows."

"Therapy helps. It gives me someone I can turn to."

"It makes me feel better to have a professional consultant."

"My therapist gave me confidence and insight."

"I learned about my illness and how to cope. It gave me someone to talk to when I couldn't talk to my family."

"Therapy is good for surviving impossible situations."

"It helped me make dramatic changes in my ability to deal with the activities of living."

"I was in psychotherapy. The counselor was dogmatic and didn't understand or sympathize with the illness. He had preconceived notions about me which were false."

"The counselor did not validate me as a person. Many times I left the office feeling worse instead of better, like the whole thing was my fault."

"It was really a waste of time. Nothing changed for me as a result of the counseling. Finally, I just stopped going."

"The counselor was not a good one for me. She was not a person I could like or relate to. I felt that she was always judging me according to her standards."

"She talked at me the whole time. She kept telling me what to do, but never gave me a chance to say what I wanted to do, or how I was feeling. I left her office feeling frustrated and confused."

I have seen several different counselors since I began to work on stabilizing my moods. The first was a male psychiatrist who talked with me and prescribed my medication. It was there that I first began to get some sense of myself as a real person with needs and abilities. Prior to that, my life had always been totally focused on others. A process of real growth began, painfully and slowly at first.

My next counselor was a young woman. She also had a profound effect on me. I was beginning to get some sense that there was a real person inside me, competent, warm, and worthy. What a revalation!

My next counselor was a psychoanalyst who was recommended to me by a close friend. This was a very confusing and frustrating experience for me. The analyst expected me to do all the talking and I wasn't used to that. Consequently not much happened. It got even worse when she attributed the motives to my actions, such as the time when I missed an 8:30 appointment because I had a bad head cold and overslept. She said I was avoiding her because I didn't want to face my problems and share with her things I had done in the past for which I felt ashamed. She said this another time when I tried to change an appointment because my mother was coming for a visit. After six months, I ended this counseling feeling angry and confused, as if I had wasted a lot of time and money: for a while, I didn't see anyone. This experience had a very negative effect on my level of trust.

Soon afterwards, I got into a really horrible second marriage. When I realized how bad it was, that the charming man I had married was actually a very abusive alcoholic, I took the advice of a friend and began seeing a highly recommended counselor. She was in her sixties, had been through a lot, and understood completely where I was coming from. She got me back on track, and during the next eight years increased my level of self-understanding, taught me stress reduction and relaxation techniques, involved me in group therapy with other women with similar self-esteem and relationship problems (some of these women became lifelong friends), and helped me get out of that very bad marriage.

During my marriage, my husband and I saw a family therapist for a short period of time to see if we could work out our maritial diffulties. This therapist said that the reason I was being abused was because my husband was jealous, and that I should stop smiling so much. Obviously, this was a very bad piece of advice. I let that counselor know my opinion, and stopped seeing him.

For the past nine years, I have been seeing a counselor who is working with me intensively on childhood issues, such as my mother's illness, sexual molestation, and the death of my friend, while supporting and advising me about current life situations. Our relationship is one of peers and is very interactive. It has given me the courage to go on when I have been discouraged and low.

What are your positive feelings about any counseling experiences you've had? _____

_____

_____

_____

_____

_____

Do you have any fears associated with going into therapy? Are there any other impediments that keep you out of therapy (such as cost)? _____

_____

_____

What can you do to overcome any fears or impediments that may be keeping you out of therapy? _____

_____

_____

The Therapy Model

Some people prefer one-on-one counseling and others prefer group therapy. Among study participants, the length and frequency of therapy also varied. Respondents had a lot of ideas about ideal counseling scenarios:

"Initially, group therapy—so that the person can see they are not the only one with these problems and that other people have made good progress. [This also] provides a network."

"Informal counseling dealing with how to get out of bed and get motivated: to do the bare minimum if depressed and to calm mania."

"Focus on education, self-care, and social skills, with periodic follow-up visits as issues present themselves. . . . making use of community resources, supporting self-monitoring, working on building a solid support system."

"A wise, insightful, knowledgeable, loving, and caring therapist or program that encourages independence and teaches you how to work with others."

"In a neutral environment with empathy. Someone who projects genuine concern and who can relate."

"Insight-oriented with supportive therapy. The more you learn about yourself, the easier it is to make adjustments when life is rough."

"Deals with the ramifications of the illness, plus supports the person. Help with problems of living. Deals with more than just symptoms."

Describe what, for you, would be the ideal counseling scenario:

Kind of therapy: _____

Frequency of appointments: _____

Length of each appointment: _____

Term: ongoing; as needed; long-term (more than one year); short-term (less than one year) _____

Other Comments: _____

_____

_____

_____

_____

_____

What, if anything, is getting in the way of this kind of counseling scenario being available to you? _____

_____

_____

What can you do about it? _____

_____

_____

_____

Peer Counseling

I recommend that everyone try peer counseling (also known as co-counseling, or reevaluation counseling): it's free, it really helps, and both people involved get time and attention devoted to their issues. Peer counseling has the added benefit of focusing at least part of your attention on your peer counseling partner's issues, a process that in itself is therapeutic.

Here's how peer counseling works. Two people who know and trust each other—that trust is critical—set up a peer counseling arrangement. They decide how often they want to meet and for how long. I suggest meeting weekly and at the same time each week. It helps you get in the habit and is often frequent enough to stay current. Divide the time you are spending together in half: if it is one hour, which is a convenient length of time, you each get half an hour. During your time, you can talk about anything you want and express any emotion you wish to express, short of hostility or unfairness toward your counseling partner. Your partner stays focused on your issues, giving positive support and advice. Criticism or negating your partner's feelings is definitely not part of the process. For the second half of the session, you focus on your partner's issues as he or she talks.

I want to try peer counseling. It sounds good to me because _____

_____

_____

People I could approach about being a peer counseling partner (remember, it has to be someone you trust): _____

_____

_____

Fill out this next section later, as events warrant.

My first peer counseling session is set for (date) _____ ,
(time) _____ , (place) _____ .

After you've met with your peer counseling partner, record your feelings about your first meeting. (Use extra paper if necessary.) _____

_____

_____

_____

_____

I plan to continue peer counseling because _____

_____

_____

_____

I do not plan to continue or pursue peer counseling because _____

_____

_____

_____

17

Building Self-Esteem and Self-Confidence

I credit myself for remarkably courageous behavior, work, and changes in attitude. I chew off small pieces and do them well, organize well, and rest frequently.

Mood disorders and other psychiaytric symptoms can have a disastrous effect on self-esteem, severely aggravating depression and mania and diminishing the quality of your life. Study participants repeatedly pointed to problems with low self-esteem. Many reported that they had high self-esteem when manic and low self-esteem when depressed.

Describe your level of self-esteem and self-confidence (and whether these correspond to your mood swings): _____

_____

_____

_____

In what ways have mood disorders contributed to lowering your self-esteem?

☐ weakened credibility

☐ feeling negative about myself

☐ feeling different from others

- ☐ failing at most things
- ☐ adversely affecting performance
- ☐ fear of interacting with others
- ☐ inability to reach goals
- ☐ inability to complete anything
- ☐ continually finding fault with myself
- ☐ rages and fits that cause self-loathing
- ☐ guilt and shame arising from actions
- ☐ inability to trust my own perceptions
- ☐ stigmatization
- ☐ inability to commit
- ☐ difficulty with self-care
- ☐ feeling as if people know there's something wrong with me, no matter what I do
- ☐ feeling like I'm not as good as others
- ☐ loss of confidence in ability to accomplish even the smallest tasks
- ☐ guilt over what family members and friends have to go through because of my mood swings

If your self-esteem is low, what do you consider to be other contributing factors? _____

_____

_____

_____

_____

These are some more comments from people in the study:

"Because of the mood swings, I suffer from the long-lasting impact of having been thrown out of a graduate program where I was doing what I love and I was competent. This was indescribably painful."

"I don't know how I will be for any occasion, so I can't plan. I'm anxious about upcoming events, can't operate under pressure anymore, can't remember or concentrate either. These are crippling for a professor and medical administrator."

"I'm terrified of demeaning myself on personal and/or professional levels due to my discrepancy in mood: I have in the past. This is not conducive to feeling self-confident and is very discouraging."

Raising your self-esteem is absolutely essential to relieving or eliminating your depression and/or symptoms of mania.

Consider the following ways used by study participants to raise their self-esteem. Which of these strategies have you tried? Think about which strategies might work for you in the future.

☐ changing my thought processes

☐ measuring and focusing on my past successes

☐ believing in myself

☐ giving myself credit for accomplishments

☐ doing things I find scary or hard

☐ determination to get more out of life

☐ self-affirmation

☐ self-acceptance

☐ doing my best at all times

☐ self-discipline

☐ lowering my perfectionist standards

☐ not getting upset over things

☐ focusing on the positive

☐ living one day at a time

☐ believing others who affirm my worth

☐ realizing that I have not quit—that I've worked through my problems

☐ partitioning myself off from the bad memories of the past

☐ knowing that the mood swings are not my fault

☐ knowing that the stigma of mental illness is no basis for shame

☐ knowing that I am the same as others

☐ accepting that it will take longer to accomplish my goals

☐ thinking of myself as a good and positive person

☐ affirming, "I think and act with self-confidence"

What are other attitudes or strategies you have developed to help raise your self-esteem and self-confidence? _____

_____

_____

_____

_____

List attitudes you do not now have but want to work on to improve your self-esteem:

_____

_____

_____

_____

Which of these actions do you want to take toward increasing your self-esteem?

☐ develop a strong support system   ☐ be a good friend

☐ take good care of myself   ☐ take classes

☐ learn new skills   ☐ work hard

☐ seek counseling   ☐ listen to good music

☐ exercise   ☐ garden

☐ take part in community activities   ☐ work as a volunteer

☐ keep my house in order   ☐ dress well

☐ use daily affirmations   ☐ be supportive of others

☐ listen to friends, family   ☐ continue my education

☐ learn more about self-help   ☐ pursue my career

☐ do work that I feel good doing   ☐ pursue hobbies and crafts

☐ write in a journal   ☐ do meditation and relaxation exercises

☐ join special interest clubs   ☐ participate in church activities

☐ take care of family, pets   ☐ keep my life in order

☐ listen to others who affirm my worth   ☐ use creative expression (draw, paint, write, dance, etc.)

☐ just keep getting out there and trying for the brass ring

☐ be goal-oriented

☐ gain success in certain areas of my life

☐ practice consistently affirmative self-talk

☐ learn all I can about mood swings

☐ educate others who have mood swings

☐ monitor and respond appropriately to my early warning signs

☐ look at why I am low or high and do something about it

☐ learn to relate to others more effectively and appropriately through self-help books, counseling, and work in my support group

☐ be around people I like and who like me—positive people who are sympathetic and uplifting

☐ avoid people who bring me down

☐ be willing to take more risks, giving myself credit when I succeed

☐ take small risks in a safe place, getting feedback from people who know me well

☐ keep cards, pictures of friends, and positive notes on bulletin boards where I will see them frequently

☐ have a special place to keep mementos and reminders of my achievements

☐ keep a list of achievements on the refrigerator door

☐ keep a list of achievements beside the bed and review them before I go to sleep at night or when I wake up in the morning

☐ before going to sleep at night, remind myself of what I have accomplished that day

☐ write down all the things that are good about myself and read them over and over

Other activities that have helped you raise your self-esteem and self-confidence: _____

_____

_____

_____

_____

Make a list of confidence-building activities that you want to try. Then commit yourself to a beginning date.

Activity	When I Will Begin

"Doing things I love helped me regain my interest in life and my self-confidence—singing, getting a professional degree and a job, and living by myself."

Author's Note. My own lack of self-esteem and self-confidence has been an inhibiting factor all my life. I have always been highly motivated, but everything I have undertaken has seemed like such a struggle. This low self-esteem started early on with messages I received from hypercritical family members. Those feelings were reinforced in traditional classroom situations, which focused my attention on the negative aspects of my performance, with little positive reinforcement. I feel as a child that I was always trying to please the adults in my life, and yet was never quite successful. In two bad marriages, I was always the brunt of extensive criticism. Our society further perpetuates such criticism through the media, which set up unrealistic standards for what we should be like. Living in a patriarchal society, in which women are not as highly regarded as men, has further exaggerated these negative self-assessments.

Through years of extensive counseling, reading various self-help books, working on cognitive therapy techniques, attending lectures and workshops, as well as making it a point to share my life with people who are supportive and validating, I have come a long way toward gaining a high level of self-confidence and respect. It has been a difficult journey, but my life is now rich, full, and beautiful.

18

New Ways of Thinking

There are thoughts that plague me, that go around and around in my head. I feel like I have no control over them. They don't do me any good, and they make me feel terrible.

Negative Thinking

I used to tell myself over and over again how worthless I am, how bad I look, and that everything is hopeless. Irrational phobias about crowds and heights limited my experience. I was plagued with unrealistic fears for my own safety and well-being, as well as that of my family and, sometimes, the whole world.

People who experience depression or manic depression and other psychiatric symptoms are often plagued by obsessive, largely irrational thoughts. The authors of *The Relaxation and Stress Reduction Workbook* note that this type of thinking is characterized by "repetitive and intrusive thoughts that are unrealistic, unproductive, and often anxiety producing."

Much of what you feel is caused by what you tell yourself, how you think, the ways in which you choose to interpret situations, and your personal point of view. Many people, when they're young, develop the habit of filling themselves with negative thoughts about themselves and the circumstances of their lives. In effect, people program themselves and their lives to be a particular way. Negative programming can be reinforced by one's family situations and by societal expectations.

Negative obsessive thoughts can take the form of self-doubt, generalized fears, and specific phobias. Participants in the study shared the negative thoughts that plague them in these three general categories Mark the thoughts that you identify with, then add your own thoughts to the list.

Self-Doubt

☐ I will never be able to get this job done.

☐ I don't look good enough for anyone to like me.

☐ I am not smart enough to figure this out.

List your own self-doubts: _____

_____

_____

_____

_____

_____

_____

Fears

☐ The house will catch on fire.

☐ We will have a bad accident and all be killed.

☐ I think I have cancer.

☐ I will never be well.

☐ I will have another deep depression and land in the hospital.

☐ I will experience all the side effects of this drug.

List other fears you have: _____

_____

_____

_____

_____

_____

_____

Phobias

☐ bugs	☐ spiders
☐ snakes	☐ dogs
☐ cats	☐ birds
☐ horses	☐ guns
☐ knives	☐ heights
☐ flying	☐ deep water
☐ darkness	☐ public bathrooms
☐ stores	☐ crowds
☐ small, enclosed places	☐ going out
☐ going out alone	☐ medications
☐ injections	☐ doctors
☐ dentists	☐ driving
☐ driving on freeways	☐ driving on dirt roads

List other phobias you have: _____

_____

_____

_____

_____

_____

_____

_____

Distorted Thinking Styles

On examination, negative thinking can very often be identified as distorted thinking. When you become aware of the distortions in your thinking, you will be able to actually change negative thoughts to positive ones, effectively eliminating the depression and anxiety that these thoughts create.

Distorted thoughts can be easily identified because they 1) cause painful emotions, such as worry, depression, or anxiety, and/or 2) cause you to have ongoing conflicts with other people. Fifteen distorted thinking styles are examined in *Thoughts and Feelings* by Matthew McKay, Martha Davis, and Patrick Fanning.

As you read through the definitions and examples that follow, think about how your own thinking has been distorted through the years. Answering the questions will help you come up with ways in which to combat your distorted perceptions. For each distorted perception, you'll be asked to come up with a rational comeback to knock it down. The examples show you how.

Filtering

Filtering entails looking at only one part of a situation to the exclusion of everything else.

Example. "Thanksgiving is going to be a disaster. I get along so horribly with my mother."

Distorted Perception. "My enjoyment of the Thanksgiving holiday depends exclusively on how I get along with my mother."

Rational Comeback. "Even though I often fight with my mother or feel hurt by her, I have a great relationship with my father and sister, brother-in-law, and nephew. They're going to be there, too, and there's a good chance that I'll have a decent time."

Think of an example when you filtered your thoughts: _____

_____

_____

Identify the distorted perception in your example: _____

_____

_____

_____

How did you feel when you filter your thoughts in this way? _____

_____

_____

_____

When you filter your thoughts does it ever cause conflict between yourself and others? Describe examples of this: _____

_____

_____

_____

Write a rational comeback to replace your distorted perception: _____

_____

_____

_____

Polarized Thinking

This distortion involves perceiving everything at the extremes, as either black or white, with nothing in between. You can understand how polarized thinking is a particular pitfall for people who have mood swings! Things are all great, or all horrible: there's no middle ground.

Example. "I had trouble scraping together the money for the rent this month. I'm a horrible spouse, and a failure as a provider."

Distorted Perception. "My financial performance this month defines my worth as a spouse and a provider."

Rational Comeback. "I had a bad month, without a lot of work. Sometimes I have much better months. My wife says that she loves me and that I'm a good husband, no matter what kind of month I've had. The economy's bad now, and we're both working hard to make ends meet."

Think of an example of when you've used polarized thinking: _____

_____

_____

Identify the distorted perception in your example: _____

_____

_____

_____

How did you feel when your thoughts were polarized in this way? _____

_____

_____

_____

When you've used polarized thinking, has it ever caused conflict between yourself and others? (Describe) _____

_____

_____

_____

Write a rational comeback to replace your distorted perception: _____

_____

_____

_____

Overgeneralization

When you overgeneralize, you reach a broad, generalized conclusion based on just one piece of evidence.

Example. "My friend rejected me, therefore nobody will ever love me."

Distorted Perception. "This one rejection is the sole determinant of whether or not I'll be loved by other people in the future."

Rational Comeback. "Just because this one friend rejected me, it doesn't mean that no one will ever love me again. It just means that the one person rejected me. Many people do like me, and I continue to make new friends."

Give an example of when you've used overgeneralization in your thinking: _____

_____

_____

Identify the distorted perception in your example: _____

_____

_____

_____

How did you feel when you overgeneralized? _____

_____

_____

_____

When you've overgeneralized in the past, has it caused conflict between yourself and others? (Describe) _____

_____

_____

_____

Write a rational comeback to replace your distorted perception: _____

_____

_____

_____

Mind Reading

Mind reading is just what it sounds like: you base assumptions and conclusions on your "ability" to know other people's thoughts.

Example. "He looked at his watch while I was in the middle of my presentation. I became afraid that I was boring everyone."

Distorted Perception. "I know what he was thinking about when he looked at his watch."

Rational Comeback. "Only he knows what he was thinking about when he looked at his watch (if it was even a conscious gesture). It more than likely had no reference to me or my presentation."

Can you think of a time when you've used the cognitive distortion of mind reading? __

_____

_____

Identify the distorted perception in your example: _____

_____

_____

_____

How did it make you feel when you assumed that you could read other people's minds (and when you saw unflattering thoughts there)? _____

_____

_____

_____

When you've fallen prey to mind reading, has it caused conflict between yourself and others? (Describe) _____

_____

_____

_____

Write a rational comeback to replace your distorted perception: _____

_____

_____

_____

Catastrophizing

When you catastrophize, as the word suggests, you turn everything into a catastrophe, always expecting the worst-case scenario.

Example. "My son has a cold that's probably going to turn into pneumonia—my God, he's going to die!"

Distorted Perception. "Colds always lead to pneumonia and, ultimately, death."

Rational Comeback. "My son is strong and healthy, and uses good judgment. He takes good care of himself. If his cold gets any worse, he'll see a doctor. He'll get antibiotics if he needs them.

Can you think of an example of catastrophic thinking on your part? _____

_____

_____

Identify the distorted perception in your example: _____

_____

_____

_____

How did it make you feel to think this way? _____

_____

_____

_____

When you've used catastrophic thinking, has it caused conflict between yourself and others? (Describe) _____

_____

_____

_____

Write a rational comeback to replace your distorted perception: _____

_____

_____

_____

Personalization

When your thinking is distorted by personalization, you interpret everything around you in ways that reflect on you and, often, your self-worth. Personalization is a double-edged sword, in that sometimes it makes you feel great—as when everyone you deal with in the course of a day is kind and cheerful, and you take this as a sign of your winning personality and charm. But the grumpy person you encounter, who isn't won over by your brightest smile, can convince you that you've lost your looks, your personality has gone flat, and you've just been fooling yourself all these years.

Example. "If I'd done a better job as a mother, my daughter wouldn't be depressed."

Distorted Perception. "I should be able to control my daughter's happiness or unhappiness."

Rational Comeback. "No one—not even a parent—can determine whether another individual is happy or unhappy. My daughter's depression is determined by many factors, and unfortunately most of these are beyond my control."

Can you think of an example of when you have used personalization? _____

_____

_____

Identify the distorted perception in your example: _____

_____

_____

_____

How did it make you feel when you've used personalization? _____

_____

_____

_____

When you've used personalization, has it caused conflict between yourself and others? (Describe) _____

_____

_____

_____

Write a rational comeback to replace your distorted perception: _____

_____

_____

_____

Control Fallacies

This distortion entails feeling either that the events in your life are totally controlled by a force outside of yourself or that you are responsible for everything.

Example 1. "What's the use of looking for work in my field? Everyone who's any good already has a job."

Distorted Perception. "No one who's competent ever has to look for a job; the work just magically appears."

Rational Comeback. "I've got to play an active role in getting work—even geniuses have to pound the pavement sometimes and knock on doors. People aren't necessarily thinking about me (and passing me over) when they hand out jobs to other freelancers. I've got to remind all my contacts in the field that I'm available."

Example 2. "How can I possibly take a vacation now? The whole office will fall apart if I leave."

Distorted Perception. "Even though lots of other people are employed at my office, I'm the one who's really doing all the work and holding things together."

Rational Comeback. "The staff has been structured so that every employee can take a vacation once a year—including me. My work is certainly important, but it's no more important than anyone else's; and it's important for me to take my vacation, too."

Can you think of an example of when you have used one or both of the control fallacies?

_____

_____

_____

_____

_____

Identify the distorted perception in your example: _____

_____

_____

_____

How have you felt when you've used this fallacy? _____

_____

_____

_____

When you've used control fallacies, has it caused conflict between yourself and others? (Describe) _____

_____

_____

_____

Write a rational comeback to replace your distorted perception: _____

_____

_____

_____

Fallacy of Fairness

When you use the fairness fallacy, you fall into the trap of judging people's actions by rules that you've concocted about what is and what isn't fair. The trouble is that in personal interactions at least, everyone has different ideas about fairness, so you're bound to wind up feeling hurt, slighted, or wronged.

Example. "If my husband really cared about my wellness, he'd take on more responsibility with the house and kids."

Distorted Perception. "How much my husband cares about my wellness is defined by the amount of housework he takes on."

Rational Comeback. "My husband does a lot of other things that show how much he cares about my wellness: he's very attentive and tender toward me, he reads to me in bed, he does all the yardwork, takes care of the dogs, and works very hard at his job (which pays my doctors' bills). I can talk to him about feeling overburdened by the housework and all the demands the kids make on me. If we work together, we might find some solutions."

Can you think of an example of when you used the fallacy of fairness? _____

_____

_____

_____

Identify the distorted perception in your example: _____

_____

_____

_____

How did you feel when you used the fallacy of fairness? _____

_____

_____

_____

When you've used this distortion, has it ever caused conflict between yourself and others? (Describe) _____

_____

_____

_____

Write a rational comeback to replace your distorted perception: _____

_____

_____

_____

Emotional Reasoning

This is the mistaken belief that everything you feel must be true.

Example. "I feel stupid, therefore I must be stupid."

Distorted Perception. "My subjective feelings always reflect reality."

Rational Comeback. "My opinions about myself change all the time, often depending on my mood. No one is *just* smart or *just* stupid. I probably make poor choices or use poor judgment sometimes, but that's just part of being human. Most people would probably say that I'm pretty intelligent."

Can you think of an example of when you have used emotional reasoning? _____

_____

_____

_____

Identify the distorted perception in your example: _____

_____

_____

_____

How did you feel when you used emotional reasoning? _____

_____

_____

_____

When you've used emotional reasoning, has it caused conflict between yourself and others? (Describe) _____

_____

_____

_____

Write a rational comeback to replace your distorted perception: _____

_____

_____

_____

Fallacy of Change

This is the assumption that other people will change to suit you if you pressure them enough. The illusion is that your happiness depends on bringing about these changes. Co-dependent behavior, which you may have read about in other contexts, relies heavily on this fallacy.

Example. "If my father would only start going to AA meetings, we could make another attempt at having a decent relationship."

Distorted Perception. "The quality of my relationship with my father depends on whether or not he goes to AA meetings."

Rational Comeback. "I have no control over whether or not Dad goes to AA meetings. The only part of our relationship that I *can* control has to do with my own thoughts and feelings and actions. To the extent that I can change these, I can change our relationship."

Can you think of an example of when you have used the fallacy of change? _____

_____

_____

_____

Identify the distorted perception in your example: _____

_____

_____

_____

How did you feel when you used the fallacy of change? _____

_____

_____

_____

When you've used this distortion, did it ever cause conflict between yourself and others? (Describe) _____

_____

_____

_____

Write a rational comeback to replace your distorted perception: _____

_____

_____

_____

Global Labeling

This is making a broad judgment based on very little evidence.

Example. "One of the mangos I bought at that store turned out to be rotten, therefore the store has rotten produce and I'm never going back there."

Distorted Perception. "It's accurate to judge the quality of this store's merchandise on the basis of one piece of fruit."

Rational Comeback. "Just because I got one bad mango does not mean that the store as a whole is no good. It just means that they had some rotten mangos. (If I go back and tell them, maybe they'll give me a refund—or a better mango!)"

Can you think of an example of when you have used global labeling? _____

_____

_____

_____

Identify the distorted perception in your example: _____

_____

_____

_____

How did you feel when you used global labeling? _____

_____

_____

_____

When you used global labeling, did it cause conflict between yourself and others? (Describe) _____

_____

_____

_____

Write a rational comeback to replace your distorted perception: _____

_____

_____

_____

Blaming

This is a very common distortion and is just what it sounds like: bad things that happen are someone's fault, either yours or someone else's.

Example. "I'm depressed because my family of origin was completely dysfunctional."

Distorted Perception. "Dysfunctional families always cause people to suffer from depression when they grow up."

Rational Comeback. "It's true that I grew up in a dysfunctional family; but my depression has also involved a lot of other factors, including choices I've made and continue to make."

Can you think of an example of when you have used the logical distortion of blaming?

_____

_____

_____

Identify the distorted perception in your example: _____

_____

_____

_____

How did you feel when you used blaming as an explanation? _____

_____

_____

_____

When you've used blaming, has it ever caused conflict between yourself and others? (Describe) _____

_____

_____

_____

Write a rational comeback to replace your distorted perception: _____

_____

_____

_____

Shoulds

This entails operating from a rigid set of indisputable rules about how everyone, including yourself, should act.

Example. "I should never feel jealous."

Distorted Perception. "My behavior should always conform to a rigid set of rules."

Rational Comeback. "I'm as subject to as wide a range of emotions as any other human being. Jealousy is one of these emotions."

What are some of your shoulds, the rigid rules that you invoke for yourself and others?

_____

_____

_____

_____

_____

_____

_____

How do you feel when you think in terms of shoulds? _____

_____

_____

_____

When you use shoulds, does it ever cause conflict between yourself and others? (Describe) _____

_____

_____

_____

Write a rational comeback to each of the shoulds you listed above: _____

_____

_____

_____

_____

Being Right

This distortion involves continually needing to justify your point of view or way of behaving. The need to be right can make it impossible for you to really listen when someone offers a new perspective or a conflicting point of view. For an example, consider the following dialogue:

Example.

Daughter: I felt so sad after our visit. I felt like you were completely indifferent to me when I arrived and when I left, even though it had been six months since we'd seen each other.

Mother: I swear to God, no matter what I do, it's never right and it's never enough. All my friends think I'm just great—it's my kids who complain about me.

Daughter: I cried as I drove away. I kept saying to myself that I'm a good person and a lovable person, even though you don't seem to think so.

Mother: I don't know what you want from me, Susan. I've tried everything, and all I get is criticism. We used to have a great relationship before you were married. I don't know what happened.

Daughter: Mom, I've been married for 17 years!

Distorted Perception.   [*Mother*] "It's impossible that I'm at fault."

Can you think of an example of when you have used being right as a cognitive distortion? _____

_____

_____

_____

Identify the distorted perception in your example: _____

_____

_____

_____

How did you feel when you used being right? _____

_____

_____

_____

Has this distortion ever caused conflict between yourself and others? (Describe) _____

_____

_____

_____

Write a rational comeback to replace your distorted perception: _____

_____

_____

_____

Heaven's Reward Fallacy

This could be called the martyr's fallacy. You believe that if you always do the right thing, you will eventually be rewarded (even if doing the right thing means ignoring your own needs).

Example. "My career comes second after my kids. Actually, I'm ready to postpone my career for 20 years, if need be, to give my children the attention they need. I may be messed up; but if it's the last thing I do, I'm going to make sure that my daughter has good self-esteem."

Distorted Perception. "My self-sacrifice will make my children into happy individuals, and I will be proved in the end to be a good mother."

Rational Comeback. "How can my daughter possibly end up with good self-esteem when she has me for a role model? I'm the family doormat! I love my kids, but it's a waste to put a successful career on hold for 20 years. I can work out a compromise between my needs and theirs—and we'll all be happier as a result!"

Can you think of an example of when you have used the heaven's reward fallacy? ____

_____

_____

_____

Identify the distorted perception in your example: _____

_____

_____

_____

How did you feel when you used the heaven's reward fallacy? _____

_____

_____

_____

Did this ever cause conflict between yourself and others? (Describe) _____

_____

_____

_____

Write a rational comeback to replace your distorted perception: _____

_____

_____

_____

A Four-Step Process for Eliminating Distorted Thoughts

There are several simple and very effective techniques for eliminating stress-producing, distorted, and negative thought patterns or changing them to positive ones. By systematically examining thought patterns and applying behavioral techniques, you can change the way you think and feel about yourself and your life. This will have a profound effect on your moods, and will greatly enhance the quality of your life. The four steps in this process involve

- Identifying your emotion

- Describing the situation that gave rise to the emotion

- Identifying the distortion in your thought process

- Refuting the distortion

Read through the example below.

1. **What emotion (or emotions) are you feeling now?**
   I am feeling angry, tense, and anxious.

2. **Describe, *in detail*, the event or situation that gave rise to your emotion.**
   I went to my friend Peter's house at 4:00 P.M., as previously arranged, to go for a walk and have dinner together. He was not at home when I got there.

3. **Describe your thoughts, and identify any distortions in your thinking.**
   Because Peter wasn't there, I decided he really didn't want to spend the time with me, that he really doesn't like me and doesn't respect my feelings. (This would fit in the category of mindreading.)

4. **Refute the distortions.**
   There was only one piece of evidence, his not being there when I arrived, that was the basis for my distortion. The truth is, Peter and I have been close friends for a long time. All evidence indicates that he likes me a lot. An emergency may have come up, he may have gone to do an errand that took longer than anticipated, he may have misunderstood the plan that we made or he may have forgotten that we made a plan (or I may have misunderstood)—any of which are acceptable reasons and do nothing to lend credence to my distorted thought. The best course of action for me would be to wait on his porch (doing relaxation exercises) until his return; or leave him a note asking him to call me when he gets in.

Practice using this four-step process to work on straightening out your distorted thoughts. For your first try, choose a situation in which the distortion in your thinking is fairly easy for you to identify. As the process becomes clearer, you can work on situations in which the distortion is more subtle (or in which there are several distortions operating at once). Use separate sheets of paper to analyze each situation.

1. What emotion (or emotions) are you feeling now? _____

_____

_____

_____

_____

2. Describe in detail the event or situation that gave rise to your emotions: _____

_____

_____

_____

_____

3. Describe your thoughts and identify any distortions in your thinking: (Refer to the descriptions of distorted thinking styles in this chapter.) _____

_____

_____

_____

_____

4. Refute the distortions: _____

_____

_____

_____

_____

As you grow more familiar with this process, it will come as second nature to you, so that you can straighten out your thought distortions before they have a negative effect on your mood.

Thought Stopping

Thought stopping is a simple way to bring thoughts to consciousness and eliminate them. By eliminating a negative thought, you can eliminate the emotions and feelings that go along with it.

Step 1. Identify a Negative Thought for Target Practice

Review the self-doubts, fears, and phobias that you listed earlier. Check off those that are currently most bothersome, cause you the most stress, and interfere the most with your life. Then choose one of these thoughts to practice on. It's best to begin with a thought whose logic is pretty easy to topple. As you grow more adept, you can tackle more and more formidable beliefs and notions.

Bothersome Thought: _____

_____

Ask yourself the following questions to determine whether this thought needs to be changed:

Is this thought realistic or unrealistic? _____

Is the thought productive or counterproductive? _____

Is this thought easy or hard to control? _____

How uncomfortable does this thought make me feel? _____

_____

How much does this thought interfere with my life? _____

_____

Sample Thought-Stopping Exercise

Bothersome Thought: *I'm afraid that I'll have another deep depression and need hospitalization.*

Is this thought realistic or unrealistic? *It is realistic, because I have had deep depressions before for which I needed to be hospitalized. However, the circumstances of my life have changed significantly since then. I understand depression. I have an excellent support system of health care workers, family members, and friends. I watch for early warning signs and get help early. Several related medical problems have been appropriately treated. I use relaxation techniques, exercise regularly, and carefully manage my diet. I have eliminated sugar and caffeine from my diet. There is limited stress in my life and I have learned to handle stress that is unavoidable.*

Is the thought productive or counterproductive? *Definitely counterproductive.*

Is this thought easy or hard to control? *At times this thought is very hard to control.*

How uncomfortable does this thought make me feel? *Very uncomfortable!*

How much does this thought interfere with my life? *It interferes a lot, because it makes me feel depressed and discouraged.*

Based on the answers to these questions, it is clear that I would benefit from eliminating this thought from my mental repertoire.

Step 2. Dwell on the Thought

Bring the thought to the level of consciousness and focus on it for several minutes. You might want to do this when you're very relaxed, or combined with a meditation.

Step 3. Interrupting the Thought

When first working with a persistent thought, it's important to stop it by means of a powerful response.

One way to do this is to set a timer for three minutes. Now think about the thought. When the timer goes off, shout "Stop!" You could also raise your hand, snap your fingers, or stand up quickly. Then empty your mind of the thought. Keep your mind blank or focused on a positive thought for at least 30 seconds. If the intrusive thought returns during that time, shout "Stop!" again.

Another way to do this is to tape record yourself shouting "Stop!" at timed intervals. Focus on the thought, then drive it from your mind each time you hear yourself shout "Stop!"

Some people wear a rubber band on their wrist to snap instead of saying "Stop!" when unwanted thoughts come up. Others pinch themselves or dig their nails into the palms of their hands. You will discover what works best for you.

Whenever you realize that you are thinking the unwanted thought, shout "Stop!" After you have done this successfully several times, you can progress to saying "Stop" in a normal tone of voice when unwanted thoughts come up. Eventually you can move on to a whisper, and finally to just saying "Stop" to yourself silently whenever negative thoughts resurface.

Step 4. Substitute a Positive or Assertive Thought for the Negative One

Whenever the negative thought comes up, immediately replace it with an alternative thought. For example, instead of thinking, "I will have a deep depression and need hospitalization," replace it with, "I am feeling fine."

Stopping a thought takes time and patience. But, gradually, you will notice that the thought recurs less and less frequently.

Exercise: Thought Stopping

Bothersome Thought: _____

_____

Is the thought realistic or unrealistic? _____

Is the thought productive or counterproductive? _____

Is the thought easy or hard to control? _____

How uncomfortable does this thought make me feel? _____

_____

_____

How much does this thought interfere with my life? _____

_____

_____

_____

Based on the answers to the above questions, do you still feel that this is an appropriate thought to stop? If your answer is no, choose another thought and begin the process again.

Bring the thought to consciousness and focus on it for several minutes. How did that feel? _____

_____

Working with either a timer or a recording, focus on the thought and then interrupt it by shouting "Stop!"

☐ *I am going to use a timer to alert me when to shout "Stop!"*

☐ *I'll use a recording of my own voice that says "Stop!"*

☐ *I'll raise my hand when I shout "Stop!"*

☐ *I'll snap my fingers when I shout "Stop!"*

☐ *I'll stand up when I shout "Stop!"*

You can use all or one of these strategies to reinforce your cognitive-behavioral change. Repeat this process until you feel ready to move on to the next step. Then interrupt the thought without using a timer or recording. Progress from shouting, to saying, to whispering, and, finally, thinking the word "Stop." **How did this work for you?** _____

When you feel ready, substitute a positive or assertive thought for the intrusive one.
The positive or assertive thought I will substitute is: _____

_____

_____

When you have become proficient at this technique, you can use it to eliminate other obsessive self-doubts, fears, and phobias. You can work on one or several thoughts at a time, whichever feels best to you. Remember to give yourself credit for your success.

Examples of Changing Negative Thoughts to Positive Ones

Many of us have gotten into the habit of thinking in ways that are inaccurate, irrational, and self-defeating. This negative "self-talk" causes unnecessary stress, anxiety, and depression. By examining these negative thoughts and changing them to positive ones, you can make great strides toward improving and stabilizing your moods and enhancing your overall well-being.

Below I've listed some commonly held belief patterns of people with mood disorders, followed by suggestions on how these patterns can be changed to have a positive effect on your feelings.

Negative Thought: *I will never be well. I will always have problems with depression and/or mania.*

The Truth: *There's no reason why I can't continue to stay well.*

My mother was in a hospital for 8 years with severe mood swings. For the rest of her life, thirty-seven years, she had only one brief episode, which was quickly brought under control through psychotherapy and short-term drug therapy.

Of people in the study, 82 expressed a belief in finding solutions to their problem with mood swings; 50 people have had times when they felt that their mood swings were over for good (these periods lasted from 1 month to 25 years).

The ways in which people achieved these results include the use of medications, appropriate treatment of medical problems, and a variety of therapies, including stress reduction and relaxation work, exercise, diet, and lifestyle changes. They did it, and you can, too!

One study participant said, "At the present time, my mood has been stabilized for over a year. It would be unrealistic to think it will never happen again, but at the same time, I don't want the anticipation of another episode to stop me from living and functioning right now. I just live with the security that if and when it happens again, I will handle it—'just like before.' I have established a solid support system."

If "I will never be well" is part of your negative self-talk, write thoughts you can use to change that negative thought pattern to thoughts that are more positive: _____

_____

_____

Negative Thought: *I am not worth anything.*

Low self-esteem plagues those of use who have experienced mood disorders. Recurring bouts of debilitating depression, sometimes countered with manic extremes, including bizarre behavior, make it difficult for people with mood disorders to maintain a positive self-image.

The Truth: *I have a great deal of value.*

To really get this one refutation programmed into your brain, spend some time reading books on positive thinking (see the Resources List).

Write here some personal positive statement of your value: _____

_____

_____

_____

Negative Thought: *I have never accomplished anything.*
The Truth: *I've already accomplished a great deal.*

Give yourself some credit! Take a few moments for some serious and honest thought about your achievements so far.

Make a list of your accomplishments. I'm providing plenty of space, as people with mood disorders tend to have high levels of achievement! You can use additional pages if you need to. Be sure to include all educational and personal achievements. Be true to yourself and give yourself a break. Don't minimize anything you have accomplished.

_____

_____

_____

_____

_____

_____

_____

Make photocopies of the list of your accomplishments, and post it in prominent places. Let it be a reminder of your self-worth whenever you are feeling as if you have never accomplished anything.

Negative Thought: *I will never accomplish anything.*

The Truth: *I have the capacity to accomplish just about whatever I want to, with the exception of a few physical restrictions.*

What is it that you would like to accomplish in your life? What are your dreams and goals? Write them here. Use additional pages if you need to. _____

_____

_____

_____

_____

_____

_____

Read your list of dreams and goals over again and again. As you reread it, you will begin taking positive steps toward the achievement of these goals. (Fantasy is a powerful tool toward the fulfillment of your hopes and dreams!) If you have setbacks, just pick yourself up, dust yourself off, and get going again.

Negative Thought: *I cannot allow myself to make mistakes.*

The Truth: *Everyone makes mistakes.*

We don't like to make mistakes, but we all do. And it's not the end of the world. No one is perfect. It doesn't mean that you are stupid or worthless if you make a mistake. It just means that you made a mistake. Acknowledge your errors, then do whatever you can to learn from them.

Negative Thought: *In order for me to be happy, everyone must love and approve of me.*

The Truth: *It would be great if I could be loved and approved of by everyone, but it just isn't the way the world works.*

Just as you don't love or approve of everyone you meet, it's not possible for everyone to love and approve of you. It doesn't mean that you are bad or that anything is wrong with you. Tastes are so diverse that no one can please everyone. The important thing is to make sure that you love and approve of yourself.

Negative Thought: *I want to die.*

This thought is all too common among people when they are depressed. I know that I have said this over and over again in my mind, literally hundreds of times a day. That is what my mother repeated constantly when she was in a deep depression. I've learned to stop this negative thought before it even surfaces.

The Truth: *I want to live and be happy.*

Replace that old, worn-out "I want to die" with "I choose life."

Take it from me, this works! I really had to work at changing this debilitating negative thought, but I have succeeded in committing myself to living, no matter what comes up.

For yourself, your loved ones, and the world, for all you can achieve, give yourself the gift of life. I have and I'm glad. Even when the going is really rough, and I don't feel like I can get out of bed one more time, I choose life. In the next moment my daughter could poke her head around the corner, a good friend could call, the swallows could return, or a beautiful sunset could paint the sky. Take a chance on what's around the corner and choose life.

☐ *I choose life.*

Negative Thought: *There is no reason for me to go on living.*

The Truth: *There are many compelling reasons why I should live my life.* Your reasons might include your loving feelings for family members, friends, and pets; flowers, trees, the ocean, the mountains; your enjoyment of skiing, skating, walking, making love, eating wonderful food; the pleasure you get from movies, television shows, art, music, and travel; the satisfaction you get from artistic and productive work, from helping others, from communicating meaningfully with others, or communing with Nature or God.

Make a list of the reasons why you should live: _____

_____

_____

_____

_____

_____

_____

_____

_____

_____

For Christmas, my three granddaughters gave me an enlargement of a wonderful picture of them all laughing, mounted on brightly colored poster board and surrounded by their hand prints. I have it displayed on a wall where I see it constantly. It gives me such a lift, I smile every time I see it. It reminds me of how much I want to go on living.

I'm going to fill my living space with the following reminders of why I should live: _____

_____

_____

_____

_____

_____

This is my personal plan for how I'm going to spend more time with people I enjoy: _____

_____

_____

_____

_____

_____

This is how I plan to make more time in my life to do the things I like to do: _____

_____

_____

_____

_____

_____

Further Positive Comebacks for Negative Thoughts

The following negative thoughts were expressed by people at a mood disorders support group I belong to. The group helped everyone develop positive thoughts to counter their negative ones. (I highly recommend this activity for support groups.)

Negative Thought: *I am lazy.*
Positive Thought: *I am a hard worker when I am feeling well.*

Negative Thought: *I don't have any goals.*
Positive Thought: *I am developing some goals for myself.*

Negative Thought: *I am unmotivated.*
Positive Thought: *I am a highly motivated person.*

Negative Thought: *I am an outsider.*
Positive Thought: *I am part of the group.*

Negative Thought: *I am unlovable.*
Positive Thought: *I am a lovable person.*

Negative Thought: *I am dysfunctional.*
Positive Thought: *I'm having a hard time right now, but I'm working hard at getting better.*

Negative Thought: *I don't have any social skills.*
Positive Thought: *I'm developing my social skills.*

Negative Thought: *I'm getting older and yet I'm not where I should be in life.*
Positive Thought: *Everyone is getting older, and everyone develops at a different rate. I'm just where I should be.*

Negative Thought: *I am all alone in the world.*
Positive Thought: *I know and love many people.*

Negative Thought: *I will always be alone.*
Positive Thought: *I might continue to be alone, but there are many people who are precious to me.*

Negative Thought: *I have wasted many years of my life.*
Positive Thought: *I have done many good things during my life.*

Negative Thought: *I am hurting my body by smoking and drinking.*
Positive Thought: *I'm working hard on giving up smoking and drinking, and I know that I will soon achieve my goal.*

Negative Thought: *I am getting older and I look like it.*
Positive Thought: *Everyone gets older—but happiness is the best cosmetic. The happier I feel, the better I'll look.*

Negative Thought: *I will never succeed, so why bother trying?*
Positive Thought: *I will succeed—that is why I am trying so hard.*

Negative Thought: *What's the use?*
Positive Thought: *Life is worthwhile.*

Negative Thought: *Even if I do succeed, I am going to die anyway.*
Positive Thought: *Of course, everyone dies; but I might as well try to make the best of my time while I'm alive.*

Negative Thought: *Nobody loves me.*
Positive Thought: *Many people love me.*

Negative Thought: *I have leaned on those who love me so much that they are sick to death of me.*
Positive Thought: *There is joy in giving as well as receiving. Those who help me do so because they want to. I'm going to give back as much as I can—but first I have to get well.*

Negative Thought: *I drag people down.*
Positive Thought: *I often make people feel better by being an understanding and sympathetic friend.*

Negative Thought: *I am a burden.*
Positive Thought: *I have lots to give.*

Negative Thought: *I am unable to love.*
Positive Thought: *I know that I can love.*

Negative Thought: *I will never be independent again.*
Positive Thought: *I've been independent before, and I'll be independent again.*

Negative Thought: *I will always be like this. It will not end. It's hopeless.*
Positive Thought: *People with the kinds of problems I have do get well, and they stay well for long periods of time.*

Negative Thought: *What's the point?*
Positive Thought: *I'm alive, so I have plenty of gifts. It's my responsibility to make the most of them.*

Negative Thought: *I blew my college education by getting fired.*
Positive Thought: *I only got fired. I did not blow my education. I'll get another job. Nothing can take away the things I learned in college.*

Negative Thought: *I don't deserve to live.*
Positive Thought: *I deserve to live.*

Negative Thought: *Why bother? Whatever I do, it won't work.*
Positive Thought: *Sometimes the things I do work out well.*

Negative Thought: *How can I succeed at suicide?*
Positive Thought: *How can I succeed at life?*

Negative Thought: *I am not as well equipped as everyone else to function in the world.*
Positive Thought: *I am just as well equipped as everyone else to function in the world. I have a good mind and a good heart.*

Negative Thought: *I am weak-willed; I have a character defect.*
Positive Thought: *I am basically a strong person. I am just having a hard time right now.*

Negative Thought: *Why me? Why am I afflicted?*
Positive Thought: *Everyone has problems. We just do the best we can with them.*

Negative Thought: *It's my fault I'm depressed. If I tried harder, I wouldn't have mood swings.*
Positive Thought: *Mood swings aren't anyone's fault, not any more than the flu or cancer. I'm doing the best I can to get well.*

Affirmations

Many people have made dramatic changes in their lives through the creation and repetition of positive affirmations. An affirmation is a statement that describes the way you would want your life (or you) to be at its very best. Although this notion may seem a bit simplistic, it really works: repeated over and over again, affirmations can have tremendous power to act as a very positive force in your life.

I have used affirmations successfully for many years, as have many people in the study. It has been interesting for me to review old affirmations from time to time to see how my life has changed. Some affirmations that were appropriate for me several years ago are not even necessary now, and I have replaced them with new ones. This is an on-going process. I keep my affirmations in a journal by my bedside and review them daily, updating them as appropriate. I keep extra lists of them handy, one in my pocketbook to review when I am waiting for an appointment and another near my exercise bicycle for me to read while I'm pedaling.

Rules for Creating Affirmations

1. **When developing an affirmation, always use the present tense.** For example: *I am healthy, I am well, I have a good job,* as if the condition already existed.

2. **Use only positive words in your affirmations.** For example, *happy, peaceful, loving, enthusiastic, warm.* Avoid using negative terms such as *worried, frightened, upset, tired, bored,* even if you're negating them (don't say "I'm not upset"; say instead, "I feel calm").

3. **Use the first person**: *I, me,* or your own name.

4. **The affirmation should create a strong picture of you, successful in whatever way you desire, right now.**

5. **Keep your affirmation short and simple.**

6. **If you have a religious or spiritual faith, use your faith to enhance this process**. For example, "I trust the perfection and goodness of the universe."

Examples of Positive Affirmations

I think and act with confidence.
I am strong and powerful.
I fully accept myself as I am.
I have many accomplishments to my credit.
I am healthy and energetic.
I deserve the time and space to heal.
I have all the resources I need to do what I want to in my life.
I am loved by many people.
I am a very valuable person.
I am safe and protected.
I am effective and efficient in stressful situations.
I am peaceful and serene at all times.
My relationships are happy and fulfilling.
I am in charge of my life.
I look and feel wonderful.
I express myself easily and comfortably.
I choose life.

Developing Affirmations

Compose some affirmations of your own. You can use this opportunity to create an idealized picture of your life and circumstances, and the ways in which you respond. It's all right for your affirmations to stretch the truth, or even be complete fabrications, as long as they represent your image of the way you'd like things to be. Imagination is a powerful precursor to reality! _____

_____

_____

_____

_____

_____

_____

_____

_____

_____

It's a good idea to keep a journal by your bedside with an updated list of the affirmations you find most helpful.

Practicing Your Affirmations

1. Once you have developed your affirmations, repeat them several times first thing in the morning and before going to sleep at night. Having your journal beside your bed will serve as a useful reminder.

2. Repeat your affirmations over and over again when you are relaxing or meditating.

3. Repeat your affirmations at any time during the day when you are not concentrating on something else (to yourself, or out loud when possible). For example, when you are doing the dishes, vacuuming, are stuck in traffic, waiting in line at the grocery store. The more you repeat your affirmations, the sooner they will reflect reality.

4. Reinforce your affirmations by writing them over and over again while repeating them silently or out loud.

5. It can help to repeat an affirmation in an overly loud tone of voice. Diminish the volume gradually until you are repeating the affirmation in a whisper and finally saying it silently inside your head. (This is a good exercise to do when you are traveling in your car.)

19

Using Relaxation to Stabilize Moods

Learning to release the tension in my body has been such a gift. I can use relaxation any time and it's free.

Relaxation and Mental Health

More and more people are using relaxation techniques—also referred to as meditation—to make themselves feel much, much better. The value of deep relaxation in achieving wellness is also being recognized increasingly by the medical community. Research shows that the benefits of practicing relaxation techniques increase dramatically over time. Many studies have found that regular relaxation can speed psychotherapy, lessen chemical addiction, and decrease anxiety.

People in the study noted that they use relaxation techniques to lift themselves out of depression and to relieve mania and other troubling symptoms. Relaxation is particularly successful at decreasing the agitation that is often a warning signal of an impending mood swing.

To be able to use relaxation techniques during a crisis, it's essential to learn how to relax when you're stable (it's pretty much impossible to learn relaxation when you're either too high or too low). Relaxation techniques can be a valuable resource in helping you work through difficult times and in lowering your stress level on an ongoing basis.

The first step is to learn how to relax. In our fast-paced society, this is not as easy as it sounds.

Learning to Relax

Because relaxation is being recognized as such an important adjunct to good health, you have many resources available for learning the state of the art in relaxation techniques. Read and practice the relaxation techniques described later in this chapter. You may also want to utilize any or all of the following supplementary tools.

Take a relaxation or meditation course. Such courses are now available in most geographical areas and are often free. In my area, a relaxation class was recently sponsored by the local hospital. Learning with others, and under the guidance of an instructor, is an excellent way to learn how to relax or meditate. Look for courses in the community calendar section of your local newspaper. Also check with your local hospital or mental health hotline (see the Resource List at the end of this workbook).

Use an instructional video. In my area, one can borrow excellent videos from the hospice office and the library on how to relax. Relaxation and meditation tapes may also be available for rent at your local video store. Several excellent relaxation videos are for sale (see the Resource List).

Listen to audio relaxation tapes. See lists of audio tapes at the back of this book. Relaxation tapes are also sometimes available at health food stores. I recommend that you buy several of these tapes. They can really help you relax at those times when it is most difficult.

Make your own audio tapes. Use the exercises in this book, or develop your own versions. You may still want to get a commercially produced tape to use as a model.

Check out other resources. There are many excellent books on learning how to relax. These are also listed in the Resource List. Some of these are available at libraries.

I, _____(your name)_____, *am committed to learning how to relax, and to practice daily, so that these skills will be available to me when I need them.*

These are the resources I'm going to use to learn how to relax: _____

_____

_____

_____

For any method of relaxation or meditation to be effective, you must practice daily at a regular time. I practice relaxation techniques for 15 minutes before I get out of bed in the morning and for 15 minutes before I go to sleep (sometimes it *puts* me to sleep). I also try to practice for half an hour after lunch, but my schedule does not always allow for this.

You will figure out for yourself the times when your house or workplace is most quiet, and when you can take a 15-minute break without interruption. Ask your family or co-workers to respect this time by keeping quiet and not disturbing you.

Locate a space or several spaces that are cozy, comfortable, and quiet. This might be in a corner, in your living room, a window seat in your bedroom, or the lunchroom at work. It's also possible to relax out of doors, in a secluded place in the woods, near a meadow, stream, by the ocean, or on a mountaintop. Churches, which are often open and empty on weekdays, are wonderful, quiet places where you can practice relaxation techniques.

Some people like to make their relaxation space special by adorning it with comfortable cushions, pictures, flowers, and candles. The only hard-and-fast rules are to make sure that the space is quiet, that you are comfortable there, and that you will not be disturbed.

I will practice relaxation in the following place or places: _____

_____

_____

_____

Set up a two-week trial period to determine how regular periods of deep relaxation will affect your life.

For two weeks I will relax _____ times daily at the following times: _____

_____

How I felt before I began this relaxation program: _____

_____

_____

_____

How I felt after I completed the two-week relaxation program: _____

_____

_____

_____

Based on what I learned through the trial period, I am going to take the following action regarding structured periods of relaxation: _____

_____

_____

_____

I am going to practice my relaxation techniques every day at the following times: _____

_____

If you miss a session now and again, don't fret. Just do the best you can. Practice relaxing until it becomes second nature, and until you can use the technique any time you begin to feel nervous, tense, or irritable.

When you notice danger signs that you are getting either manic or depressed, spend more time using your relaxation techniques and practice more often during the day. At these times, it can be salvational to use an audio or video tape that has a guided meditation exercise (you may be too subject to distraction to meditate or relax on your own).

Relaxation Techniques

Breathing

Proper breathing habits and simple breathing exercises relax the body and mind. People who practice these exercises daily, either by themselves or before beginning a meditation session with others, find that breathing properly can alleviate depression and mania, enhance the meditation experience, and create a greater sense of overall well-being. Read through the techniques described below and decide which might work best for you. You may want to try them all.

Breathing Awareness

Lie down on the floor with your legs flat or bent at the knees, your arms at your sides, your palms up, and your eyes closed. Breathe through your nose if you can. Focus on your breathing. Place your hand on the place that seems to rise and fall the most as you breathe. If this place is on your chest, you will need to practice breathing more deeply so your abdomen rises and falls most noticeably. (When we are nervous or anxious, we tend to breathe short, shallow breaths in the upper chest.) Now place both hands on your abdomen and notice how it rises and falls with each breath. Notice if your chest is moving in harmony with your abdomen. Continue to do this for several minutes. Get up slowly. This exercise is something you can do during a break at work. If you can't lie down, you can do it sitting in a chair.

How I felt before I did the breathing awareness exercise: _____

_____

_____

How I felt after doing the breathing awareness exercise: _____

_____

_____

_____

Practice deep breathing every day for two weeks, then assess how it's affecting your moods and state of mind.

How I felt after practicing the breathing awareness exercise once or twice a day for two weeks: ___

_____

_____

_____

Deep Breathing

This exercise can be practiced in a variety of body positions; however, it's most effective if you can do it lying down with your knees bent and your spine straight. After lying down, scan your body for tension. Place one hand on your abdomen and one hand on your chest. Inhale slowly and deeply through your nose into your abdomen to push up your hand as much as it feels comfortable. Your chest should only move a little in response to the movement in your abdomen. When you feel at ease with your breathing, inhale through your nose and exhale through your mouth, making a relaxing whooshing sound as you gently blow out. This will relax your mouth, tongue, and jaw. Continue taking long, slow, deep breaths that raise and lower your abdomen. As you become more and more relaxed, focus on the sound and feeling of your breathing. Continue this deep breathing for five to ten minutes at a time, once or twice a day. At the end of each session, scan your body for tension. As you become used to this exercise, you can practice it wherever you happen to be, in a standing, sitting, or supine position. Use the exercise whenever you feel tense.

How I felt before I did the deep breathing exercise: _____

_____

_____

How I felt after doing the deep breathing exercise: _____

_____

_____

Practice deep breathing awareness every day for two weeks, then assess how it's affecting your moods and state of mind.

How I felt after doing the deep breathing exercise once or twice a day for two weeks: _____

_____

_____

_____

The Relaxing Sigh

Do you notice yourself sighing or yawning during the day? This is usually a sign that you are not breathing deeply enough to get enough oxygen. The sigh or yawn helps to remedy the situation and also releases tension. When you feel the need to relax, sit or stand up straight. Sigh deeply, letting out a sound of deep relief as the air rushes out of your lungs. Then let the air return to your lungs slowly and naturally. Repeat eight to twelve times whenever you feel tense or anxious.

How I felt before I did the relaxing sigh exercise: _____

_____

_____

How I felt after doing the relaxing sigh exercise: _____

_____

_____

_____

Practice the relaxing sigh every day for two weeks, then assess how it's affecting your moods and state of mind.

How I felt after doing the relaxing sigh exercise once or twice a day for two weeks: _____

_____

_____

_____

Complete Natural Breathing

This way of breathing will become second nature as you practice it.

Sit or stand up straight. Breathe through your nose. While inhaling, fill the lower section of your lungs (your diaphragm will push your abdomen out to make more room for the air). Now fill the middle part of your lungs with air as your lower ribs and your chest move forward slightly. Then fill the upper part of your lungs with air as you raise your chest slightly and draw in your abdomen a little. With practice these steps can be performed in one continuous, smooth inhalation in a few seconds. Hold your breath for a few seconds. Exhale slowly, pulling your abdomen in slightly and lifting it up slowly as your lungs empty. When you have exhaled completely, relax your abdomen and chest. Repeat this sequence at least five times, raising your shoulders and collarbone occasionally after the inhalation to be sure that the very top of your lungs is filled with fresh air.

Purifying Breath

This exercise cleans your lungs while stimulating and toning your entire breathing process and refreshing your body. It can be used with the other breathing exercises.

Sit or stand up straight. Inhale a complete natural breath, as described in the previous exercise. Hold this breath for several seconds. Exhale a little of the air with force through a small opening in your lips. Stop exhaling for a moment, then blow out more air. Repeat this procedure until you have exhaled the air. Practice for several minutes.

Tap Away Tension

This is a good exercise to relax you quickly while making you feel more alert.

Stand up straight with your hands at your sides. As you inhale slowly, lightly tap your chest with your fingertips, moving your hand around so that your entire chest is tapped. When you have inhaled as much air as feels comfortable, hold your breath and pat your chest with your palms. Exhale using the purifying breath described in the previous exercise. Practice a few more purifying breaths and then repeat the tap-away-tension exercise as many times as it feels comfortable. After you have repeated this exercise several times, try tapping the areas of your back that you can reach with your hands.

How I felt before I tried complete natural breathing, the purifying breath exercise, and the tap-away-tension exercise: _____

_____

_____

How I felt after trying these exercises: _____

_____

_____

_____

Practice complete natural breathing, the purifying breath, and the tap-away-tension exercises every day for two weeks, then assess how it's affecting your moods and state of mind.

How I felt after practicing these exercises every day for two weeks: _____

_____

_____

_____

The Bracer

This is a good exercise when your energy is low. It will stimulate your breathing, circulation, and nervous system.

Stand up straight with your hands at your sides. Inhale and hold a complete natural breath as described above. Raise your arms straight out in front of you, using just enough energy to keep them up and relaxed. Gradually bring your hands to your shoulders while contracting your hands into fists, so that when they reach your shoulders they are clenched as tight as you can make them. Keep your fists clenched as you push your arms out straight very slowly. Pull your arms back to your shoulders and straighten them out, fists tense, as fast as you can several times. Release your fists and let your arms drop to your sides, exhaling forcefully through your mouth. Practice a few purifying breaths as described previously. Repeat this exercise several times until you feel its purifying effects.

The Windmill

This is a good exercise to revive you when you feel overworked and tense.

Stand up straight with your arms in front of you. Inhale and hold a complete natural breath as described previously. Swing your arms backward in a circle several times and then reverse directions. You may also try rotating them like a windmill. Exhale forcefully through your mouth. Practice several purifying breaths as described earlier. Repeat the exercise several times.

Bending

This is another exercise that will relieve tension when you have been working hard. It will also stretch your torso and make it more flexible.

Stand straight with your hands on your hips. Inhale and hold a complete natural breath as described before. Letting the lower part of your body remain stiff, bow forward as far as you possibly can while exhaling slowly through your mouth. Stand up straight again, inhale, and hold another complete natural breath. Bend backwards while slowly exhaling. Stand up straight again and hold another complete breath. Repeat this exercise, bending to the left and right. After each round of four bends, practice one purifying breath. Do four full rounds.

How I felt before I tried the bracer, the windmill, and the bending exercises: _____

_____

_____

How I felt after trying these exercises: _____

_____

_____

_____

Practice the bracer, windmill, and bending exercises every day for two weeks, then assess how you feel.

How I felt after practicing these exercises every day for two weeks: _____

_____

_____

_____

Complete Natural Breathing and Imagination

Lying down, place your hands on your solar plexus (across your lower ribs) and practice complete natural breathing for several minutes. Imagine that with each incoming breath, energy is rushing into your lungs and being immediately stored in your solar plexus. As you exhale, imagine that this energy is flowing to all parts of your body. Practice daily for at least five to ten minutes. You can also use this exercise to imagine sending energy to a place in your body where there is pain, moving one hand from your solar plexus to the place on your body that hurts.

Alternate Breathing

This is an excellent relaxation exercise. Some people also find that it alleviates tension and sinus headaches.

Sit in a comfortable position with good posture. Rest the index and second finger of your right hand on your forehead. Close your right nostril with your thumb. Inhale slowly and soundlessly through your left nostril. Close your left nostril with your ring finger while opening your right nostril by removing your thumb. Exhale slowly, quietly, and as thoroughly as possible through your right nostril. Inhale through your left nostril. Close your right nostril with your thumb and uncover your left nostril. Exhale then inhale through your left nostril. Begin by doing 5 cycles of alternate breathing. Gradually increase the number of cycles to 10 or 25.

How I felt before I tried complete natural breathing and imagination, and alternate breathing exercises: _____

_____

_____

How I felt after I did these exercises: _____

_____

_____

_____

Practice complete natural breathing and imagination, and the alternate breathing exercises every day for two weeks, then assess what effect they've had on your moods and your state of mind.

How I felt after practicing these exercises every day for two weeks: _____

_____

_____

_____

Many of these exercises are adapted from yogic breathing techniques, and can be practiced and perfected by taking a yoga class (yoga classes are available in most communities around the country).

Progressive Muscle Relaxation

The purpose of progressive muscle relaxation is to focus on body sensations and how relaxation feels by systematically tensing and then relaxing different muscle groups in your body. Make a tape recording of this exercise so that you can use it when you need to. Be sure you leave yourself time on the tape to tense and relax your muscles.

Find a quiet space where you will not be disturbed. You can do this exercise either lying on your back or sitting in a chair, as long as you are comfortable.

Close your eyes. Now clench your right fist as tightly as you can. Be aware of the tension as you do so. Keep your fist clenched for a moment. Now relax. Feel the looseness in your right hand and compare it to the tension you felt previously. Tense your right fist again, then relax it; notice the difference between tension and relaxation.

Now clench your left fist as tightly as you can. Be aware of the tension as you do so. Keep your fist clenched for a moment. Now relax. Feel the looseness in your left hand and compare it to the tension you felt previously. Tense your left fist again, relax it, and again notice the difference.

Bend your elbows and tense your biceps as hard as you can. Notice the feeling of tightness. Relax and straighten out your arms. Let the relaxation flow through your arms and compare it to the tightness you felt before. Tense and relax your biceps again.

Wrinkle your forehead as tightly as you can. Now relax it and let it smooth out. Feel your forehead and scalp becoming relaxed. Now frown and notice the tension spreading through your forehead again. Relax and allow your forehead to become smooth.

Close your eyes now and squint them very tightly. Feel the tension. Now relax your eyes. Tense and relax your eyes again. Now let them remain gently closed.

Now clench your jaw, bite hard, and feel the tension. Now relax your jaw. Your lips will be slightly parted. Notice the difference. Clench and relax again.

Press your tongue against the roof of your mouth. Now relax. Do this again.

Press and purse your lips together. Now relax them. Repeat this.

Feel the relaxation throughout your forehead, scalp, eyes, jaw, tongue, and lips.

Hold your head back as far as it can comfortably go and observe the tightness in your neck. Roll your head to the right and notice how the tension moves and changes. Roll your head to the left and notice how the tension moves and changes. Now straighten your head and bring it forward, pressing your chin against your chest. Notice the tension in your throat and the back of your neck. Now relax and allow your shoulders to return to a comfortable position. Allow yourself to feel more and more relaxed. Now shrug your shoulders and hunch your head down between them. Relax your shoulders. Allow them to drop back, and feel the relaxation moving through your neck, throat, and shoulders; feel the lovely, very deep relaxation.

Give your whole body a chance to relax. Feel how comfortable and heavy it is.

Breathe in and fill your lungs completely. Hold you breath and notice the tension. Let your breath out and let your chest become loose. Continue relaxing, breathing gently in and out. Repeat this breathing several times and notice the tension draining out of your body.

Tighten your stomach and hold the tightness. Feel the tension. Now relax your stomach. Place your hand on your stomach and breathe deeply into your stomach, pushing your hand up. Hold for a moment and then relax. Now arch your back without straining, keeping the rest of your body as relaxed as possible. Notice the tension in your lower back. Now relax deeper and deeper.

Tighten your buttocks and thighs. Flex your thighs by pressing your heels down as hard as you can. Relax and notice the difference. Do this again. Curl your toes down, making your calves tense. Notice the tension. Relax. Bend your toes toward your face, creating tension in your shins. Relax and notice the difference.

Feel the heaviness throughout your lower body as the relaxation gets deeper and deeper. Relax your feet, ankles, calves, shins, knees, thighs, and buttocks. Let the relaxation spread to your stomach, lower back, and chest. Let go more and more. Experience deeper and deeper relaxation in your shoulders, arms, and hands, deeper and deeper. Notice the feeling of looseness and relaxation in your neck, jaws, and all your facial muscles.

How I felt before I did the progressive relaxation exercise: _____

_____

_____

How I felt afterwards: _____

_____

_____

_____

Practice progressive muscle relaxation every day for two weeks; then see whether it's made a difference in the way you feel.

How I felt after practicing progressive muscle relaxation once or twice a day for two weeks: _____

_____

_____

_____

Body Scan

This exercise will help you become more aware of how you are feeling right now. As you become aware of your body, mind, and emotions in a nonjudgmental way, you will begin to experience a new clarity and self-acceptance that will help you relax deeply. Do your very best not to judge yourself as you are doing this exercise. Just allow yourself to complete the body scan without worrying about the results.

Get into a comfortable position, either sitting up or lying down in a place where you won't be disturbed.

Gently close your eyes and focus your complete attention on your breathing. Notice the cool air as it is breathed in through your nose, and the warm air as it is breathed out. Focus your full attention on each breath, cool air being breathed in, warm air being breathed out. Just breathe naturally, noticing each breath. Let each breath flow into the next without trying to make anything happen. If your mind strays away from your breath with thoughts about something else, just bring your focus gently back to the breath.

Focus all your attention on your feet and toes. Simply notice how they are feeling.

Now, with all your attention on your toes and feet, allow these areas to relax, release, and then let go. Don't try to make anything happen—just allow it to happen.

Focus your attention on your legs—the lower legs, knees, and upper legs. Notice how they are feeling without making any judgment. Are there any sensations in your legs—tightness, tingling, itching, warmth, cold? Feel whatever it is you feel. Now allow your legs to fully and completely relax. Just let go and let them relax.

Focus your attention on your buttocks and lower abdomen. Notice how they feel. Comfortable, warm, relaxed, loose, whatever. Just notice how they feel. Are there any tight or tense areas? With your mind completely focused on these areas, allow them to fully and completely relax.

Focus your attention on your stomach, chest, and back. Notice any sensations in these areas. Is there any tightness or discomfort present? Feel whatever it is you feel in these areas. Then let go; simply and completely let go.

Now put your full attention on how your hands, arms, shoulders, and neck are feeling. Are there areas of discomfort here? Notice and feel whatever you feel. Then, simply and completely, let go.

Focus your attention on your mouth, nose, face, eyes, and head. Are you experiencing any tightness or discomfort in these areas? Completely feel whatever you are feeling. Relax your mouth, nose, face, eyes, and head. Your jaw and eyelids may begin to droop with relaxation.

Notice how the relaxation is penetrating every organ, every muscle, and every cell of your body. Let your whole body and mind completely relax. Enjoy this feeling of deep relaxation throughout your body. Notice how good it feels. Appreciate yourself for allowing this to happen.

Focus your attention again on your breath, noticing the cool air come in as you inhale, and the warm air go out as you exhale. Stay focused on each breath as it goes in and out, breath by breath. Notice how relaxed, refreshed, and energetic you feel. This relaxation and feeling of renewed energy will stay with you as you get on with the things you do. Slowly get up and resume your activities. Remember that each time you do this exercise, you will relax more fully and deeply, continuing to enhance your wellness.

How I felt before I did the body scan exercise: _____

_____

_____

How I felt after I did the body scan exercise: _____

_____

_____

_____

Practice the body scan exercise every day for two weeks; then assess how this practice has affected your moods and state of mind.

How I felt after doing the body scan exercise once or twice a day for two weeks: _____

_____

_____

_____

Meditation

Meditation is described in *The Relaxation and Stress Reduction Workbook* as "the practice of uncritically attempting to focus your attention on one thing at a time." You can choose to meditate on anything that appeals to you. Gazing at an object, such as the second hand on a wristwatch, a candle flame, a flower, or a favorite picture, will focus your attention. Or you may choose to repeat, either aloud or to yourself, a syllable, word, or group of words.

It can be helpful before meditating to bring yourself into a quieter frame of mind by reading an inspiring passage from a book that means a great deal to you. I sometimes use this quote from *The Power of Myth* by Joseph Campbell:

> One thing that comes out of myths is that at the bottom of the abyss comes the voice of salvation. The black moment is the moment when the real message of transformation is going to come. At the darkest moment comes the light.

Some people refer to Kahlil Gibran's chapter "On Love" in *The Prophet*. You might spend a few moments studying a flower, plant, rock, piece of jewelry, or picture. Use your creativity and you will come up with plenty of inspirations to launch your meditation.

As you attempt to focus your mind, you will find that it wanders from one thought to another. When you realize this, notice the new thought, then bring your focus back to your breathing.

How to Meditate

The following step-by-step instructions will show you how to begin.

Select a position that is comfortable for you:

- Sit in a chair with your feet flat on the floor, your knees relaxed, and your hands resting in your lap.

- Sit cross-legged, tailor fashion, on the floor, with a cushion under your bottom.

- Kneel on a cushion, with another cushion between your feet and the floor.

Your back should be comfortably straight with the weight of your head balanced on top of your spinal column (pull your chin in a bit) and an arch in the small of your back. Now rock from side to side and from front to back until your torso feels balanced on your hips. Close your mouth, breathe through your nose, and have your tongue in the roof of your mouth.

Now spend several minutes getting in touch with yourself. With your eyes closed, focus on the places where your body touches the chair, cushion, or floor. Notice what this feels like. Now notice those places where one body part touches another. Pay attention to the sensations at these places of contact. Notice how much space your body takes up. Feel the boundary between your body and the space around it.

Take several deep breaths and notice your breathing. Notice whether your breathing is fast or slow, deep or shallow, and where your breath goes in your body (high up in your chest, near your stomach, or down low in your abdomen). Now practice moving your breath from one place to another, breathing first into your chest, then down into your stomach area, then down into the lower parts of your torso. Notice your abdomen expanding and contracting. This deep breath is the most relaxing one to use when meditating. This may be hard at first, but it will become easier as you practice.

Maintain a passive attitude when meditating. Remember that you will have many intrusive thoughts when you first begin to meditate, but your moments of fixed attention will increase as your ability to let go of stray thoughts improves. Don't worry about whether you are doing things correctly or well enough. Realize that whatever happens is what is supposed to happen.

You may want to spend some time practicing the process of letting go of intrusive thoughts. I often do this when I am having a hard time quieting down enough to sleep. Take several deep breaths. As you have a thought or perception, imagine that you are enclosing that thought or perception in a bubble. Then just watch the bubble float away. You may think of other images that are easier for you to use, such as puffs of smoke or leaves floating down a stream.

For some meditations in which you are not gazing at a particular object, you may close your eyes, or keep them focused on a particular spot on the floor or wall. Maintain the meditation for as long as feels comfortable to you. You can start out with just a 5-minute meditation. As you become more accustomed to meditating, you will want to spend more time—up to 20 or 30 minutes, twice a day, at regularly scheduled times. You may want to find a group to meditate with on a regular basis.

Different Styles of Meditation

There are many different ways to meditate—but all ways lead to the same result. Choose the style or styles you think you will most likely be able to practice on a regular basis. I use all of the meditations described below, and find them to be very helpful in stabilizing my moods. I have found that I can use these techniques to relax myself in many different situations, not just when I am in a quiet place and in the right position—such as before surgery or other medical treatments, when stuck in traffic, or when I'm feeling anxious about someone or something.

Mantra Meditation

Select a syllable, word, or group of words that you enjoy saying: this is your mantra. Many people use the neutral sound *om*. Say your mantra over and over again to yourself or out loud, whichever feels better to you. Let your mantra find its own rhythm as you repeat it. Try to stay aware of the mantra with each repetition. Notice any sensations in your body. If your mind wanders, acknowledge this, then bring your attention back to your mantra.

How I felt before trying mantra meditation: _____

_____

_____

How I felt after trying mantra meditation: _____

_____

_____

_____

Practice the mantra meditation twice a day for two weeks; then think about whether it has affected your mood or state of mind.

How I felt after practicing the mantra meditation twice a day for two weeks: _____

_____

_____

_____

Breath-Counting Meditation

Take several deep breaths, focusing your attention on each part of the process (inhale, the point at which you stop inhaling and begin exhaling, exhaling, and before breathing again). Pay attention to the pause and use that time to notice any sensations in your body. Now count your breaths, counting one for the inhale and two for the exhale. If you lose count, simply start over again. Note any thoughts that intrude, but just let them float away. Always bring your focus back to your breathing.

How I felt before trying the breath-counting meditation: _____

_____

_____

How I felt after doing the breath-counting meditation: _____

_____

_____

_____

Practice the breath-counting meditation twice a day for two weeks; then think about whether you feel any different as a result.

How I felt after doing the breath-counting meditation once or twice a day for two weeks: _____

_____

_____

_____

Gazing

Set the object of your choice on a surface that is at eye level and about a foot or two away from you. Choose something simple: a flower, a candle, a stone—something without a lot of emotional associations for you. Now gaze at the object while keeping your eyes relaxed. Notice everything about it: texture, size, color, shape. Trace the edge of the object with your eyes; see all the minute details that you wouldn't usually take the time to notice. If you become distracted, simply return your gaze to the object.

How I felt before trying the gazing meditation: _____

_____

_____

How I felt after trying the gazing meditation: _____

_____

_____

_____

Practice the gazing meditation twice a day every day for two weeks; then think about whether it has affected your mood or state of mind.

How I felt after practicing the gazing meditation for two weeks: _____

_____

_____

_____

Other Styles of Meditation

Below are ten additional meditations you can try. With each one, repeat the pattern of two weeks of practice, then make an assessment of how you feel. Testing in this way will allow you to find the styles of meditation that work best for you. All of these meditations can be used as a mix-and-match resource, depending on your mood.

Almost any activity that doesn't consciously engage your brain can become a meditation. All you need to do is concentrate on every action and every sensation. You can meditate as you eat, walk, garden, wash the dishes, make a bed, dust the furniture, wash your car, and so on.

The Moving Band Meditation

Imagine that a three-inch-wide band is around the top of your head. Focus all your attention on that part of your head. Notice the sensations. If there is any tension, try to release it. Now mentally lower the band three inches and again focus your attention on the area encompassed by the band. What does it feel like? Again, try to relax any tension in this area. Continue to "move" the band slowly down your body in this way. Have it circle each leg or arm individually. Sometimes you may want to move this imaginary band very slowly. At other times it will feel more relaxing to move it more quickly.

The Inner Exploration

Pick one part of your body on which to focus all your attention. Explore that part of your body in detail with your mind. What are the sensations in this part of your body? How does it move? What does it do? Is it tense? If it is tense, practice relaxing this part of your body in isolation. You may want to choose parts of your body that tend to be tense, such as the neck, shoulders, jaw, forehead, or lower back. Or you may choose internal areas that tend to be tense, such as the stomach or chest. Another idea is to focus on body parts that you rarely think about, such as your toes, your elbows, or behind your knees.

Softening

We all tend to respond to pain, irritation, and discomfort by tensing all or part of our body, even though this automatic reaction tends to increase the pain or level of discomfort. The more it hurts, the more we respond with tension. This is a good meditation to do when you're tense or in pain. Get relaxed, then focus on the feeling of pain, irritation, or discomfort. Reassure yourself that everything is all right. Now consciously focus on relaxing (softening) the muscles you had been tensing.

Don't Move

Make an agreement with yourself that you will not move for a predetermined period of time—this can range from one to ten minutes. As you meditate, you will notice that some part of your body is moving without your realizing it. Just notice this movement and keep meditating. As you proceed you will begin to anticipate your need to move. Is it in response to an itch? Sore muscles? Identify the uncomfortable sensation and, rather than move, consciously soften around the sensation. Soften any muscle groups that feel tense. Be sure that you are breathing deeply. When your time is up, allow your body to move to whatever position is comfortable. Focus on what that feels like. Is the relief immediate or gradual? Release any tension in you body before resuming your activities.

Lifted Arm

Place your left hand on your lap, bend your right arm at the elbow (as in signaling for a right-hand turn), and lift that arm so the tips of your fingers are level with the top of your head. As the right arm begins to tire, focus your attention on the sensation of tiredness. See if you can find a way to relax the muscles in your arm without dropping it. Check out the rest of your body for tension. Relax any areas that feel tense. If you notice that you are beginning to feel anxious, take several deep breaths and remind yourself to relax. When you have finished meditating, lower your arm very slowly. Focus on what your arm feels like. How does the discomfort or tiredness change as you lower your arm? Relax any tension you feel in other parts of your body before you resume your activities.

Warming Up and Cooling Down

Meditate in an area that is slightly warmer or cooler than you would normally prefer. As the extra warmth or coolness becomes noticeable, focus on your body's reaction to it. Is your body tensing? Are you starting to sweat or shiver? See if you can find a way to relax your body's reaction to the temperature. Does focusing on your object of meditation help? When you have finished meditating, spend a few minutes in an area that has a comfortable temperature and notice how your body adjusts to this change.

Responding to Irritation

Use any irritating sound or sensation as the focus of your meditation. It could be a barking dog, a printer, the noise of traffic, or an itch. Notice what your body does in reaction. Then relax any tension that your body has formed in response to the irritant. (This is a good meditation to use when you're in a place where it would normally be difficult to meditate because of noise or other distractions.)

Being Present in the Moment

Most of the stress in our lives comes from thinking about the past or worrying about the future. When all your attention is focused in the present moment, it is difficult to feel either stress or worry. Get relaxed, then focus all your attention on what you are doing right now. When other thoughts intrude, just turn your awareness back to the present moment of meditation. It is not necessary to be alone in a special place to do this meditation. Try it when you are feeling irritated waiting in a line, stopped at a street light, stuck in traffic, or feeling overwhelmed or worried. Notice how focusing on the present moment makes you feel.

Eating Meditation

Sit down in front of your food. Take several deep breaths. Notice the color, shape, and texture of the food. Notice how looking at the food makes you feel. Reach slowly for your food. Now begin eating very slowly. Stay aware of how you are feeling and what you are tasting all the time you are eating. Eat as if you were eating in slow motion, being very conscious of each bit of food and each motion involved in eating it. How do your teeth and tongue feel? What does it feel like to swallow? Can you feel the food moving down your esophagus and into your stomach? When other thoughts intrude, notice them and return your attention to eating.

Walking Meditation

Stand up and relax your body all over. Take several deep, focused breaths. Now begin walking. Be aware of every process involved in moving. Try to match you breathing rhythm to your walking in a way that is comfortable to you. Pay attention to all the sensations of walking. Notice your muscles contracting and relaxing as you move. How do the various parts of your body feel as you walk? After you've scanned the feelings in you body, become aware of everything you can see as you walk. Then become aware of everything you can hear and everything you can smell. As thoughts intrude, let them go and notice everything about the experience of walking instead.

Reactions of People in the Study

Nineteen people in the study have effectively used meditation. The benefits they noted are listed below. **Which of these would you like to achieve?**

- ☐ relaxation
- ☐ sense of control
- ☐ lifting of symptoms
- ☐ grounding
- ☐ clearer thinking
- ☐ enhanced sense of life
- ☐ feeling of safety
- ☐ relief from depression
- ☐ enhanced ability to sleep
- ☐ calmness
- ☐ inner peace
- ☐ balance
- ☐ ability to keep mania within bounds
- ☐ refreshment of the mind
- ☐ feeling free
- ☐ relief from manic episodes
- ☐ increased ability to deal with symptoms
- ☐ diminished tension

One of the great advantages of meditation is that it doesn't depend on the presence of anyone or anything; it's a therapeutic tool that is *always* available to you.

Other benefits you'd like to achieve from meditation: _____

_____

_____

_____

_____

Three Calming Exercises

Guided Imagery Meditation

Guided imagery focuses your imagination on relaxing and healing images. A detailed example is given below, but you can make up your own healing and peaceful scenarios. The important thing is to include as much sensory detail as possible. Try to include all five senses: touch, taste, smell, hearing, and sight. Try the following guided imagery meditation.

Get in a very comfortable sitting or lying position. Make sure that you are warm enough but not too warm, and that you will not be interrupted by the phone, doorbell, or the needs of others. You might want to make a tape recording of these instructions.

Stare at a spot above your head on the ceiling (if you're lying down) or stare straight ahead. Take a deep breath to a count of eight, hold it for a count of four, let it out for a count of eight.

Again—in to a count of eight; hold for a count of four; exhale for a count of eight.

Again—in to a count of eight; hold for a count of four; exhale for a count of eight.

Now close your eyes, but keep them in the same position they were in when you were staring at a spot on the ceiling or in front of you.

Breathe in to a count of eight; hold for a count of four; exhale for a count of eight.

Now focus on your toes. Let them completely relax. Now move the feeling of relaxation slowly up your legs, through your heels and calves to your knees. Now let the warm feeling of relaxation move up your thighs. Feel your whole body relaxing. Let the relaxation move very slowly through your buttocks, lower abdomen, and lower back. Now feel it moving, very slowly, up your spine and through your abdomen. Now feel the warm relaxation flowing into your chest and upper back.

Let this relaxation flow from your shoulders, down your arms, through your elbows and wrists, out through your hands and fingers. Now let the relaxation go slowly through your throat and up your neck, letting it all soften and relax. Let the feeling move up into your face. Feel the relaxation fill your jaw and cheek muscles, and surround your eyes. Relax your eyes. Let the feeling of relaxation move up into your forehead. Now let your whole scalp relax and feel warm and comfortable. Your body is now completely relaxed, with the feeling of relaxation filling every muscle and cell of your body.

Picture yourself walking on the beach on a sunny day. As you stroll along, you feel the warmth of the sun on your back. You lie down on a soft towel in the sand. The sand molds to your body and you feel warm and comfortable. The sun warms your skin, the salt air smells fresh. You can still taste the fresh-squeezed juice you just drank, the juice that a friend made for you because she knows how much you like it. You hear the waves breaking against the shore in a steady rhythm. The sound of seagulls calling overhead completes your feeling of blissful contentment.

As you lie here you realize that you are perfectly and completely relaxed. You feel safe and at peace with the world. You know you have the power to relax yourself completely at any time you need to. By completely relaxing, you are giving the body the opportunity to stabilize itself, and that when you wake up you will feel calm, relaxed, and able to get on with your tasks for the day.

Now slowly wiggle your fingers and toes. Gradually open your eyes and resume your activities.

Focusing on Detail

For a quick relaxer when your day gets hectic, focus on detail. If you are at home, keep several picture postcards or greeting cards with lots of attractive detail handy. I recommend the book *Animalia* by Graeme Base. It is filled with detailed pictures which are very interesting to study. When you start to feel rushed or agitated, sit down in a quiet, comfortable spot, and focus on the detail in your chosen picture for ten minutes. Notice if you feel calmer afterwards.

You can do this exercise anywhere by just focusing on your surroundings. It can keep you from getting irritated when you're waiting in line or stuck in traffic. If you are waiting in a doctor's office, focus on the detail in a picture in a magazine.

Checking In

Every so often throughout the day, take a brief break, take several deep breaths, and get back in touch with how you feel. Check yourself out all over. And then imagine the tightness flowing out of the tense places in your body. Let your mind take a brief but complete break.

20

Diet

When I stick to a diet that is high in grains and vegetables, I feel better and my moods are more stable. Junk foods that are high in fat, sugar, and salt deepen my depressions and make me more hyper.

What You Eat Affects the Way You Feel

My own personal experience has shown me clearly that what I eat affects the way I feel. It is very important for me to avoid sugar. It makes me feel lethargic, foggy, bloated, and uncomfortable. Caffeine speeds me up, so I avoid it if I'm already going faster than is comfortable and am working to slow myself down. I have learned that I cannot digest dairy foods; so I avoid all except yogurt.

Thirty-eight of the people in the survey said they had particular eating habits that affect their moods. I know that number would be even higher if people were paying more attention to what they eat and how they feel after they eat it. Many of the study participants say that food allergies make them feel worse.

Avoid eating any one food excessively or exclusively. You need a varied diet to get all the nutrients necessary to keep you healthy. People with ups and downs of mood need to be particularly cautious, because they are so easily thrown out of balance. Especially if an undetected food allergy is in the picture, a varied and healthy diet can go a long way toward minimizing symptoms.

If you're like so many others, you often crave particular foods in excess. People in the study most frequently mentioned craving foods that are high in sugar (especially chocolate), carbohydrates, such as bread or pasta, beverages that contain caffeine, and salty foods. Often the foods we crave are the ones we should avoid (a craving can indicate a food allergy!). With a healthy diet, these cravings diminish.

I recommend *The Zone* and *Mastering the Zone* (adapted for your special needs) for making the transition to a good diet. They contain information on how foods affect moods and gives a variety of simple recipes that you can alter to suit your tastes and lifestyle. It's a lot of work to get into the mode of eating well, but it's a change that is definitely worthwhile.

You don't have to be super strict. Allow yourself to splurge occasionally and have a treat. Note how you feel afterward. Any negative symptoms you feel may keep you from splurging too often. Eventually you will get used to the foods in your new, healthy diet, and some of them will seem like treats.

Keep on hand healthy foods that are easy to fix or ready to eat—and that you enjoy eating—so you don't stop eating when you are feeling too low to cook.

Weight Control

Half the people in the study reported that they are significantly overweight. They often blamed this on the drugs they are taking and/or the bingeing or lethargy that can accompany mood swings.

Food is sometimes the only thing you can find that relieves the low feeling, at least while the food is still in your mouth.

Besides being unhealthy, excess weight makes people feel self-conscious and unattractive, lowering their self-esteem and further complicating their depression.

I myself have been significantly overweight. At one time I weighed 30 pounds more than the weight suggested for a woman of my age and build. This was at a time when I was experiencing a lengthy depressive episode and was in an abusive marital situation. I found that I craved sweets and salty foods. As I needed to buy bigger and bigger clothes, I felt worse and worse about myself and my appearance, further aggravating my depression. When I realized that I was using food to numb my pain, I started to take better care of myself, avoiding sweets and fast foods, and treating myself to a good, healthy diet along with a regular program of exercise. I lost most of the weight, but find that it's a constant battle to keep it off. While I realize that it's best for my health if I control my weight, I am also learning to like my body and the way I look, no matter how much I weigh.

Many of the people in the study reported talking to their doctor about the relationship between weight gain and the drug or drugs they're taking. Based on the doctor's recommendation, and using all the resources available to them, they made a decision about the best and safest course of action relative to continuing or changing their drug treatment program.

Some have gone on a weight reduction diet and exercise program based on the best available information. If you have health problems or take medications, it's imperative that you get your doctor's advice before making any changes in your eating or exercise routine. Many study respondents said that they go to weight control support groups such as Overeater's Anonymous or Weight Watchers.

Because feelings about food often have strong emotional connections, many of the people who have successfully lost weight and kept it off have worked closely with a therapist and read resource books about problems with food addiction.

Several people in the study said that they have made the decision to live with their extra weight. They're determined not to let it get in the way of living a full and satisfying life. One woman said: "The effect of my excess weight is diminishing to nothing. About three years ago, I decided I was going to stop feeling inferior, stop talking about it, wear attractive clothes, and go swimming."

Another respondent said that her weight directly correlates with her self-image and level of self-esteem. She has recently lost weight, is still losing, and feels great about it.

Another person, who lost 130 pounds, found that it was scary going from heavier to so much lighter; but the weight loss helped relieve a back injury, as well as her mania and depression.

Hypothyroidism, or low thyroid function, can cause weight gain and make it difficult to lose unwanted pounds. If you are overweight, make sure you have a complete battery of thyroid tests (see the chapter entitled "Possible Causes of Mood Disorders").

If you've decided that your weight is a problem that needs to be addressed for reasons of health or to enhance your self-esteem, what is your weight goal? _____ pounds

How many pounds less is this than your present weight?_____

How long are you going to give yourself to lose these pounds?_____

Be easy on yourself. Remember—it is never healthy to lose more than two pounds a week. And weight loss does not usually progress evenly, no matter what you do. Don't be discouraged if you hit a plateau that lasts for a while. Be patient. Your weight will eventually continue to drop if you still have more to lose.

If you give in to temptation, don't give up. You haven't done anything serious. Just get back on the diet and stick to it as best as you can. And be sure to give yourself a pat on the back for every good day.

Weight Loss Plan

Recommendations of doctor or health professionals: _____

_____

_____

Results of a complete battery of thyroid tests showed that:

☐ my thyroid is fine

☐ I need further testing

☐ I need treatment for a thyroid disorder

Based on these findings, I am going to take the following action: _____

_____

_____

_____

I plan to attend a weight loss support group (when) _____ *(where)* _____ .
(Local newspapers usually list these groups.)

Resources I plan to use (books, videos, classes, etc.)*:* _____

_____

_____

Sugar

The number one food culprit for many people is sugar. One study participant described it as "a mood-altering substance that should be avoided by all people with mood disorders, as it can be very dangerous." Other descriptions of the effects of sugar include mood elevation, hyperactivity, fatigue, increased pulse rate, mood instability, depression, loss of control, headaches, irritability, agitation, distorted and exaggerated anxiety, exaggerated moods, and worsened depression.

Many people in the study said that they avoid sugar in any form. It's useful to bear in mind that 100 years ago sugar was a rare and occasional treat. Now it is a standard ingredient used to enhance flavor in most of the prepared foods we buy. Our bodies seem to be having trouble adapting to this increased sugar load.

Sugar Blues by William Dufty describes in detail the effects of sugar on the body. *The Yeast Connection Cookbook* by William C. Crook looks at the role of sugar in medical problems involving the yeast *Candida albicans*, and gives dietary solutions. Medical doctors are becoming more aware that excess yeast in the system can cause or worsen mood instability, depression, inability to concentrate, and mental fogginess.

As an experiment, eliminate all sugar from your diet for two weeks. You'll really have to read labels! Closely monitor how you feel—keeping a daily journal will make this easier.

Did eliminating sugar from your diet affect the way you feel? Note whether the symptoms below were aggravated, alleviated, or remained unchanged.

Symptoms	Aggravated	Alleviated	Unchanged
Depression			
Mania			
Food cravings			
Bloating			
Heartburn			

Constipation			
Diarrhea			
Headaches			
Sinus problems			
(Other)			

If you noticed significant positive changes as a result of two weeks without sugar, you may want to continue on a low- or no-sugar diet. I eat very little sugar. When I am tempted and give in, I only have to eat a small amount of sugar before I begin to notice symptoms. The first symptom I notice is an intense feeling of fatigue.

Because of what I have learned about the effects of sugar on my body, I have decided to take the following action regarding the use of sugar in my diet: _____

_____

_____

_____

Artificial sweetners are not a good substitute for sugar. Evidence is mounting that they may be responsible for many health problems. Small amounts of an herb, stevia, found in health food stores is an effective and safe sweetner. In addition, you can satisfy your sweet tooth with fruit and sweet vegetables like carrots and winter squash.

Caffeine

Many people in the study noted that limiting the caffeine in their diet lessens the intensity of their mood swings. Caffeine can cause mood elevation, nervousness, hyperactivity, jitteriness, irritability, insomnia, anxiety, shakiness, restlessness, pounding heart, sluggishness, headaches, and overstimulation. Before you ingest foods containing caffeine, look at it as a drug and give it the same level of consideration.

Caffeine is not only in coffee. It is found in tea, various soft drinks, cocoa, and chocolate products. The caffeine content of various foods, taken from the *Wellness Encyclopedia*, is listed below. Of course, these figures can vary according to product and method of preparation.

per 5-ounce serving:

Coffee, drip	110–150 mg.
Coffee, perk	60–125 mg.
Coffee, instant	40–105 mg.
Coffee, decaffeinated	2–5 mg.

Tea, steeped for 5 minutes	40–100 mg.
Tea, steeped for 3 minutes	20–50 mg.
Hot cocoa	2–10 mg.
per 12-ounce serving:	
Cola drinks	45 mg.
per 1-ounce serving:	
Milk chocolate	1–15 mg.
Bittersweet chocolate	5–35 mg.
per slice:	
chocolate cake	20–30 mg.

There are many decaffeinated products on the market that can be used as substitutes but, as you can see, even decaf coffee contains some caffeine!

Check labels to determine the caffeine content of foods and drinks. Being aware of the possible effects of caffeine allows you to make appropriate decisions about when and in what amounts to use it.

It can be very difficult to give up caffeine. People who withdraw abruptly from using all caffeine often experience unpleasant reactions, such as a mild but persistent headache, a general feeling of tiredness, an inability to focus mentally, and a constant temptation to "have another cup of coffee." These symptoms decrease over time, but may last up to two weeks. Cutting out caffeine may not be something you can do when you are trying to make many other changes in your life. Gradual withdrawal is an answer for most people.

After I drink caffeine I feel _____

_____

_____

I intend to make the following changes with regard to the use of caffeine in my diet: _____

_____

_____

Dairy Products

People respond to dairy products in different ways. Some people say they help relieve mood swings. Positive effects cited by people in the study include soothing, leveling, inducing sleep, and a feeling of well-being. Negative effects include fatigue, irritability, acne, racing pulse, thick mucus, sinus congestion, and intensification of premenstrual syndrome. I find that I can no longer digest dairy products at all. I suffer severe digestive symptoms when I give in to the temptation of these delicious foods. Yogurt, mercifully, is an exception, and satisfies my desire for dairy products.

It's a good idea to test your reaction to dairy products by eliminating them from your diet for two weeks, just as you did with sugar. (Don't try both experiments at the same time, as you won't be able to tell which food type has been causing what set of symptoms.)

Which of these symptoms do you associate with your intake of dairy products?

- ☐ fatigue
- ☐ irritability
- ☐ acne
- ☐ racing pulse
- ☐ sinus congestion
- ☐ worsened PMS
- ☐ (other) _____

- ☐ gas
- ☐ bloating
- ☐ heartburn
- ☐ constipation
- ☐ diarrhea

Go through the list again after you've eliminated dairy products from your diet for two weeks. **Was there a difference?** _____

Eliminating dairy products from my diet for two weeks made the following changes in how I feel:

_____

_____

_____

I have decided to take the following action regarding my use of dairy products: _____

_____

_____

_____

Other Foods That Might Be Causing Problems

People in the study reported on other kinds of food that seem to aggravate their mood swings. Foods mentioned include wheat products, fermented foods, eggs, meat, and tomatoes. You can use the two-week experiment with any that you feel might be aggravating your mood swings or compromising your health. Each experiment will require careful reading of product labels and conscientious monitoring of your reactions in a daily journal. The advantage of this method is that you can eliminate offending foods from your diet one at a time, rather than going on an oppressively restrictive diet with the vague idea that some foods might be bad for you.

Changing Your Diet

Let me emphasize that making dietary changes is not easy. Your new diet may require more cooking. It may require separate meals for yourself and other people you live with. It certainly requires changes in habits that have developed over a lifetime. Your new diet may even seem costlier at first, as you stock up on new staples and find out where to buy everything you need.

See a Nutritionist

A good nutritionist or naturopathic physician can give you dietary information and make recommendations on the use of food supplements that are tailored to meet your personal needs. They may want to do testing to see if any deficiencies might be causing or worsening your condition.

Again, be gentle with yourself. Give yourself a pat on the back for a job well done, and don't be too hard on yourself for a little backsliding. Change is always difficult. But, believe me, it's worth the effort.

21

Exercise: Do It

Exercise lifts my moods and makes me feel, overall, more confident and secure.

There was universal agreement among study participants that exercise makes them feel better. If they are depressed, exercise improves their mood. If they are manic, gentle exercise, such as a leisurely walk, helps calm them down.

Caution: Some people in the study noted that strenuous or very active exercise, such as heavy labor or fast running, can worsen symptoms. Choose mild forms of exercise when you have signs of mania.

"I do hard-work toning consisting of water aerobics and low-impact dance aerobics. It gets the heart rate up, increases my sense of well-being, and the body benefits, too. This is most effective if in a class where one has rapport with other class members. The classes are also good for structure. Exercise is a necessity for me. I benefit by having small, medium, and large depressions lifted right out of my mind."

According to *The Anxiety and Phobia Workbook* (see Resource List), the physiological benefits of regular exercise include:

- Reduced skeletal muscle tension

- Increased metabolism of excess adrenaline and thyroxin in the bloodstream (excess adrenaline and thyroxin tend to keep you in an uncomfortable state of arousal and vigilance)

- Discharge of pent-up frustration

- Enhanced oxygenation of the blood and the brain, increasing alertness and concentration

- Stimulated production of endorphins, which increase your sense of well-being

- Increased energy level through increased acidity of the blood

- Improved circulation

- Improved digestion

- Improved elimination from the skin, lungs, and bowels

- Decreased cholesterol levels

- Decreased blood pressure

- Suppressed appetite and consequent weight loss

- Improved regulation of blood sugar

In addition to these physiological benefits, people who exercise notice the following psychological benefits:

- Increased feeling of well-being

- Reduced dependence on alcohol and drugs

- Reduced insomnia

- Improved concentration and memory

- Alleviation of depression symptoms

- Greater control over feelings of anxiety

- Increased self-esteem

These factors are ample reason for anyone to begin exercising regularly. However, most people find it very difficult to exercise when they're depressed. Typically, during depression your energy level and motivation are low. The chronic physical aches and pains that often accompany depression can make the prospect of a workout even less appealing. The tendency to isolate yourself can also be an inhibiting factor if your exercise of choice involves classes or appearing in public.

I find it easier to exercise when I am depressed if exercise is already an established part of my daily wellness routine, like brushing my teeth and eating breakfast. Every day, over the lunch hour, I take a 20-minute walk or bicycle ride. You may prefer to walk in the morning or evening (the season may make a difference in the time of day you exercise if you exercise outdoors) and for a shorter or longer period of time. If I'm low, I make my exercise session as easy for myself as possible. I choose places to go where I am not likely to meet many people, and where the trails are flat and unchallenging. I have a stationary bicycle that I ride indoors if the weather is bad. I often ride it while watching something pleasant on TV or reading to break the monotony. Aerobic exercise records, tapes, and television programs are another good way I have found to get the exercise I need indoors at home.

Varying the kind of exercise you do from day to day may make the regimen more interesting for you. On the other hand, when you're depressed, the same thing over and over, every day, can feel easier and more comfortable. Whatever works best for you is what you need to do.

Some people find it easier to exercise in a group. Your local newspaper or recreation department is a good resource for locating exercise groups or classes. When you're really depressed, you may not feel comfortable in a group—so make whatever arrangements necessary to make exercise palatable. Exercising with a friend can also enhance your motivation and make the experience more pleasurable.

I always found it hard to exercise the first day or two after making some change in my drug treatment program. I found myself tiring quickly, and feeling short of breath. Pay attention to what your body is saying, and act accordingly. Don't force yourself to exercise when you feel ill or overstressed, or when you are experiencing some unexplained physical symptoms. (This is a good time to try relaxation techniques.)

Again, it helps to have a regularly scheduled time to exercise. If you exercise consistently, you'll reap enormous benefits.

If you miss a day or two, don't give yourself a hard time about it. Just do the best you can. Be sure to give yourself a pat on the back when you *do* exercise. I always reward myself with a short rest and sometimes with a piece of fruit when I finish exercising.

Remember, it is always a good idea to get your doctor's approval before increasing your activity level, especially if you have a medical condition requiring treatment.

If you have a hard time exercising when you are depressed, why do you think it is a problem for you? _____

_____

_____

_____

_____

_____

_____

What could you do for yourself that would make it easier to exercise when you are depressed? _____

_____

_____

_____

_____

I find that even very slow exercise, such as neck rolls, leg lifts, and yoga, can help lift depression. Physical therapists, and people who do therapeutic body work or massage (sometimes known as body workers or body counselors), have good advice to offer on gentle exercise that can help lift depression. These are the kinds of exercise most enjoyed by study participants. Check those which you participate in already, and those which you would like to try.

Exercise	Do It Now	Plan To Try
Walking		
Jogging		
Swimming		
Hiking		
Gardening		
Yoga		
Ice skating		
Outdoor physical work (such as mowing the lawn)		
Speed walking		
Biking		
Skiing		
Working out at a gym		
Dancing		
Aerobics classes or *Jazzercise*		
Roller skating		

Other forms of exercise I plan to try: _____

_____

It helps to have a regularly scheduled time to exercise. Walking for half an hour at lunchtime works for some people. Others prefer to exercise early in the morning or in the late afternoon. If you exercise consistently at a particular time, the regime becomes a habit. Even if you miss a day or two a week, you'll still reap enormous benefits.

Many people find it easier to exercise in a group. Your local newspaper or recreation department is a good resource for locating exercise groups or classes.

Remember: It is always a good idea to get your doctor's approval before increasing your activity level, especially if you have a medical condition requiring treatment.

How would you rate your current fitness level?

☐ *I feel that I already get all the exercise I need.*

☐ *I feel that I need to increase the amount of exercise I get. I will do it*
(how long) _____ (days per week) _____

☐ *I am going to join an exercise group or class (where)* _____
(when) _____

You can determine if you are really out of shape and need more exercise by considering the following symptoms. Check the ones that apply to you.

☐ Out of breath after walking up a flight of stairs or climbing a hill

☐ Takes a long time to recover after walking up a flight of stairs or climbing a hill

☐ Feeling exhausted after short periods of exertion

☐ Chronic muscle tension

☐ Poor muscle tone

☐ Obesity

☐ Muscles are cramped and ache for days after participating in a sport

☐ Generally tired, lethargic, and bored

Other symptoms you have which might be due to lack of exercise: _____

_____

_____

_____

_____

If you feel that you're out of shape, I suggest that you commit yourself to a regular program of exercise. Check in with your doctor to determine the kind and duration of exercise that would be best for you, especially if you have not been exercising for some time.

☐ *I feel that I am already in good shape, and plan to stick to the exercise program I have.*

☐ *I commit myself to a regular program of exercise.*

☐ *I am going to join an exercise group (when)* _____
(where) _____

Exercise at the same time each day. Choose the time of day that fits into your schedule—early in the morning, during your lunch break, or early in the evening. Your work schedule and family responsibilities may need to be considered. Avoid exercising within 90 minutes of a meal, or just before going to bed.

I *am going to exercise at* (time) _____ *on the following days*:

_____

_____

_____

    Enjoy yourself while exercising. Don't consider your exercise session as something you *have* to do or a chore, but rather as something you *want to do.* Consider this as special time that you are giving to yourself and your body.

    If you have not been exercising regularly, start slowly and increase your time and exertion gradually. At first you may be able to exercise for only five minutes. Age and physical shape make a difference. Try adding five more minutes of exercise each week if you feel comfortable doing so.

    When you first begin to exercise, you will notice some aches and pains that you didn't have before. These will go away in several days. A warm bath after exercising always helps.

    Use the chart at the end of this chapter to monitor your exercise program and help you answer the following questions:

How I felt before I began a program of regular exercise: _____

_____

_____

_____

_____

How I felt after exercising regularly for two weeks: _____

_____

_____

_____

_____

After exercising when depressed I felt: _____

_____

_____

_____

_____

After exercising when manic I felt: _____

_____

_____

_____

_____

My long-term exercise goals are: _____

_____

_____

_____

_____

Use this daily chart to keep track of your exercise program (copy it for future use).

Daily Exercise Record

Week of: _____

Date	How long I exercised	Type of exercise	How I felt before	How I felt afterwards

22

Light, Electromagnetic Radiation, and the Biological Clock

I started getting outside for a few minutes every day, just sitting on the porch because it was so hard for me to move or be seen and, like a miracle, my deep depression started to lift.

The Importance of Full-Spectrum Light

Overwhelming scientific evidence shows that exposure to light through the eyes affects mental as well as physical health. It turns out that people need full-spectrum light—that is, light that contains all the wavelengths of sunlight. Not getting enough full-spectrum light, or prolonged exposure to distorted spectrum light from fluorescent bulbs, seems to affect mental outlook, moods, and health in general. This has been borne out by generations of bleak suicide statistics and high rates of alcoholism in northern countries whose inhabitants are deprived of sunlight for months at a time.

Recently dubbed "seasonal affective disorder" (SAD), these winter doldrums have been shown to be highly responsive to supplemental doses of full-spectrum light.

Research has shown that students in classrooms illuminated with full-spectrum light have one-third fewer sick days than students in classrooms lit with distorted spectrum lights. The full range of health benefits from full-spectrum lights continues to be revealed.

Full-spectrum light has two distinguishing characteristics: it contains 1) the same rainbow colors and 2) the same amount of near-ultraviolet light as sunlight. There are two sources for full-spectrum light: sunlight and specially designed full-spectrum light bulbs. Full-spectrum light bulbs—*Vita-Lite* bulbs (the same lights used as "grow" lights for indoor gardening)—can be purchased in hardware stores, some specialized nurseries and, sometimes, in health food stores. These bulbs can be used to replace the distorted spectrum light bulbs that are usually found in fluorescent light fixtures. If your hardware store does not have the size bulbs you need, have them special ordered. *Vita-Lite* is a trade name; these bulbs are currently the only ones of their kind on the market. A chromolux bulb gives off light that is close to full spectrum but can fit in your incandescent socket. It is available at health food stores.

Studies have shown that full-spectrum light, in order to be effective, must be absorbed through the eyes. You do not need to look directly at the source, however (in the case of the sun, this is certainly to be avoided). Exposure on the skin is not effective; and, as is well known, prolonged exposure to the sun may be harmful. Although it is not yet known precisely how light works to affect moods, it seems clear that it has a physiological effect on the nervous, immune, and endocrine systems.

More and more people are reporting success using light—either sunlight or supplemental full-spectrum light from specially made bulbs or in light boxes.

Light: A Natural Mood Elevator

In the last hundred years, our lifestyles have changed rapidly and significantly. Exposure to full-spectrum light has been drastically reduced because

- People spend much more time indoors, working and playing. Some people work the night shift and sleep during the day.

- Changes in our modes of transportation—from walking and riding in a buggy to traveling by car, train, and plane—have further reduced the time we spend out of doors.

- Office buildings and factories often have only a few small windows or none at all. Indoor lighting, which is almost always distorted spectrum light (because it is the least expensive), has replaced windows as a light source.

- People wear glasses, sunglasses, and contact lenses, which block part or, in the case of hard contact lenses, all of the near-UV light.

- Sulphur dioxide and ozone in the air block near-UV light.

These factors make it necessary to pay particular attention to the amount and kinds of light you are exposed to. Some people seem to need more light than others. The amount of full-spectrum light received through the eyes is reduced on cloudy days and by window glass (up to 50 percent).

I first became aware of the usefulness of supplemental light when I attended a workshop on light therapy. I was suffering from a deep episode of major depression at the time, and it was all I could do just to get out to this one-hour workshop. I decided that I didn't have anything to lose from trying this simple, inexpensive, and noninvasive treatment.

Based on what I learned, I purchased a shop light: a simple, hanging-type light fixture that is usually used in garages, basements, and indoor nurseries, requiring two four-foot fluorescent bulbs. The cost for this was $12 at the hardware store. I replaced the distorted spectrum bulbs the fixture contained with two full-spectrum fluorescent light bulbs ($15 each). Then I set the fixture on the table in the room where I spent most of my time, and used it as my light source. After several days, I noticed a significant improvement in my depression. It isn't necessary to sit right in front of the fixture: just use it as your light source.

Because this initial experiment was so successful, I had my son build me a light box. He made a bank of lights by mounting three shop light fixtures on a piece of plywood, again replacing the distorted spectrum bulbs with full-spectrum bulbs. I set this up in the room where I spend the most time, and noticed that I was feeling better and better. This alternative is much less expensive than purchasing a commercially built full-spectrum light box and, although cumbersome, is perfectly acceptable.

Commercial full-spectrum light boxes cost over $200. I use one of these in my office. I like it because it is smaller than my homemade version (reflectors are used to increase the amount of available light), more attractive, and I can take it with me when I travel. The intensity of the light from these fixtures is low, not nearly enough to get a suntan.

I am now much more aware of my needs for full-spectrum light, especially on cloudy days and through the dark days of late fall and early winter.

Ways to Get the Light You Need

Glasses, especially tinted glasses, block some wavelengths from the sun. If you can, exercise out of doors without glasses. If you can't see well enough to do this safely, then simply sit outside with your glasses off for half an hour every day.

Avoid tinted glasses (but consult with your eye doctor to make sure that you get adequate protection from ultraviolet rays, which can promote the formation of cataracts). Hard contact lenses block all the full-spectrum light; soft contacts block 50 to 90 percent of it. If you wear contact lenses, spend some time outdoors every day without them.

Spend at least a half hour a day outside, even on cloudy days. Avoid the hours between 10 A.M. and 2 P.M. in the middle of summer, as the sun's rays are too intense then and can cause skin cancer, especially if you are fair. Never look directly at the sun.

This is the cheapest and usually the most convenient way to get the light you need. Being near windows helps, but 50 percent of the full-spectrum rays are blocked by window glass, and you won't get the same benefit as from being out of doors.

Supplement your sources of artificial light with full-spectrum fixtures.

- Replace the bulbs in your fluorescent fixtures with Vita-Lite bulbs. Ask to have the fluorescent bulbs in your office replaced with full-spectrum bulbs. Point out to your employer the health benefits of such a change. If your employer won't pay for them, you could replace the distorted spectrum bulbs at your own cost, and then take the bulbs with you if you change jobs.

- Purchase one or more shop-light fixtures, replace the fluorescent bulbs with Vita-Lite bulbs, and use these to light your work and living space.

- Buy a full-spectrum light box. Avoid using the light box when you are feeling hyperactive or manic.

Try the cheapest and simplest method first: get outside for at least half an hour every day. If this has a noticeable effect on your mood, make the investment and try the full-spectrum bulbs. Depending on the results, you may want to purchase a light box. They are portable, attractive, and provide a lot of light.

Assessing Your Own Reactions to Light

Read through the statements below, then spend as much time as you need to determine whether or not they're true for you. You might want to consult old journals and calendars in thinking about your answers.

☐ *I notice that I have more problems with depression in the late fall and early winter.*

☐ *I notice that my mood is lower on cloudy days and worsens when there is a series of cloudy days.*

☐ *I notice that I feel better on bright sunny days and when I get some light during the day.*

☐ *I plan to be outside for at least half an hour every day (I can get both the exercise and light I need during a half-hour walk).*

My plan for increasing the amount of my exposure to full-spectrum light: _____

_____

_____

After two weeks of increased exposure to full-spectrum light, I've noticed the following changes:

_____

_____

_____

After two months of increased exposure to full-spectrum light, I've noticed the following changes:

_____

_____

_____

I intend to make the following changes in my daily routine based on my observations of how I felt after two months of increased exposure to full-spectrum light: _____

_____

_____

_____

_____

The Dangers of Electromagnetic Radiation

I have become aware that some of the scientific advances we take for granted and we trust can really be very harmful.

Nobody really knows what the scoop is on electromagnetic radiation. But new and more compelling evidence surfaces daily that exposure to electromagnetic fields poses significant health risks.

This is really startling in light of our universal exposure to electromagnetic fields, from the transformers that flank our houses to the electrical appliances we use every day. Some researchers believe that electromagnetic radiation can be held responsible for the tremendous increases we're seeing in cancer; other equally distinguished scientists believe the whole thing to be a lot of hooey. What is certain, though, is that the safety of electromagnetic radiation is becoming a critical health issue. It is thought that the production of melatonin in the body decreases with exposure to electromagnetic radiation. Melatonin regulates the biological body rhythms, enhances the immune system, and inhibits tumor growth-enhancing hormones.

Depression and/or agitation are included in the list of effects of overexposure, or, in some cases, any exposure, to this type of radiation. Some people in the survey noted an increase in their level of agitation and a general uneasiness with overexposure to low-frequency (ELF) electromagnetic radiation. I noticed a marked decrease in these symptoms when I stopped using an electric blanket. I had always felt an uneasiness about electric blankets that I should have paid attention to before science confirmed my intuition. It is interesting to note that the sale of electric blankets has been plummeting ever since information was made public on the hazards of their use.

There are three factors that affect the health risk of your exposure to electromagnetic fields:

1. The strength of the electromagnetic field

2. How close you are to the source of the field

3. Length of exposure

Here are some general guidelines to follow:

Avoid using electric blankets. Even when an electric blanket is switched off, surges of power can course through its wires. You can use your electric blanket to warm up the bed before you get in; then unplug it, or switch it off at a power bar surge protector (these are available at hardware and electronics stores). If the blanket is kept on when you are in bed, you are exposed for a long time to a strong electromagnetic field close to the source of emission. Use a warm, cuddly comforter instead.

Avoid electrically heated waterbeds. If you must use a waterbed, heat it up before you get into it, then turn the heater off. A power bar surge protector is also a good way to turn off the heater, as well as protect you from power surges.

Minimize your exposure and keep a safe distance from computer terminals, copying machines, and video display terminals, even if they are on the other side of a wall. Stay 28 inches from the front and three to four feet from the back and sides. If you work at a video display terminal, move the keyboard as far away from the screen as practical, and spend at least 10 minutes of every hour away from your work station. This may require some negotiation if you work for someone else.

Avoid wearing battery-operated watches. Although such watches have a relatively weak field, your exposure to them is prolonged. Consider also your length of exposure to beepers and personal stereos. Do not keep a digital or electric clock by the head of your bed. Use a battery-operated clock instead, and keep it two to three feet from the bed.

Avoid sitting closer than six to eight feet from the front or sides of your TV or VCR. Most TVs have an instant-on feature and VCRs have a digital clock, so that even when they're off, they're giving off a magnetic field. These features can be bypassed by unplugging the sets or having them plugged into a power bar, which turns these appliances off when not in use (however, you will lose the programming on your VCR if you unplug it).

Stay three feet away from fluorescent lights and one to three feet away from electrical appliances, if possible, when they are on. Turn off electrical devices when they are not in use. This limits your exposure and also helps alleviate depression by lowering your electric bill!

Make sure that no one in your household sleeps or spends a great deal of time where low-voltage power lines from the street come into your house.

If electricity in your house is grounded to water or plumbing pipes, they will generate an electromagnetic field; they should be grounded into the earth. Have this checked by an electrician.

Watch newspapers and magazines and check the Internet for the most current findings on the health effects of electromagnetic radiation.

Milligauss is a measure of the frequency and wavelength of electromagnetic fields. It is not yet clear how much exposure is unsafe, but some people try to avoid prolonged exposure to fields stronger than two to three milligauss, which is the level that has been linked in some studies to an increased risk of childhood cancer.

Here are the electromagnetic "doses" associated with some common household appliances, measured in milligauss:

Blender	5.2 at 1 ft.
Electric can opener	30 at 225 ft.
Clothes dryer	1 at 24 ft.
Dishwasher	1 at 15 ft.
Freezer	1 at 3 ft.

Garbage disposal	1 at 5 ft.
Iron	1 at 3 ft.
Microwave oven	3 at 40 ft.
Mixer	5–100 at 1 ft.
Electric oven	1 at 8 ft.
Refrigerator	1 at 8 ft.
Electric stove or range	1 at 8 ft.
Toaster	0.6 at 1 ft.
Vacuum cleaner	1.2 at 18 ft.
Computer	1 at 25 ft.
Ceiling fan	1 at 11 ft.
Fluorescent desk lamp	6–20 at 1 ft.
Sewing machine	1 at 23 ft.
Typewriter	1 at 23 ft.
Electric clock	5 at 10 ft.
Electric blanket	3 at 50 ft.
Waterbed heater	1 at 9 ft.
Electric shavers	50 at 300 ft.
Fluorescent light fixture	2 at 32 ft.
Hair dryer	1 at 75 ft.
Baseboard heater	3 at 2 ft. for a 4-foot-long heater
Portable heater	2.5 at less than 3 ft.
Television	1.5 or less at 3 ft.
Electric drill	56 at 194 ft.

(Source: *Associated Press/Valley News*)

The Biological Clock

In the hypothalamus of the brain there is a "biological clock" that controls your body's daily rhythms. For example, your temperature is lowest in the morning and highest in the evening. Another rhythm is the natural tendency to sleep at night and be awake in the daytime. Several hormones that are associated with depression and mood stability, such as cortisol, melatonin, and thyroid-stimulating hormone, have similar biological rhythms.

Apparently, the body's biological clock is set for a 25- instead of a 24-hour day. You are constantly resetting this "clock" through sleep and exposure to light: going to bed at the same time each day, getting up at the same time, and getting exposure to full-spectrum light.

When this clock does not get reset properly—for instance, if you sleep late on a weekend morning, have a job that keeps you up all night, or are indoors all day and don't get any full-spectrum light—you may notice an increase in depression and mood instability, accompanied by a loss of your sense of well-being.

You need to think about resetting your biological clock if you have trouble getting to sleep at night and trouble getting up in the morning.

I have trouble falling asleep at night.   ☐ Yes   ☐ No

I have trouble getting up in the morning.   ☐ Yes   ☐ No

If you answered yes to either of these questions, you should think about making the following suggested adjustments in your schedule and routine to allow for resetting your biological clock.

Early to bed and early to rise. Go to bed at the same time each day, by 10:00 or 11:00, and get up at the same time each day, by 7:00 A.M.

Occasionally get up an hour or two earlier than usual to raise your mood.

Get plenty of bright, full-spectrum light, particularly before noon.

Exercise daily. For some reason, this seems to help keep the biological clock in good order.

Avoid prolonged exposure to electromagnetic fields. Again, not all the data has come in—but such exposure seems to throw your body's clock off schedule.

Make adjustments in your schedule to compensate for changes to daylight savings or standard time. To anticipate the spring change, go to bed and get up a half hour earlier during the week before the time changes. The change is not as noticeable in the fall, but it would help to reverse that process, going to bed and getting up half an hour later the week before the time changes.

Late-afternoon naps are good for you. Many people find it very easy to fall asleep between 2:00 and 4:00; during these hours, efficiency is normally lower, and more accidents occur. The tendency to want to take a siesta is more than just a Latin tradition: the impulse is internally generated by the human brain. Consider taking a half-hour nap in the afternoon between 2:00 and 4:00 P.M. If this is not possible because of your work schedule, plan your day so that the time you need to be most alert and creative is in the morning. (I feel much better in the evening if I get a short nap in the afternoon.)

I am going to make the following adjustments to my schedule to allow for "resetting my biological clock" for two weeks: _____

_____

_____

_____

_____

How I felt before I made these adjustments to my schedule and routine: _____

_____

_____

_____

_____

How I felt afterwards: _____

_____

_____

_____

_____

I intend to make the following changes in my daily routine based on what I learned from my two-week experiment: _____

_____

_____

_____

_____

I plan to take the following action with regard to my exposure to low frequency electromagnetic radiation: _____

_____

_____

_____

PART IV

Looking at Suicide

23

Suicide: The Tragedy of Mood Instability

The reality is that depression does end. It does not go on forever. There is light at the end of the tunnel. Life is rewarding and worthwhile. I have experienced many depressive episodes, they have ended, and I am glad I am alive.

The tragedy of depression and manic depression is that so many people who suffer from these illnesses end their lives through suicide.

Of the 120 people who took part in the survey, 77, or just over 64 percent, have thought seriously about or made plans to commit suicide. Fifty-five respondents (46 percent) have made serious attempts to end their life. Sixteen percent of people who are diagnosed as having some type of mood disorder eventually commit suicide. These figures are far too high to ignore.

Twenty-one survey participants have a close family member who has committed suicide. One person said of her suicide attempt, "I was scared because I realized that my grandmother had done the same thing." The fear of eventually committing suicide weighs heavily on the minds of those who have experienced mania or depression.

One respondent said that the only reason she attempted suicide was because she was in a panic: she just wanted help, and could not arrange to get into the hospital on time. Others said they had attempted suicide so that someone would pay attention to their pain. As people moved toward wellness, the great majority were grateful to still be alive.

I tried to commit suicide several times. Suicidal ideation and planning was my constant companion through numerous deep depressions and agitated depressive states. It truly seemed like the only way out of the hopelessness and pain. Now, after many years of stability, I am leading a happy and productive life. I'm glad to be here. Take it from me—choose life.

I asked study participants to describe what it is that triggers suicidal thoughts. Their responses fit into 12 categories:

hopelessness	depression
desperation	low self-esteem
loneliness	guilt
bad memories	seasonal triggers
psychosis	fatigue
chemical imbalance	exposure to chemical vapors

Hopelessness

Many people cited hopelessness as a trigger for their suicide attempt. **Have you ever had these feelings?**

☐ no hope for the future

☐ no hope that things will ever change

☐ no hope that I will ever be well and/or stable

☐ no hope that I will ever be able to meet my goals in life

☐ no hope I will ever be able to have a successful relationship or career

☐ no hope that I will ever be able to accomplish anything

☐ no point in being alive

☐ no control over my life

The truth is, even though in this state of profound depression a person can rarely see reality clearly, there is hope. After many years of suffering from this illness, I am quite well and have been happy for a long time. My mother was diagnosed with manic depression and spent 8 years in a psychiatric ward for the incurably insane. After she left the hospital at the age of 45, she worked for 20 years as a dietician. When she retired she became involved in numerous volunteer activities and enjoyed her 28 grandchildren. She became a respected member of the community.

Fifty people in the survey had extended periods of time (up to 25 years) with no mood swing problems. Nineteen others felt that their problem with mood swings is gone for good.

The educational levels of survey participants, their areas of expertise, and the significant achievements in their lives would be exemplary even if they had no emotional problems. All of these people have spent long periods of time completely incapacitated, periods when their lives were in constant turmoil. And yet they got well, or got things under control. There is no such thing as a "hopeless case" of depression or manic depression. By taking charge of your life, you can and will accomplish your goals.

Have you ever felt hopeless? _____ **Describe this feeling:** _____

_____

_____

_____

_____

What is the positive reality of your situation and your life? (For instance, do you have a pleasant place to live, a good job, a nice family, a good education, friends, a loving partner, good physical health, a pet, a talent, a hobby?) _____

_____

_____

_____

_____

Depression

Many people feel that suicide is the only way to end the deep, horrible, overwhelming despair of depression, agitated depression, or agitated mania. The pain and blackness inside are so overwhelming that suicide is seen as a relief. The need to stop this excruciating pain becomes overwhelming.

The reality is that depression does end; it does not go on forever. There truly is light at the end of the tunnel.

How long have your episodes of depression lasted? _____

Do you remember feeling as if the depression would never end? _____

Repeat these affirmations over and over to yourself whenever you need to: *Depression Ends. Life is worth living.* Write them on 3 by 5 cards to carry with you and post in prominent places around your home or where you work. Use them as a mantra as you fall asleep at night.

Desperation

People with suicidal thoughts often feel totally overwhelmed, that they have too many problems all at once, that others are expecting more from them than they can possibly accomplish (this may be the result of promises made during a mania). Sometimes suicide appears to be the only way out. You may have the feeling that you are trapped and that there is no other alternative.

The reality is that there is always a way out other than death, no matter how dreadful or complicated the situation. You may have to tell people you are sick and can't do what you said, that you need to take some time off to get well, that you need to reduce your stress level to control your illness—whatever it takes. Enlist the help of people in your support system to work out compromises and solutions. Get whatever help you need to work out your problems. Sometimes the thorniest problem only requires a fresh perspective.

Describe times in your life when you have felt desperate: _____

_____

_____

_____

_____

How did you work yourself out of these desperate situations? _____

_____

_____

Now remember: you have done it before; you can do it again.

Low Self-Esteem

The low self-esteem that accompanies depression and manic depression is a key contributory factor to suicide. Despite any rise in self-esteem during manic episodes, mood swings themselves rob people of their sense of self-worth.

Some people in the study expressed the opinion that the world would be a better place without them. Self-accusation and guilt go hand in hand with such perceptions. We feel that we are complete failures in every sense of the word and that there is no point in being alive. We become obsessed with memories of past failures and feelings of inadequacy.

Wait a minute. Take a good and honest look at yourself. Make a list of all your accomplishments, all the people you've ever befriended or helped, all your acts of compassion and kindness. Don't forget that you achieved these things in spite of obstacles greater than most people face. You deserve a pat on the back.

Dedicate yourself to raising your self-esteem (see "Building Self-Esteem and Self-Confidence"). Make a habit of noticing the good things about yourself. There are many excellent books that can help you in this very important learning process; some of these are noted in the Resource List.

Loneliness

An overwhelming feeling of loneliness and isolation is also a contributing factor in suicides. People who experience depression and manic depression feel that no one cares for them, and sometimes have the mistaken notion that their family and friends wish they were dead. One person in the study felt that suicide was a way of "getting back" at her family for not wanting her. Everyone experiences these feelings at times, but when depressed, the feelings are greatly exaggerated.

Depression is often accompanied by a deep fear of desertion by friends, family, and other support system members. A number of suicide attempts alluded to in the study coincided with the ending of a close relationship, either by death, separation, or abandonment. Difficulty sustaining close, lasting relationships plagues and discourages people who experience mood disorders.

Your family and friends really do care about you. And if for some reason they aren't there to support you, get involved in a support or advocacy group, a church, or a special interest group; or volunteer for a worthy cause. Your circle of friends will widen. You will find that you are not alone.

Who are the people in your life about whom you really care and who care about you?

_____

_____

_____

_____

_____

If you can't put five people on this list, refer to "Building a Strong Support System" and start working on setting up a support system for yourself.

I do not yet have five people in my support system. Therefore I am going to begin developing my support system in the following ways: _____

_____

_____

_____

_____

Guilt

When people come down from mania and realize what they have done, suicide often seems like the only way to escape the embarrassment, guilt, financial havoc, and other repercussions.

How do you cope when you realize that you've cheated on a beloved mate, run naked through the streets, spent large sums of money frivolously, created huge credit card debts, or announced to the public that you've found the cure to a dread disease?

One study participant wrote: "You won't be hearing from me again. This is just too much for me and my family. I have been picked up again for shoplifting." Luckily, she did not carry through with her threat.

The reality is that the guilt is hard to deal with, but you can pick up the pieces, make amends where you have to, and go on. The world is much more forgiving than you would expect. Believe me, I know. I've done these things, too. And so have the many other survey participants who have learned to let go of guilt and embarrassment and get on with their lives.

I feel guilty and embarrassed because I _____

_____

_____

_____

What I need to do to pick up the pieces or make amends for my out-of-control behavior: _____

_____

_____

_____

Get help from your counselor and other members of your support system to let go of the guilt and embarrassment and to move on. With their help and through your own efforts, you will go far toward preventing further hard times.

Bad Memories

Depression combined with feeling overwhelmed by bad memories, particularly those associated with childhood abuse, can act as a trigger to suicide.

The following techniques can help you let go of bad memories:

Counseling. Short- or long-term therapy with a competent counselor is a very effective way to release the hold that bad memories can have on your life. (See the chapter called "How About Counseling?")

Alternative health care workers. There are many skilled people who do various types of massage and physical release work that can be part of your effort to overcome bad memories. Get good references from people you trust about the competency of these practitioners in your area.

Journal writing. Writing can be cathartic. Use a notebook to write down all your thoughts and feelings associated with a particular memory, recalling as much detail as you feel comfortable including. This process helps put the memory into perspective, and also helps you let go. As an alternative to the journal, you can write about each memory on separate sheets of paper and then throw them away or burn them as a way of symbolically ridding yourself of burdensome feelings. Remember, you don't have to write neatly, spell accurately, or worry about grammar: these notes are for your use only (unless you choose to share them with your therapist).

Talking it out. Scrutinize bad memories with a trusted friend, family member, therapist, or health care worker (but make sure that you choose someone who can listen without feeling uncomfortable). Peer counseling, group therapy, and support groups can all provide an appropriate forum. Whatever avenue you choose, you should be able to talk about the memory as much as you need to without fear of judgment, criticism, trivialization of its importance, or correction of details by your listeners. You may need to talk about the same memory over and over again until you get it out of your system. If you are using peer counseling or talking to a group, be sure to give the other participants time to share their experiences, too.

Creative arts. You don't have to be an artist to be able to use visual images as a way to unlock old memories. Many people in the study found it useful to work with crayons, magic markers, water colors, acrylics, and clay. In my town, they held an art show called "Heartworks" of art created by people who are healing from the pain of sexual abuse. Look for art therapy clinics in your area, or sign up for an art or ceramics class at your local community college—whatever it takes to give color, shape, and texture to your feelings.

Confrontation. People who were harmed by adults when they were children sometimes feel that confronting the perpetrator of the abuse can be a healing experience. Consider this carefully: In some cases it is not a good idea—in fact it may be a very bad idea. **It is absolutely essential to plan any such confrontation carefully to protect yourself, and to be working closely with a competent counselor, and have a strong support network before undertaking such a meeting.**

Self-help resources. Use the Resource List in this book for help in locating appropriate self-help books, tapes, and organizations.

Your doctor, counselor, support group, or some of the great self-help literature in your library or bookstore can help you let go of these memories and have them become a part of the past that doesn't affect the present.

Eye movement desensitization. This new noninvasive technique often successfully reduces the anxiety associated with bad memories. It is simple and safe, but it must be done by a person who is trained in the use of this technique. Ask your doctor or therapist for information.

Bad memories I need to let go of: _____

_____

_____

_____

_____

_____

How I plan to work at letting go of bad memories so they no longer diminish the quality of my life:

_____

_____

_____

Seasonal Triggers

The holiday season, when it seems as if everyone else is having such a great time and experiencing the joys of togetherness, can be the worst time of year for you if you're depressed. Couple this with the reduced daylight hours during the winter season and you have a recipe for suicidal ideation. As anyone who has ever worked on a suicide hotline will tell you, the Christmas holidays are a time when many suicide attempts are made.

Despite the difficulties, there are things you can do to make the holiday season less stressful. Don't overplan, overextend yourself, or spend more money than you can reasonably afford. Plan pleasant times with people you enjoy—eating simple foods and sharing simple pleasures. Call on members of your support system. If your family upsets you, explain as diplomatically as you can, and then plan to spend the holidays with people who make you feel good.

Things that have made the holidays hardest for me in the past: _____

_____

_____

_____

My plan for the holiday season this year: _____

_____

_____

_____

The darkness of the season may have a lot to do with feeling badly during the Christmas season. Full-spectrum lighting, described in the chapter on light, is now being used extensively to overcome winter doldrums. If you can't afford full-spectrum lighting, be sure that you get outside every day for at least 20 minutes without your contact lenses or glasses. If your vision is sufficiently keen, combining this with a walk is a great idea.

I plan to increase the light in my life by: _____

_____

_____

_____

Psychosis

Severe psychosis, particularly when accompanied by hearing voices, was another precipitator of suicide attempts cited by people in the study. Suicide can seem like the only way to get rid of the voices telling you how bad you are, or to do dangerous things. It may also seem like the only way of getting rid of "things" swirling around in your head, the things you see that aren't there, the experiences you have that aren't real, and the other delusions that accompany severe episodes of psychosis.

Psychosis is very dangerous for you and others—get help and support immediately. At the earliest onset of even the most mild psychotic symptoms, ask someone in your support system to stay with you, or arrange for other people to stay with you, until all your symptoms are gone. You should never be alone when you are psychotic.

Psychosis can be experienced by people with either depression or mania and depression in either the manic or depressive phase. The key for people in either of these categories is to monitor their symptoms, get treatment at the earliest onset of symptoms, and formulate a plan in a time of wellness for how your psychosis will be handled when and if it occurs.

Psychosis can be effectively treated. It's a terrible thing to experience, but you can get through it with support. If you can't get help for yourself, tell trusted members of your support system to be alert to your symptoms and to get help for you if necessary.

If I become psychotic, my plan for getting the help that I need is: _____

_____

_____

_____

I will ask the following members of my support system for assistance if I become psychotic: _____

_____

_____

In the event that these people become aware that I am psychotic, I give them permission and expect them to take the following action in my behalf: _____

_____

_____

Fatigue

Many people in the study noted a correlation between being very tired and suicidal ideation. If your fatigue is due to a depressive episode, let someone in your support system know how you feel, especially if you are thinking about suicide. Have him or her arrange for someone to be with you at all times until your suicidal feelings pass.

Eat foods that are high in complex carbohydrates; get plenty of full-spectrum light—just sitting outside, even on a porch will help. Get some exercise if you can.

Instead of thinking about suicide when you are overtired, take a break. Make sure that your lifestyle and career allow you to take good care of yourself. Even if you can't take a vacation, take some sick time and get rested up. Check in with your medical doctor to see if a physical problem might be contributing to your fatigue. Check in with yourself, your support system, and your counselor to see if you are overdoing it. If you are, take action. Get more rest if you're overworking; schedule activities for yourself if you're simply tired all the time without a reason. Full-spectrum light can have a tonic effect on fatigue; some people have also reported success with acupuncture. The important thing is to strike the right balance for yourself between rest and activity, work time and play time, responsibility and relaxation. When you notice that you're tired all the time, do something about it! Fatigue can be dangerous.

When I notice that I am feeling very fatigued, I will take the following action: _____

_____

_____

_____

Exposure to Chemical Vapors

I recall vividly a harrowing experience one afternoon in winter when, with all the windows closed, my landlady was varnishing the stairs of my apartment. Feeling suddenly very strange, I decided to leave and walk to a friend's house. When I got there, I very calmly went in the bathroom and looked for something sharp to use to cut my wrists. Prior to exposure to the chemical vapors my mood had been stable. These vapors plummeted me to a deep suicidal level within half an hour.

Other study and workshop participants have related similar experiences with exposure to noxious vapors. It may be that those of us who are prone to mood swings are hypersensitive to the effects of these kinds of chemicals. I don't know; but why take any chances?

Steer clear of noxious vapors. When things start to smell bad, hit the road! If you have to work with toxic paints or chemicals, work outside, open as many windows as possible, or wear a respirator.

☐   *I plan to be observant of the effects of noxious vapors on my moods and to remove myself from situations that might be causing or increasing my mania, anxiety, or depression.*

Treatment After a Suicide Attempt

Most people have trouble knowing how to act and what to say following the suicide attempt of a close friend or family member. Perhaps you might have been victimized by this ignorance and bewilderment in the past. People in the study noted that others treated them in the following ways following a suicide attempt. **Which descriptions match your own experience?**

- ☐ with deep understanding
- ☐ I was avoided
- ☐ others became detached and cool
- ☐ like I was a freak
- ☐ with compassion
- ☐ with irritation
- ☐ others were rejecting
- ☐ with resentment
- ☐ with denial
- ☐ others were shocked
- ☐ people were overprotective of me
- ☐ others were judgmental

- ☐ with helpfulness
- ☐ with indifference
- ☐ with disgust
- ☐ with a lack of understanding
- ☐ with sympathy
- ☐ people were afraid of me
- ☐ like I was stupid
- ☐ others seemed puzzled and confused
- ☐ with caution
- ☐ others were angry
- ☐ they acted guilty

- ☐ others were unable to believe or understand my wish to die
- ☐ others knew that I was ill and that this phenomenon is part of the illness
- ☐ I was treated no differently than before the suicide attempt
- ☐ members of my support system were angry

In what other ways have you been treated after a suicide attempt? _____

_____

_____

_____

One person in the study commented:

"My support group ignored the attempt, saying, 'There really isn't a problem with you, you just need some rest.' But even worse than others discounting it were those I trusted and believed were friends becoming a menagerie of silent acquaintances, instantly acting as though I was never there. . . . Over the last 10 years I have had only two friends who have come back when I've started getting better, and they were in two different hospitals for long periods of time. But even these people became distant when I really began the struggle again."

People in the study expressed their preferences for the behavior of family and friends following a suicide attempt.

- ☐ to be treated with understanding   ☐ to be treated with love

☐ to be treated with compassion   ☐ to be treated in a positive manner

☐ others to give me encouragement to live while recognizing the depth and validity of my despair

☐ acknowledge most of what has happened without dwelling on it

☐ to have opportunities to talk with someone I'm very close to and trust about my feelings, someone who can be objective and helpful

☐ that special help that comes from people who don't want me to make another attempt on my life and are committed to seeing that I don't

☐ to be treated normally—I'd prefer that the suicide attempt weren't mentioned, as if it hadn't happened

☐ to be left alone

Describe how you would like to be treated by others after a suicide attempt: _____

_____

_____

_____

_____

_____

Another person from the study commented:

"After being in a four-day coma from a suicide attempt, I had incredible support from my church (70 cards) and so many visitors I would send them away because I was tired out. This greatly influenced my present stability."

24

Preventing Suicide

Suicide can best be prevented if taken seriously, if I can talk to someone I can trust, and they care: if they'll listen, be there, try to help, or get the help I need. If I ask for a call and I don't answer, or don't answer the door, something needs to be done. People need to believe, not just ignore me.

Caution: Anyone who is talking about, contemplating, or making unusual arrangements that might precede a suicide attempt needs help immediately. This should be treated as an emergency situation.

When I was depressed, I was often overwhelmingly obsessed with thoughts of suicide.

In the early stages of suicidal ideation, I was still able to talk with others in my support system and would listen as they tried to convince me not to take my life.

At some point I crossed a threshold—very quickly—where I decided that I was definitely going to take my life. I'm not sure what convinced me of this; I think it was an imagined slight or rejection from someone I really cared about, or a feeling of being extremely isolated or in severe psychic or physical pain. It was as if I went into a different mode. My suicide plans became much more detailed. I decided how, where, and when I would end my life. I figured out who I wanted (the police) and who I didn't want (my family and support people) to find me. I stopped talking to anyone about my suicide intentions. I acted as if there were nothing wrong.

When others asked me how I was feeling, I tried to convince them that I was feeling "very well and stable." I became devoid of emotion. I usually gave myself away at these times by totally rejecting the person I imagined had slighted me (this was always someone who was very close). This person, or another member of my support system, ended up intervening by confronting me and forcing me to get help, thus thwarting my plan. Perhaps I set this dynamic up intentionally; I'm not sure.

Having been very suicidal many times, having made several attempts to take my life, and looking back from a vantage point of many years of stability, I urge anyone who has a tendency toward mood swings and/or suicide to set up the following system when they are stable. Learn relaxation techniques, set up a suicide support system, and take precautionary measures concerning medications, firearms, and your car. These things are described in greater detail below.

Learn Relaxation Techniques

There are many breathing and relaxation techniques that take one into a deep meditative state. Refer to the chapter on relaxation in this book. Study these techniques until they are second nature. I also recommend taking a course in relaxation techniques or meditation. Some people have found it difficult to learn relaxation techniques on their own, but very easy with the guidance of a good teacher.

My plan to learn relaxation techniques: _____

_____

_____

_____

Practice every day, at least once a day, but several times if you can. Ten or fifteen minutes at a stretch is long enough. Have several set times for relaxation. Do it at other times or more frequently if you begin to feel frantic, if you want to, or if you are having trouble sleeping. You will notice that when you are in a relaxed state you are not depressed. The more you practice, the better it works. Practice regularly; but if you miss one of your set times, don't panic or give up on relaxation. Just do it the next time you have scheduled.

☐ I plan to relax daily at _____ , _____ , _____ (times of day).

☐ I will use relaxation when I notice early warning signs of mania or depression, when I feel frenetic, or when I am having trouble sleeping.

You can use this wonderful time in a relaxed state to review your past accomplishments, think pleasant thoughts, focus on inspirational readings or works of art, meditate on your affirmations (see "New Ways of Thinking"), or whatever makes you feel best. Relaxation really takes the pressure off.

When I am in a relaxed state I will think of:

Past accomplishments: _____

_____

Pleasant thoughts: _____

_____

Inspirational readings, works of art, etc.: _____

_____

Affirmations: _____

_____

_____

You may have heard people recommend that you make one sound or say one thing over and over when you're relaxing. If you're troubled with suicidal ideation, you might want to repeat the affirmation, "I choose life." This replaces "I want to die" (the thought that used to keep repeating itself over and over in my head during depressive episodes). If you really stick to it, *I choose life* becomes so firmly implanted in your brain that you can't say, "I want to die." The strategy is simple, cheap, safe, and noninvasive.

☐ *When I am in a relaxed state, I will repeat over and over the affirmation, "I choose life."*

Give yourself a "Live!" message. Obviously, you can't be relaxing all the time. But you can constantly reaffirm your decision to live. Make the decision that you don't want to die, and then don't allow yourself to consider dying as a possibility. Just forbid it. Take control of your life. Contemplating suicide is a habit. Change the habit, just as you have changed other bad habits like biting your nails, sucking your thumb, or smoking. You can replace the habit of suicidal thoughts with a good habit, such as looking at pictures of your children or grandchildren or playing with your dog.

Instead of contemplating suicide, I will _____

_____

_____

_____

_____

Set Up a Suicide Support System

Make a list of the people you like and trust the most, with whom you're most comfortable, and by whom you're best understood. These people should be very familiar with mood disorders (you can teach them, if necessary). People in your support group are often good choices because they understand what you are experiencing. However, when they are having mood instability problems themselves, call on other people. Ideally, your support system should include stable and understanding family members, your health care professionals (doctor, counselors, etc.), and the staff at the local mental health or emergency phone line. Choose at least five people who are most accessible as potential members of your suicide support team.

Ask the people whom you've chosen whether they would be willing to be on your support team. If they are, spend some time with them individually, educating them about the problem, sharing your individual experience, explaining what possible scenarios might arise when their assistance and support would be needed, and the kinds of action you would like them to take on your behalf. If they are willing to take on this responsibility, share with them as much information as you possibly can about your illness and your feelings. Arrange for these designated people to visit with your doctor or other health care professionals if you think this would be useful.

It is also very helpful to get everyone in your support system together for a group meeting so that they know each other and feel comfortable being in contact and working cooperatively when the need arises. Arrange this as a simple gathering at your home or even in a cafe when you are feeling well, in anticipation of the time when you may not be doing well and support will be needed. An informal discussion of what you would like the group to do is all that is required.

You need at least five people to ensure that one is available in case of a crisis. You should never expect any one person to be available to you at all times.

Ideally, people in your suicide support system will know you so well that they may be able to spot your mood swings even before you do, and will promptly assist you in taking evasive action.

The five people in my suicide support system are:

Name _____ phone number _____

Name _____ phone number _____

Name _____ phone number _____

Name _____ phone number _____

Name _____ phone number _____

My plan for how I will educate members of my suicide support team and facilitate their support:

_____

_____

_____

Make a pact with these people that you will contact them when you are feeling suicidal. Have them arrange for someone to stay with you until you start to feel better, and to get you help. Give them permission ahead of time to do whatever they have to do to keep you safe. Remember, these are people you trust and who really care about you. In exchange for their promise to be part of your suicide support system, you promise them that you will call one of them without fail at times when you feel suicidal.

☐ *I promise to contact someone on my suicide support team if I am feeling suicidal or having suicidal ideation.*

☐ *I give members of my suicide support team permission to take the following actions on my behalf to protect me and prevent me from committing suicide.*

_____

_____

Regulate the Medications You Have on Hand

Many people with mood disorders keep old prescription medications hidden away in case they want to commit suicide at some later time. Medications are all too easy to accumulate. When the doctor changes prescriptions—which for some of us is often—patients often keep the leftovers from the old prescription.

In most cases, there is no system in place for tracking what happens to leftover medications. Neither the druggist nor the doctor may remember to monitor excess pills. People with mood swings need to do this for themselves.

Clean all the old drugs out of your house (even those in your bottom drawer you keep just in case). Flush them down the toilet. Get rid of them all. And tell the members of your support team what you have done.

☐ *I have flushed all my old medications down the toilet. I only keep on hand small quantities of the medications I use regularly.*

Talk honestly to your doctor about any suicidal tendencies you may feel. For your own protection, request that prescriptions be filled in small quantities. Although even a week's worth of a prescription could prove lethal under certain circumstances, depending on what the medication is, it may be hard, costly, and inconvenient to get less than that amount. It is therefore essential that other suicide prevention mechanisms be in place. When I was suicidal, members of my support system kept my medications for me, giving me only the appropriate dose at the right time, and watched me take it.

☐ *I will discuss suicidal thoughts and ideation with my doctor and request prescriptions be filled in small quantities.*

Talk the situation over with your pharmacist, too. (Be sure that you have a good pharmacist who understands, knows you, and is truly interested in your welfare.) Drugstores keep records (often on computer) of just what drugs they have sold to you and when. If they sold you a month's supply of one drug, and two weeks later the doctor changes your prescription (as so often happens), have the pharmacists require you to return the amount you should have left over from the previous prescription before you can pick up the new one.

My pharmacist told me that, if requested, they can place a special marker by a person's name in their records to cue the computer program if it appears that the person has too much of any medication on hand. The pharmacist can then take some action (such as requiring that the old medication to be turned in) before the new medication is dispensed. My pharmacist expressed the opinion that any druggist would be glad to provide a similar service.

☐ *I will talk with my pharmacist about working together to prevent me from having a potentially dangerous amount of medications on hand.*

Members of your support system should know what medications you are taking, their expected side effects, and where you keep them in the house. There should be no secrets between you on this score. The issue is too serious. (If you need further incentive, it is unsafe to have these old medications around, because a child or another member of the family might take them either by mistake or on purpose.)

☐ *I will educate all members of my support system about the medications I'm taking, where I keep them, and possible side effects.*

Get Rid of All Firearms

No firearm should be kept in a home where there is anyone who has a tendency to be suicidal. They are a quick, easy-to-use, drastic, and horrible resolution to a temporary situation. Find an alternative if you have rationalized keeping a gun for purposes of self-defense (get a dog, carry a can of mace, take a course in martial arts, move to a safer neighborhood).

☐ *I will dispose of all firearms in my home or give them to a member of my support team for safekeeping.*

   If people you live with collect firearms or use firearms in sports activities, ask them to store the firearms somewhere outside the home, where they are locked away and inaccessible to you.

☐ *I will ask anyone I live with to store firearms outside our home and to keep them locked away.*

Be Cautious About Driving

When you have early warning signs of depression or are starting to feel suicidal, give your car keys to a member of your support team. If you must get to work, ask someone on your support team to take you. You could also take public transportation or carpool with other workers. This is not a safe time for you to be driving. Give members of your support team permission to take your car keys away if you seem depressed or suicidal.

☐ *I will give my car keys to a member of my support team if I have early warning signs of depression or feel suicidal. I will ask others to take me to work, will take public transportation, or will join a carpool.*

☐ *I give members of my support team permission to take my car keys away if I seem depressed or suicidal.* (Remember, these are people whose judgment you trust.)

Express Your Emotions

Talk to a member of your support team. Let all your feelings out. Cry, scream, kick, carry on, hit pillows—whatever it takes to get rid of that black tension (short of hurting yourself, someone else, or some thing). Do this as often as possible. Members of your support team will want to take turns, as the experience of witnessing so much emotional release can be draining and exhausting. But keep at it, for at least an hour a day. (See the chapter "How About Counseling?")

☐ *When I get depressed, I will spend at least one hour a day expressing my emotions to a member of my support team.*

Get Support

Don't allow yourself to be alone when you're having suicidal thoughts, even though you may really want to be alone. Have someone with you around the clock, no exceptions. It's hard, but it's critical. You may wish that everyone would just go away; but don't let them.

Your life at these times depends on the presence of others. You will have to educate members of your support team that you are not to be left alone when you are feeling suicidal.

☐ *I will not allow myself to be alone when I am feeling suicidal. I will tell members of my support team to arrange for someone always to be with me at these times.*

Remind Yourself How Good You Are, and How Good It Is to Be Alive

Hang pictures of your favorite people (children, grandchildren, parents, friend, partner) and places all around the house. Post special letters, awards, diplomas, and all other honors where you can easily see them. Keep a list of your accomplishments on your refrigerator door, and another next to your bed. Keep mementos of special times in obvious places. When you feel like committing suicide, just look around at all these reminders of why you should live.

I have a bureau in my hallway—a place that I pass many times every day—which is decorated with favorite family pictures, special cards that I received, and mementos of special times and events. This display has helped me through many rough times.

What I will do to keep reminding myself how good I am, and how good it is to be alive: _____

_____

_____

_____

Recommendations from Study Participants

Suicide Prevention: Choices You Have to Make

Stay on prescribed medications. People don't like taking medications. They often make you feel lousy and have miserable side effects. However, many of the survey participants rely on medication, as I did for a long time, to protect themselves. Be sure that you and members of your support team educate yourselves fully about any medication that a doctor recommends for your treatment.

Take action at the first sign of depression. Letting the depression get out of hand is not a good policy. Don't wait until you are really low.

Schedule regular appointments with your health care professionals. Keep your appointments no matter how good or awful you are feeling. Remember that these appointments are just as much a matter of prevention as they are of cure.

Get together with your trusted counselor and talk, talk, talk. Get together with trusted friends and family and talk, talk, talk. It works. Just being with others and enjoying a meaningful exchange can lift your spirits and help you feel less alone.

Writing often helps people work through suicidal episodes. Write anything you want, anything you feel. No one is grading your work. No one is looking over your shoulder or judging you. You don't have to worry about correct spelling or grammar. Just remain open and honest emotionally (even if you're writing fiction or poetry). Drawing or painting can work in the same way to ease painful emotions.

Pray. Lots of people do it. And lots of people feel that it works.

Many people attend a support group or 12-step programs and find them to be helpful and supportive. Attendance at such a group may be a lot to expect of yourself when you feel like committing suicide; but if you can possibly get out, do it. (Have someone else drive you.)

You might want to make a "suicide contract" with your health care professionals and members of you support group. This means that you promise to call them before you attempt to take your life.

Overall Life Changes to Prevent You from Becoming Suicidal

Learn everything you can about mood disorders and any other troubling symptoms you may have. Scour the library and bookstores. (See the Resource List at the end of this book.)

Set up a lifestyle for yourself that causes you as little stress as possible. This is hard to do in this day and age, but it can be done. There are many helpful hints throughout this workbook.

Love yourself. (See "Building Self-Esteem and Confidence.")

Make provisions when you are feeling well so that you will be safe when you are suicidal. Take all the precautions you need to regarding medications, firearms, car keys, etc.

Ask for help when you need it.

Exercise, eat right, get plenty of rest and light. In essence, take good care of yourself in every way. Don't let up. Those of us who have mood disorders need to be very disciplined about this. (See chapters on exercise, diet, and light)

Keep your faith, whatever it is. Many participants feel that a strong spiritual support system is essential to their well-being.

Change your attitude. Think positively. Appreciate what you can do, and don't give yourself a hard time about what you can't do. (See "New Ways of Thinking.")

Work on improving your interpersonal relationships. Get help on this from your health care professionals or members of your support group. It feels good to get along with others, and it makes life worth living.

Regularly attend a support group that is appropriate for you. Play an active role in the group when you can. (See the chapter on support groups.)

Additional thoughts about suicide from study participants:

"I keep my medications in balance and am very aware of particular external things which precipitate depression. I continue learning about my illness and educate those close to me so they will recognize my shifts before I do."

"I do everything I can—diet, socialize, take medications, see doctors, whatever—to feel I am in mastery of my illness and my fate."

"I don't know if I was actually attempting to end my life. I remember just wanting to go to sleep, to get away from the bad feelings. I had constant feelings that I was causing everyone too many problems and we would all be better off if I were dead. I even had a master plan, but it wasn't an overdose. I really believe I was just trying to temporarily escape at the time I took the overdose. The more I took, the more out of touch I became, and it just got out of control. I just wanted to stop the pain. Afterwards, when I realized what I had done, I felt even worse. I felt very guilty for putting my close friends and family through that. It took a long time to get over it and establish trust from everyone."

Resource List

Books, Audiotapes and Videos (listed by topic)

Addiction

Appleton, N. 1996. *Lick the Sugar Habit.* Santa Monica, CA: Choice Publishing.

Bireda, Martha. 1990. *Love Addiction: A Guide to Emotional Independence.* Oakland, CA: New Harbinger Publications, Inc.

Birkedahl, Nonie. 1990. *The Habit Control Workbook.* Oakland, CA: New Harbinger Publications, Inc.

Catalano, E. M., and N. Sonenberg. 1993. *Consuming Passions: Help for Compulsive Shoppers.* Oakland, CA: New Harbinger Publications, Inc.

Jampolsky, Lee. 1991. *Healing the Addictive Mind: Freeing Yourself from Addictive Patterns and Relationships.* Berkeley, CA: Celestial Arts.

Roth, G. 1997. *Why Weight? A Guide to Ending Compulsive Eating.* New York: Dutton.

———. 1992. *When Food Is Love: Exploring the Relationship Between Eating & Intimacy.* New York: NAL/Dutton

———. 1993. *Breaking Free From Compulsive Eating.* New York: NAL/Dutton.

Santoro, J., and R. Cohen. 1997. *The Angry Heart: Overcoming Borderline and Addictive Disorders.* Oakland, CA: New Harbinger Publications, Inc.

Stevic-Rust, L., and A. Maxmin. 1996. *The Stop Smoking Workbook: Your Guide To Healthy Quitting.* Oakland, CA: New Harbinger Publications, Inc.

Anger

Black, J., and G. Enns. 1998. *Better Boundaries: Owning and Treasuring Your Life.* Oakland, CA: New Harbinger Publications, Inc.

Lerner, H. 1997. *The Dance of Anger.* New York: HarperCollins.

McKay, M., P. Rogers, and J. McKay. 1997. *When Anger Hurts.* Oakland, CA: New Harbinger Publications, Inc.

McKay, M., K. Paleg, P. Fanning, and D. Landis. 1996. *When Anger Hurts Your Kids: A Parent's Guide.* Oakland, CA: New Harbinger Publications, Inc.

Potter-Efron, Ron 1994. *Angry All the Time: An Emergency Guide to Anger Control.* Oakland, CA: New Harbinger Publications, Inc.

———. 1998. *Working Anger: Preventing and Resolving Conflict on the Job.* Oakland, CA: New Harbinger Publications, Inc.

Potter-Efron, Ron, and Pat. 1995. *Letting Go of Anger.* Oakland, CA: New Harbinger Publications, Inc.

Rubin, T. 1998. *The Angry Book.* New York: Touchstone

Scott, Gini Graham. 1990. *Resolving Conflict.* Oakland, CA: New Harbinger Publications, Inc.

Anxiety

Bourne, E. 1995. *The Anxiety & Phobia Workbook,* Second Edition. Oakland, CA: New Harbinger Publications, Inc.

———. 1998. *Healing Fear: New Approaches to Overcoming Anxiety.* Oakland, CA: New Harbinger Publications, Inc.

Brown, Duane. 1996. *Flying Without Fear.* Oakland, CA: New Harbinger Publications, Inc.

Copeland, M. E. 1998. *The Worry Control Workbook.* New York, NY: Barnes and Noble Books.

Desberg, Peter. 1996. *No More Butterflies: Overcoming Shyness, Stagefright, Interview Anxiety, and Fear of Public Speaking.* Oakland, CA: New Harbinger Publications, Inc.

Markway, B., C. Carmin, C. A. Pollard, and T. Flynn. 1992. *Dying of Embarrassment: Help for Social Anxiety and Social Phobia.* Oakland, CA: New Harbinger Publications, Inc.

Zuercher-White, Elke. 1998. *An End To Panic: Breakthrough Techniques for Overcoming Panic Disorder.* Oakland, CA: New Harbinger Publications, Inc.

Anxiety Audio Tapes

Acquiring Courage. Oakland, CA: New Harbinger Publications, Inc.

Cognitive Therapy

Beck, A., J. Rush, B. Shaw, and G. Emery. 1979. *The Cognitive Therapy of Depression.* New York: Guilford Press.

Burns, D. 1999. *Feeling Good.* New York: William Morrow.

———. 1999. *The Feeling Good Handbook.* New York: William Morrow.

Ellis, T., and C. Newman. 1996. *Choosing to Live: How to Defeat Suicide Through Cognitive Therapy.* Oakland, CA: New Harbinger Publications, Inc.

McKay, M., M. Davis, and P. Fanning. 1998. *Thoughts and Feelings: The Art of Cognitive Stress Intervention.* Oakland, CA: New Harbinger Publications, Inc.

McKay, M., and P. Fanning. 1991. *Prisoners of Belief: Exposing and Changing Beliefs That Control Your Life.* Oakland, CA: New Harbinger Publications, Inc.

Cognitive Therapy Audio Tapes

Covert Modeling and Covert Reinforcement. Oakland, CA: New Harbinger Publications, Inc.

Distorted Thinking. Oakland, CA: New Harbinger Publications, Inc.

Systematic Desensitization and Visualizing Goals. Oakland, CA: New Harbinger Publications, Inc.

Thought Stopping. Oakland, CA: New Harbinger Publications, Inc.

Depression

Clayton, Lawrence, and Sharon Carter. 1995. *Coping with Depression.* New York: Rosen Publishing Group.

Colbert, Ty. 1995. *Depression and Mania: Friends or Foes?* Santa Ana, CA: Kevco Publishers.

Copeland, Mary Ellen. 1994. *Living Without Depression and Manic-Depression: A Workbook for Maintaining Mood Stability.* Oakland, CA: New Harbinger Publications, Inc.

———. 1997. WRAP: *Wellness Recovery Action Plan.* W. Dummerston, VT: Peach Press. (To order, call: 802-254-2092)

———. 1999. *Winning Against Relapse: A Workbook of Action Plans for Recurring Health and Emotional Problems.* Brattleboro, VT: Peach Press.

Copeland, M.E., and S. Copans. 1998. *The Adolescent Depression Workbook.* W. Dummerston, VT: Peach Press. (To order, call: 802-254-2092)

DePaulo, J., and K. Ablow. 1996. *How to Cope with Depression.* New York: McGraw-Hill.

Karp, D. 1996. *Speaking of Sadness: Depression, Disconnection, and the Meaning of Illness.* New York: Oxford University Press

Mondimore, F. 1997. *Depression: The Mood Disease.* Baltimore, MD: The Johns Hopkins University Press.

Papolos, J., and D. Papolos. 1988. *Overcoming Depression.* New York: Harper & Row.

Rogers, Sherry. 1997. *Depression Cured At Last!* Sarasota, FL: SK Publishing.

Slagle, P. 1994. *The Way Up from Down.* New York: St. Martin's Press.

Diet, Nutrition, and Natural Medicine

Balch, J., and P. Balch. 1997. *Prescription for Nutritional Healing.* New York: Avery Publishing Group.

Braverman, E., with C. Pfeiffer, K. Blum, and R. Smayda. 1997. *The Healing Nutrients Within.* New Canaan, CT: Keats Publishing.

Crook, W. G., and M. H. Jones. 1989. *The Yeast Connection Cookbook.* Jackson, TN: Professional Books.

Elkins, R. 1995. *Depression and Natural Medicine.* Pleasant Grove, UT: Woodland Publishing.

Fanning, P. 1990. *Lifetime Weight Control: Seven Steps to Achieving and Maintaining a Healthy Weight.* Oakland, CA: New Harbinger Publications, Inc.

Nash, Joyce. 1999. *Binge No More.* Oakland, CA: New Harbinger Publications, Inc.

Prevention Health Books, eds. 1993. *Doctor's Book of Home Remedies II.* Emmaus, PA: Rodale Press.

Rector-Page, L. 1994. *Healthy Healing: An Alternative Healing Reference.* Healthy Healing Publications, P.O. Box 436, Carmel Valley CA 93924.

Sandbek, T. J. 1993. *The Deadly Diet: Recovering from Anorexia and Bulimia.* Oakland, CA: New Harbinger Publications, Inc.

Sears, B., and W. Lawren. 1995. *The Zone: A Dietary Road Map.* New York: HarperCollins Publishers.

Sears, B. 1997. *Mastering The Zone.* New York: Harper Collins Publishers.

Turner, Kristina. 1987. *The Self-Healing Cookbook: A Macrobiotic Primer for Healing Body, Mind and Moods with Whole, Natural Foods.* Vashon Island, WA: Earthtones Press (P.O. Box 411, Vashon Island, WA 98070.

Electromagnetic Radiation

Becker, R. O. 1990. *Cross Currents.* Los Angeles: J. P. Tarcher.

Morgan, G. *Electric and Magnetic Fields for 60-Hertz Electric Power: What Do We Know About the Possible Health Risks?* Department of Engineering and Public Policy, Carnegie Mellon University, Pittsburgh, PA 15213. (This brochure is available from many electric utility companies.)

Families

Becker, Marilyn. 1993. *Last Touch: Preparing for a Parent's Death.* Oakland, CA: New Harbinger Publications, Inc.

Brown, E. M. 1989. *My Parent's Keeper: Adult Children of the Emotionally Disturbed.* Oakland, CA: New Harbinger Publications, Inc.

———. 1994. *Stepfamily Realities: How to Overcome Difficulties and Have a Happy Family.* Oakland, CA: New Harbinger Publications, Inc.

Lauer, J., and R. 1999. *How to Survive and Thrive in an Empty Nest: Reclaiming Your Life When Your Children Have Grown.* Oakland, CA: New Harbinger Publications, Inc.

Mueser, K., and S. Gingerich. 1994. *Coping with Schizophrenia: A Guide for Families.* Oakland, CA: New Harbinger Publications, Inc.

Focusing

Cornell, Ann Weiser. 1996. *The Power of Focusing: A Practical Guide to Emotional Self-Healing.* Oakland, CA: New Harbinger Publications, Inc.

Gendlin, Eugene. 1982. *Focusing.* New York: Bantam.

Gay and Lesbian

Hardin, K. 1999. *The Gay and Lesbian Self-Esteem Book: A Guide to Loving Ourselves.* Oakland, CA: New Harbinger Publications, Inc.

Johnson, B. 1997. *Coming Out Every Day: A Gay, Bisexual, and Questioning Man's Guide.* Oakland, CA: New Harbinger Publications, Inc.

Light

Czeisler, C. A., et al. 1990. "Exposure to bright light and darkness to treat physiologic maladaption to night work." *New England Journal of Medicine* 322:1253-59.

Hyman, J. 1990. *The Light Book.* Los Angeles: J. P. Tarcher.

Rosenthal, N. 1998. *Winter Blues: Seasonal Affective Disorder: What It Is & How to Overcome It.* New York: Guilford Press.

Loss and Grief

Caplan, S., and G. Lang. 1995. *Grief's Courageous Journey: A Workbook.* Oakland, CA: New Harbinger Publications, Inc.

Harris, Maxine. 1995. *The Loss That Is Forever: The Lifelong Impact of the Early Death of a Mother or Father.* New York: Dutton.

Staudacher, Carol. 1987. *Beyond Grief: A Guide for Recovering from the Death of a Loved One.* Oakland, CA: New Harbinger.

———. 1992. *Men and Grief.* Oakland, CA: New Harbinger Publications, Inc.

Loss and Grief Audiocassettes

Medema, K., and J. W. Nadeau. 1993. Where Do I Go From Here? A Musical Dialogue in the Journey of Loss and Grief. St. Paul, MN: Color Song Productions.

Medema, K., and J. W. Nadeau, with B. Walton. 1995. Why Do I Feel Like This? Midlife in Word and Song. St. Paul, MN: ColorSong Productions.

Medications and Treatments

Barnhart, E. R., ed. 1990. *Physicians' Desk Reference* (PDR). Montvale, NJ: Medical Economics Company.

Bezchlibnyk-Butler, K., and J. Jeffries. 1996. *Clinical Handbook of Psychotropic Drugs.* Toronto: Hogrefe & Huber Publishers.

Consumer Guide, ed. 1995. *Prescription Drugs.* NewYork: NAL/Dutton.

Gorman, J. 1995. *The Essential Guide to Psychiatric Drugs.* New York: St. Martin's Paperbacks.

Preston, J., J. O'Neal, and M. Talaga. 1999. *Consumer's Guide to Psychiatric Drugs.* Oakland, CA: New Harbinger Publications, Inc.

———. 1999. *Handbook of Clinical Psychopharmacology for Therapists.* Oakland, CA: New Harbinger Publications, Inc.

Schou, M. 1993. *Lithium Treatment of Manic Depressive Illness: A Practical Guide.* New York: Karger.

Thueson, David. 1995. *Thueson's Guide to Over-the-Counter Drugs.* Oakland, CA: New Harbinger Publications, Inc.

Men's Issues

Diamond, Jed. 1994. *The Warrior's Journey Home: Healing Men, Healing the Planet.* Oakland, CA: New Harbinger Publications, Inc.

Fanning, P., and M. McKay. 1993. *Being a Man: A Guide to the New Masculinity.* Oakland, CA: New Harbinger Publications, Inc.

Staudacher, Carol. 1992. *Men and Grief.* Oakland, CA: New Harbinger Publications, Inc.

Mental Health and Wellness

Affinito, Mona Gustafson. 1999. *When to Forgive.* Oakland, CA: New Harbinger Publications, Inc.

American Psychiatric Association. 1994. *Diagnostic and Statistical Manual of Mental Disorders* (DSM-IV). Washington, DC: American Psychiatric Association.

Borysenko, J. 1993. *Minding the Body, Mending the Mind.* Redding, MA: Addison-Wesley.

Breggin, P. 1991. *Toxic Psychiatry: Why Therapy, Empathy, and Love Must Replace the Drugs, Electrochock, and Biochemical Theories of the "New Psychiatry."* New York: St. Martin's Press.

Center for Substance Abuse Prevention, SAMHSA. 1997. *National Clearinghouse for Alcohol and Drug Information Publications Catalog.* Washington, DC: Center for Substance Abuse and Mental Health Services Administration (SAMHSA).

Colbert, T. 1996. *Broken Brains or Wounded Hearts: What Causes Mental Illness.* Santa Anna, CA: Kevco Publishers.

Copeland, M. E. 2000. *The Loneliness Workbook.* Oakland, CA: New Harbinger Publications, Inc.

———. 2000. *The Worry Control Workbook.* New York, NY: Barnes and Noble Books.

———. 1999. *Winning Against Relapse: A Workbook of Action Plans for Recurring Health and Emotional Problems.* Brattleboro, VT: Peach Press.

———. 1997. *WRAP: Wellness Recovery Action Plan.* W. Dummerston, VT: Peach Press. (To order, call: 802-254-2092)

Copeland, M. E., and S. Copans. 1998. *The Adolescent Depression Workbook.* W. Dummerston, VT: Peach Press. (To order, call: 802-254-2092)

Copeland, M. E., and M. Harris. 2000. *Healing the Trauma of Abuse: A Woman's Workbook*. Oakland, CA: New Harbinger Publications, Inc.

Gil, E. 1988. *Outgrowing the Pain*. New York: Dell.

Goodwin, F., and K. R. Jamison. 1990. *Manic-Depressive Illness*. New York: Oxford University Press.

Hyman, Bruce, and Cherry Pedrick. 1999. *The OCD Workbook: Your Guide to Breaking Free from Obsessive-Compulsive Disorder*. Oakland, CA: New Harbinger Publications, Inc.

Kushner, H. 1987. *When All You've Ever Wanted Isn't Enough*. Boston: G. K. Hall.

New Harbinger Publications. *Self-Help Catalog*. Oakland, CA: New Harbinger Publications, Inc. 1-800-748-6273.

Reed, M., ed. 1994. *Healthcare Resource Directory: An Information Guide to American Medical and Social Services*. Houston, TX: Medical Productions, Inc.

Seigel, B. 1990. *Love, Medicine and Miracles*. New York: Harper & Row.

———. 1990. *Peace, Love and Healing*. New York: Harper & Row.

Sheldon, M., ed. 1991. *The Wellness Encyclopedia*. Berkeley, CA: University of California Press.

Starlanyl, D., and M. E. Copeland. 1996. *Fibromyalgia & Chronic Myofascial Pain Syndrome: A Survival Manual*. Oakland, CA: New Harbinger Publications, Inc.

Steketee, Gail, and Derrin White. 1990. *When Once Is Not Enough: Help for Obsessive Compulsives*. Oakland, CA: New Harbinger Publications, Inc.

Whitfield, C. 1990. *A Gift to Myself*. Deerfield Beach, FL: Health Communications, Inc.

———. 1987. *Healing the Child Within*. Deerfield Beach, FL: Health Communications, Inc.

Colbert, Ty. 1993. *Why Do I Feel Guilty When I've Done Nothing Wrong?* Nashville, TN: Thomas Nelson Publishers.

Mental Health Video and Audio Tapes

Copeland, M. E. 1999. *Winning Against Relapse Program*. Step-by-step WRAP audio tape. Oakland, CA: New Harbinger Publications.

Copeland, M. E. 1994. *Living with Depression*. Oakland, CA: New Harbinger Publications.

Copeland, M. E. 1994. *Strategies for Living with Depression and Manic Depression*. Oakland, CA: New Harbinger Publications.

Relationships

Beattie, M. 1996. *Beyond Codependency*. New York: Harper & Row.

———. 1996. *Codependent No More*. New York: Harper & Row.

Bireda, M. 1990. *Love Addiction: A Guide to Emotional Independence*. Oakland, CA: New Harbinger Publications, Inc.

Bugen, L. A. 1990. *Love & Renewal: A Couple's Guide to Commitment*. Oakland, CA: New Harbinger Publications, Inc.

Heitler, Susan. 1997. *The Power of Two: Secrets to a Strong and Loving Marriage*. Oakland, CA: New Harbinger Publications, Inc.

Hendrix, Harville. 1990. *Getting the Love You Want: A Guide for Couples*. New York: Harper Perennial.

Jampolsky, Lee. 1991. *Healing the Addictive Mind: Freeing Yourself from Addictive Patterns and Relationships*. Berkeley, CA: Celestial Arts.

Kahn, Michael. 1995. *The Tao of Conversation: How to talk about things that really matter, in ways that encourage new ideas, deepen intimacy, and build effective and creative working relationships*. Oakland, CA: New Harbinger Publications, Inc.

Kinghma, D. R. 2000. *Coming Apart: Why Relationships End and How to Live Through the Ending of Yours*. Oakland, CA: New Harbinger Publications, Inc.

Markway, B. and G. 1996. *Illuminating the Heart: Steps Toward a More Spiritual Marriage*. Oakland, CA: New Harbinger Publications, Inc.

McKay, M., M. Davis, and P. Fanning. 1995. *Messages: The Communication Skills Book,* Second Edition. Oakland, CA: New Harbinger Publications, Inc.

McKay, M., P. Fanning, and K. Paleg. 1994. *Couple Skills: Making Your Relationship Work.* Oakland, CA: New Harbinger Publications, Inc.

McKay, M., P. Rogers., J. Blades, and R. Gosse. 1999. *The Divorce Book: A Practical and Compassionate Guide.* Oakland, CA: New Harbinger Publications, Inc.

McKinley, R. 1989. *Personal Peace: Transcending Your Interpersonal Limits.* Oakland, CA: New Harbinger Publications, Inc.

Scott, G. G. 1990. *Resolving Conflict: With Others and Within Yourself.* Oakland, CA: New Harbinger Publications, Inc.

Weyburne, Darlene. 1998. *What to Tell the Kids About Your Divorce.* Oakland, CA: New Harbinger Publications, Inc.

Viorst, J. 1998. *Necessary Losses.* New York: Simon & Schuster.

Woititz, Janet Geringer. 1986. *Struggle for Intimacy.* Pompano Beach, FL: Health Communications, Inc.

Relationship Audio Tapes

Assertiveness Training. Oakland, CA: New Harbinger Publications, Inc.

Becoming a Good Listener. Oakland, CA: New Harbinger Publications, Inc.

Conflict Resolution for Couples. Oakland, CA: New Harbinger Publications, Inc.

Effective Self-Expression. Oakland, CA: New Harbinger Publications, Inc.

Fair Fighting. Oakland, CA: New Harbinger Publications, Inc.

Making Contact. Oakland, CA: New Harbinger Publications, Inc.

Sexual Communication. Oakland, CA: New Harbinger Publications, Inc.

Relaxation and Stress Reduction

Benson, H., and W. Proctor. 1994. *Beyond the Relaxation Response.* New York: Berkeley.

Benson, H., and M. Clipper. 1990. *The Relaxation Response.* New York: William Morrow.

Birkedahl, N. 1990. *The Habit Control Workbook.* Oakland, CA: New Harbinger Publications, Inc.

Borysenko, J. 1990. *Guilt Is the Teacher, Love Is the Lesson.* New York: Warner Books.

Bricklin, M., M. Golin, D. Grandenetti, and A. Leiberman. 1990. *Positive Living and Health.* Emmaus, PA: Rodale Press.

Carlson, R., and B. Shield. 1989. *Healers on Healing.* Los Angeles: J. P. Tarcher.

Davis, M., Elizabeth Robbins Eschelman, and Matthew McKay. 1995. *The Relaxation & Stress Reduction Workbook,* Fourth Edition. Oakland, CA: New Harbinger Publications., Inc

Davis, M. 1995. *Leader's Guide to Relaxation & Stress Reduction Workbook,* Fourth Edition. Oakland, CA: New Harbinger Publications, Inc.

Easwaran, E. 1991. *Meditation.* Petaluma, CA: Nilgiri Press.

Fanning, Patrick. 1994. *Visualization for Change.* Oakland, CA: New Harbinger Publications, Inc.

Gawain, S. 1982. *Creative Visualization.* New York: Bantam Books.

Hanh, T. 1992. *The Miracle of Mindfulness! A Manual on Mediation.* Boston: Beacon Press.

Harp, D. 1990. *The New Three Minute Meditator.* Oakland, CA: New Harbinger Publications, Inc.

Hay, L. 1994. *Heal Your Life and Body.* Santa Monica, CA: Hay House.

Kabat-Zinn, J. 1990. *Full Catastrophe Living.* New York: Delacorte Press.

Matthews, S., O. C. Simonton, and J. L. Creighton 1992. *Getting Well Again.* New York: Bantam Books.

McKay, Matthew. 1997. *The Daily Relaxer.* Oakland, CA: New Harbinger Publications, Inc.

Nuernberger, P. 1981. *Freedom from Stress: A Holistic Approach.* Honesdale, PA: Himalayan International Institute of Yoga Science and Philosophy.

O'Hara, Valerie. 1996. *Five Weeks to Healing Stress.* Oakland, CA: New Harbinger Publications, Inc.

Seigel, B. 1990. *Love, Medicine and Miracles.* New York: Harper & Row.

———. 1990. *Peace, Love and Healing.* New York: Harper & Row.

Taylor, D., and M. Rock. 1987. *Gut Reaction: How to Handle Stress and Your Stomach.* New York: Berkeley.

Relaxation and Stress Reduction Audio Tapes

Applied Relaxation Training. Oakland, CA: New Harbinger Publications, Inc.

Autogenics and Meditation. Oakland, CA: New Harbinger Publications, Inc.

Body Awareness and Imagination. Oakland, CA: New Harbinger Publications, Inc.

Mindfulness Meditation Practice Tapes (2 tapes) by J. Kabat-Zinn, which include a guided body scan meditation, a guided sitting meditation, and two sides of very slow and simple yoga meditation exercise. Write to: Stress Reduction Tapes, P.O. Box 547, Levington, MA 02173.

Progressive Relaxation and Breathing. Oakland, CA: New Harbinger Publications, Inc.

Relaxations. Oakland, CA: New Harbinger Publications, Inc.

Ten Minutes to Relax, volumes 1 and 2, based on The Stress Reduction & Relaxation Workbook. Oakland, CA: New Harbinger Publications, Inc.

Yoga with Valerie. Oakland, CA: New Harbinger Publications, Inc.

Relaxation Video Tapes

Relaxation: An anti-tension workout. CA: American Health. Karl Lorimar Home Video, 1986.

Seigel, B. Innervision: Visualizing Super Health. (A catalogue of books, audio tapes, video tapes, and workshops by Dr. Seigel and others whom he recommends is available by writing to ECAP, 1302 Chapel St. New Haven, CT 06511; or call 203-865-8392.)

Self-Discovery

Bolles, R. 1996. *What Color Is Your Parachute.* 1997. Berkeley, CA: Ten Speed Press.

Kahn, M. 1995. *The Tao of Conversation.* Oakland, CA: New Harbinger Publications, Inc.

Grotberg, Edith Henderson. 1999. *Tapping Your Inner Strength: How to Find the Resilience to Deal with Anything.* Oakland, CA: New Harbinger Publications, Inc.

McDermott, D., and C. R. Snyder. 1999. *Making Hope Happen: A Workbook for Turning Possibilities into Reality.* Oakland, CA: New Harbinger Publications, Inc.

McKinley, R. 1989. *Personal Peace: Transcending Your Interpersonal Limits.* Oakland, CA: New Harbinger Publications, Inc.

Meyerson, M., and L. Ashner. 1999. *Six Keys to Creating the Life You Desire.* Oakland, CA: New Harbinger Publications, Inc.

Miller, T. 1998. *Wanting What You Have: A Self-Discovery Workbook.* Oakland, CA: New Harbinger Publications, Inc.

Potter-Efron, Ron. 1998. *Being, Belonging, and Doing: Balancing Your Three Greatest Needs.* Oakland, CA: New Harbinger Publications, Inc.

Rutledge, T. 1998. *Earning Your Own Respect: A Handbook of Personal Responsibility.* Oakland, CA: New Harbinger Publications, Inc.

Self-Discovery Audio Tapes

Meyerson, M., and L. Ashner. 1999. Designing the Life of your Dreams: A Guided Visualization for Creating the Life You Desire. Oakland, CA: New Harbinger Publications, Inc.

Rutledge, T. 1999. Practice Makes Practice: From Self-Judgment to Self-Compassion. Oakland, CA: New Harbinger Publications, Inc.

Self-Help and Coping Skills

Alderman, T. and Marshall, K. 1998. *Amongst Ourselves: A Self-Help Guide to Living with Dissociative Identity Disorder.* Oakland, CA: New Harbinger Publications, Inc.

Anthony, Martin, and Richard Swinson. 1998. *When Perfect Isn't Good Enough: Strategies for Coping with Perfectionism.* Oakland, CA: New Harbinger Publications, Inc.

Branden, N. 1988. *How to Raise Your Self-Esteem.* New York: Bantam Books.

Cash, T. 1997. *The Body Image Workbook: An 8-Step Program for Learning to Like Your Looks.* Oakland, CA: New Harbinger Publications, Inc.

Copeland, Mary Ellen. 1998. *Winning Against Relapse.* Brattleboro, VT: Peach Press.

————. 1999. *Winning Against Relapse Program* (audiotape). Oakland, CA: New Harbinger Publications, Inc.

Fanning, Patrick. 1990. *Lifetime Weight Control.* Oakland, CA: New Harbinger Publications, Inc.

————. 1994. *Visualization for Change,* Second Edition. Oakland, CA: New Harbinger Publications, Inc.

Finney, Lynne. 1997. *Clear Your Past, Change Your Future: Proven Techniques for Inner Exploration and Healing.* Oakland, CA: New Harbinger Publications, Inc.

Goodwin, Cathy. 1999. *Making the Big Move: How to Transform Relocation into a Creative Life Transition.* Oakland, CA: New Harbinger Publications, Inc.

Hadley, Josie, and Carol Staudacher. 1996. *Hypnosis for Change,* Third Edition. Oakland, CA: New Harbinger, Inc.

Harp, D., and N. Feldman. 1996. *The Three Minute Meditator,* Third Edition. Oakland, CA: New Harbinger Publications, Inc.

Hyman, Bruce, and Cherry Pedrick. 1999. *The OCD Workbook: Your Guide to Breaking Free from Obsessive-Compulsive Disorder.* Oakland, CA: New Harbinger Publications, Inc.

Kenyon, Julian. 1996. *Acupressure Techniques: A Self-Help Guide.* Rochester, VT: Healing Arts Press.

Kirschenbaum, D. 1994. *Weight Loss Through Persistence.* Oakland, CA: New Harbinger Publications, Inc.

McKay, M., P. Fanning, C. Honeychuch, and C. Sutker. 1999. *The Self-Esteem Companion.* Oakland, CA: New Harbinger Publications, Inc.

McKay, M., and P. Fanning. 1993. *Self-Esteem,* Second Edition. Oakland, CA: New Harbinger Publications, Inc.

Roberts, Susan. 1995. *Living Without Procrastination.* Oakland, CA: New Harbinger Publications, Inc.

Roberts, S., and G. Jansen. 1997. *Living with ADD: A Workbook for Adults with Attention Deficit Disorder.* Oakland, CA: New Harbinger Publications, Inc.

Rutledge, T. 1997. *The Self-Forgiveness Handbook: A Practical and Empowering Guide.* Oakland, CA: New Harbinger Publications, Inc.

Sandbek, T. 1993. *The Deadly Diet,* Second Edition. Oakland, CA: New Harbinger Publications, Inc.

Savage, Elayne. 1997. *Don't Take It Personally! The Art of Dealing with Rejection.* Oakland, CA: New Harbinger Publications, Inc.

Weiss, Lillie. 1999. *Practical Dreaming: Awakening the Power of Dreams in Your Life.* Oakland, CA: New Harbinger Publications, Inc.

Sleep

Catalano, E. 1990. *Getting to Sleep.* Oakland, CA: New Harbinger Publications, Inc.

Substance Abuse

Althauser, Doug. 1998. *You Can Free Yourself from Alcohol & Drugs: Work a Program That Keeps You in Charge.* Oakland, CA: New Harbinger Publications, Inc.

Fanning, P., and J. O'Neill. 1996. *The Addiction Workbook: A Step-By-Step Guide to Quitting Alcohol & Drugs*. Oakland, CA: New Harbinger Publications, Inc.

Hazelden Foundation. 1993. *The Dual Disorders Recovery Book: A Twelve Step Program for Those of Us with Addiction and an Emotional or Psychiatric Illness*. Center City, MN: Hazelden Education Materials.

Kinney, Jean, and Gwen Leaton. 1991. *Loosening the Grip: A Handbook of Alcohol Information*. St. Louis, MO: Mosby Year Book.

Tanner, Laurie. 1996. *The Mother's Survival Guide to Recovery: All About Alcohol, Drugs and Babies*. Oakland, CA: New Harbinger Publications, Inc.

Woititz, J. 1990. *Adult Children of Alcoholics*. Pompano Beach, FL: Health Communications.

Suicide

Beattie, M. 1991. *A Reason to Live*. Wheaton, IL: Tyndale House Publishers, Inc.

Ellis, T., and C. Newman. 1996. *Choosing to Live: How to Defeat Suicide Through Cognitive Therapy*. Oakland, CA: New Harbinger Publications, Inc

Support Groups

White, Barbara, and Edward Madara. 1995. *The Self-Help Sourcebook: Finding and Forming Mutual Aid Self-Help Groups*. Denville, NJ: American Self-Help Clearinghouse.

Samples, P., D. Larson, and M. Larson. 1991. *Self-Care for Caregivers: A Twelve Step Approach*. Cork, Ireland: Hazelden.

Trauma and Sexual Abuse

Adams, C., and J. Fay. 1990. *Free of the Shadows: Recovering from Sexual Violence*. Oakland, CA: New Harbinger Publications, Inc.

Alderman, Tracy. 1997. *The Scarred Soul: Understanding and Ending Self-Inflicted Violence*. Oakland, CA: New Harbinger Publications, Inc.

Copeland, M.E., and M. Harris. 2000. *Healing the Trauma of Abuse*. Oakland, CA: New Harbinger Publications, Inc.

Enns, G., and J. Black. 1997. *It's Not Okay Anymore: Your Personal Guide to Ending Abuse, Taking Charge, and Loving Yourself*. Oakland, CA: New Harbinger Publications, Inc.

Finney, L. 1990. *Reach for the Rainbow: Advanced Healing for Survivors of Sexual Abuse*. Park City, UT: Changes Publishing.

Matsakis, A. 1999. *Survivor Guilt: A Self-Help Guide*. Oakland, CA: New Harbinger Publications, Inc.

———. 1998. *Trust After Trauma: A Guide to Relationships for Survivors and Those Who Love Them*. Oakland, CA: New Harbinger Publications, Inc.

———. 1996. *I Can't Get Over It: A Handbook for Trauma Survivors*. Oakland, CA: New Harbinger Publications, Inc.

———. 1991. *When the Bough Breaks: A Helping Guide for Parents of Sexually Abused Children*. Oakland, CA: New Harbinger Publications, Inc.

Parnell, L. 1997. *Transforming Trauma: EMDR, the Revolutionary New Therapy for Freeing the Mind, Clearing the Body and Opening the Heart*. Lutherville, MD: Sidran Foundation Bookshelf.

Shapiro, F., and M. S. Forrest. 1998. *EMDR: The Breakthrough Therapy for Overcoming Anxiety, Stress and Trauma*. Lutherville, MD: Sidran Foundation Bookshelf.

Women's Issues

Boston Women's Health Book Collective. 1998. *Our Bodies, Ourselves for the New Century.* New York: Touchstone.

Boynton, Marilyn, and Mary Dell. 1995. *Goodbye Mother, Hello Woman.* Oakland, CA: New Harbinger Publications, Inc.

Chesler, P. 1997. *Women and Madness.* New York: Avon Books.

Clegg, Eileen. 1999. *Claiming Your Creative Self: True Stories from the Everyday Lives of Women.* Oakland, CA: New Harbinger Publications, Inc.

Clegg, Eileen, and Susan Swartz. 1998. *Goodbye Good Girl.* Oakland, CA: New Harbinger Publications, Inc.

Dalton, K. 1980. *Once a Month: The Original PMS Handbook.* Oakland, CA: New Harbinger Publications, Inc.

DeRosis, Helen. 1998. *Women & Anxiety: A Step-by-Step Program for Managing Anxiety and Depression.* New York: Hatherleigh Press.

Doress-Worters, P., and D. Siegal, in cooperation with the Boston Women's Health Collective. 1996. *The New Ourselves Growing Older: Women Aging with Knowledge and Power.* New York: Peter Smith Press.

Harris, Maxine. 1998. *Trauma Recovery and Empowerment: A Clinician's Guide for Working with Women in Groups.* New York: The Free Press.

Louden, Jennifer. 1997. *The Woman's Retreat Book: A Guide to Restoring, Rediscovering, and Reawakening Your True Self—in a Moment, an Hour, a Day, or a Weekend.* San Francisco, CA: HarperSanFrancisco.

Lush, J., and P. Rushford. 1990. *Emotional Phases of a Woman's Life.* Old Tappen, NJ: Fleming H. Revell Co.

Nelson, Miriam. 1997. *Strong Women Stay Young.* New York: Bantam Books.

Raskin, Valerie Davis. 1997. *When Words Are Not Enough: The Women's Prescription for Depression and Anxiety.* New York: Broadway Books.

Ravicz, Simone. 1998. *High on Stress: A Woman's Guide to Optimizing the Stress in Her Life.* Oakland, CA: New Harbinger Publications, Inc.

Scarf, M. 1989. *Unfinished Business: Pressure Points in the Lives of Woman.* New York: Doubleday.

Silverstein, Brett, and Deborah Perlick. 1995. *The Cost of Competence: Why Inequality Causes Depression, Eating Disorders, and Illness in Women.* New York: Oxford University Press.

Mental Health Organizations

Center for Mental Health Services
Substance Abuse and Mental Health Services Administration
5600 Fishers Lane, Room 15-99
Rockville, MD 20857
CMHS Knowledge Exchange Network 800-789-2647
Publications, information, and services

CONTAC (Consumer Organizational National Technical Assistance Center)
1036 Quarrier St., Suite 208A
Charleston, WV 25301
800-598-8847
Teaches recovery leadership skills as well as providing technical assistance to adults with psychiatric disability throughout the United States.

International Association of Psychosocial Rehabilitation Services (IAPSRS)
10025 Governor Warfield Parkway, Suite 301
Columbia, MD 21044-3357
410-730-7190, TTY: 410-730-1723

E-Mail: iapsrs33@aol.com

IAPSRS is a nonprofit organization that promotes, supportes, and strengthenes community-based psycho-social rehabilitation services and resources. Publishes a journal, newsletters, and a Resource Catalogue.

Lithium Information Center
Dean Foundation
2711 Allen Blvd.
Middleton, WI 53562
608-827-2390

The Lithium Information Center does computer searches on lithium information for a fee. Information is also available through the mail.

Mental Illness Education Project
P.O. Box 470813
Brookline, MA 02447
617-562-1111

MIEP makes educational videos about various aspects of mental health.

National Alliance for the Mentally Ill (NAMI)
200 North Glebe Rd., Suite 1015
Arlington, VA 22203-3754
800-950-NAMI (HELPLINE)

NAMI is a support and advocacy organization of people who experience psychiatric symptoms, families, and friends of people with mental illnesses, which emphasizes the biological view of causes and treatments.

National Depressive and Manic-Depressive Association (NDMDA)
730 North Franklin St., Suite 501
Chicago, IL 60610-3526
800-826-3632

A membership organization that provides direct support services to people who experience depression and/or depression and mania and their families, legislation and public policy advocacy, litigation to prevent discrimination, public education, and technical assistance to local affiliates.

National Empowerment Center
599 Canal St.
5th Floor East
Lawrence, MA 01840
800POWER2U (800-769-3728)

Provides information, programs and materials, with a focus on recovery. Newsletter and audio-visual materials.

National Institute for Mental Health (NIMH)
Information, Resources & Inquiries Branch
5600 Fishers Lane
Rockville, MD 20857
301-443-4513; TDD 301-443-8431
800-421-4211 (Depression/Awareness, Recognition, and Treatment Information)
E-mail: NIMHPUBS@nih.gov

Provides a list of free publications on depressive and other mental disorders, including a comprehensive listing of resources for help.

National Mental Health Association
1021 Prince St.
Alexandria, VA 22314-2971

Information Center 800-669-NMHA
Through its national office, state, and regional chapters, NMHA sponsors public education programs, develops and disseminates resources, and advocates for mental health issues.

National Mental Health Association (NMHA)
1021 Prince St.
Arlington, VA 22314-2917
800-969-6642
Provides information and referral.

National Mental Health Consumers' Self-Help Clearinghouse
1211 Chestnut Street, Suite 1207
Philadelphia, PA 19107
800-553-4539 (phone); 215-636-6312 (fax)
web: http://www.mhselfhelp.org; e-mail: info@mhselfhelp.org
Provides information about psychiatric disorders, technical support for existing or newly starting self-help groups, and a free quarterly newsletter. Spanish language services.

SPAN   (Suicide Prevention Advocacy Network)
5034 Odin's Way
Marietta, GA 30068
888-649-1366
Website: http://www.spanusa.org; E-mail: act@spanusa.org
National advocacy organization for the development of effective suicide prevention.

Support Group Coalition International
454 Williamette, #216
PO Box 11284
Eugene, OR 97440-3484
Focuses on advocacy, psychiatric oppression and exploring options for self-determination and humane assistance.

Well Mind Association of Greater Washington, Inc.
11141 Georgia Avenue, Suite 326
Wheaton, MD 20902
301-949-8282
Information on physiological causes of psychiatric disorders and how they can be treated.

Web Sites

Mary Ellen Copeland, http://www.mentalhealthrecovery.com and
   http://www.maryellencopeland.com.
   mentalhealthrecovery@yahoogroups.com

Most of the following resource list has been gathered from the National Mental Health Consumers' Self-Help Clearinghouse publication "Advocacy and Recovery Using the Internet." Their Web site is at http://www.mhselfhelp.org. Their mailing address is listed under Mental Health Organizations a few pages back.

Ratings and Research:
U.S. News and World Report has an in-depth study of health care providers each year and publishes its ratings at http://www.usnews.com

You can find information about a specific physician, such as training and prior disciplinary actions, through search services such as http://www.askmedi.com. Similar information may be available on your state medical board's Web site. To find your state's medical board, go to http://www.docboard.org.

American Self-Help Clearinghouse at http://mentalhelp.net/selfhelp.
For doing research on your own rather than using information that has been prepared for you:
   Library of Congress, http://lcweb.loc.gov
   National Library of Medicine's MEDLINE service, http://www.nlm.nih.gov

Mental Health/General Health:

Better Health, http://www.betterhealth.com
Center for Mental Health Services, http://www.mentalhealth.org
Dr. Koop, the former Surgeon General, http://www.drkoop.com
Internet Mental Health, Dr. Philip Long, http://www.mentalhealth.com
iVilliage, http://www.onlinepsych.com.
Healthy Healing, http://www.healthyhealing.com
Mary Ellen Copeland, http://www.mentalhealthrecovery.com and
      http://www.maryellencopeland.com.
Mental Health Net, http://mentalhelp.net
Support-Group.com, http://www.support-group.com

National Mental Health Organizations:

Bazelon Center for Mental Health Law, http://www.bazelon.org
International Center for Clubhouse Development, http://www.iccd.org
MacArthur Research Network on Mental Health and the Law,
      http://ness.sys.virginia.edu/macarthur
Mad Nation, http://www.madnation.org
National Alliance for the Mentally Ill (NAMI), http://www.nami.org
National Association of Protection and Advocacy Systems,
      http://www.protectionandadvocacy.com
National Association of State Mental Health Program Directors, http://www.nasmhpd.org
National Depressive and Manic Depressive Association (NDMDA), http:/www.ndmda.org
National Empowerment Center, http://www.power2u.org
National Mental Health Association (NMHA), http://www.nmha.org
National Mental Health Consumers' Self-Help Clearinghouse, http://www.mhselfhelp.org
National Stigma Clearinghouse, http://community.webtv.net/stigmanet
People Who Net, http://www.peoplewho.net
The Madness Group, http://peoplewho.net/Madness

Government Resources:

Health Care Financing Administration, http://www.hcfa.gov
Knowledge Exchange Network (Center for Mental Health Services),
      http://www.mentalhealth.org
Library of Congress, http://lcweb.loc.gov
MEDLINE (National Library of Medicine), http://www.nlm.nih.gov
President's Committee on Employment of People with Disabilities, http://www50.pcepd.gov
Thomas: Legislative Information on the Internet (Library of Congress), http://thomas.loc.gov
U.S. House of Representatives, http://www.house.gov
U.S. Senate, http://www.senate.gov
The White House, http://www.whitehouse.gov

Newsgroups:

http://www.deja.com
http://www.liszt.com

Message Boards:

http://forums.mentalhelp.net
http://www.betterhealth.com/allhealth/boards
http://www.support-group.com/support.htm

Chat Rooms:

http://mentalhelp.net
http://www.drkoop.com
http://www.support-group.com

For a catalog of e-mail mailing lists:

http://www.liszt.com
http://www.onelist.com

Job-hunting:

http://www.careerbuilder.com
http://www.careermart.com
http://www.careermosaic.com
http://www.hotjobs.com
http://www.mhselfhelp.org (jobs for consumers)
http://www.yahoo.com (to find a particular city's newspaper for job listings)

Advocacy Groups:

Bazelon Center for Mental Health Law, http://www.bazelon.org
Center for Mental Health Services State Resources Guides,
      http://www.mentalhealth.org/publications
Mad Nation, http://www.madnation.org
Madness Group, "Act-Mad" e-mail list, http://www.peoplewho.net/Madness
National Alliance for the Mentally Ill (NAMI), http://www.nami.org
National Association of Protection and Advocacy Systems (NAPAS),
      http://www.protectionandadvocacy.com
National Depressive and Manic-Depressive Association (NDMDA), http://www.ndmda.org
National Mental Health Association (NMHA), http://www.nmha.org

Some Other
New Harbinger Titles

The End of-life Handbook, Item 5112 $15.95

The Mindfulness and Acceptance Workbook for Anxiety, Item 4993 $21.95

A Cancer Patient's Guide to Overcoming Depression and Anxiety, Item 5044 $19.95

Handbook of Clinical Psychopharmacology for Therapists, 5th edition, Item 5358 $55.95

Disarming the Narcissist, Item 5198 $14.95

The ABCs of Human Behavior, Item 5389 $49.95

Rage, Item 4627 $14.95

10 Simple Solutions to Chronic Pain, Item 4825 $12.95

The Estrogen-Depression Connection, Item 4832 $16.95

Helping Your Socially Vulnerable Child, Item 4580 $15.95

Life Planning for Adults with Developmental Disabilities, Item 4511 $19.95

Overcoming Fear of Heights, Item 4566 $14.95

*Acceptance & Commitment Therapy for the Treatment of Post-Traumatic Stress Disorder &
    Trauma-Related Problems*, Item 4726 $58.95

But I Didn't Mean That!, Item 4887 $14.95

Calming Your Anxious Mind, 2nd edition, Item 4870 $14.95

10 Simple Solutions for Building Self-Esteem, Item 4955 $12.95

The Dialectical Behavior Therapy Skills Workbook, Item 5136 $21.95

The Family Intervention Guide to Mental Illness, Item 5068 $17.95

Finding Life Beyond Trauma, Item 4979 $19.95

Five Good Minutes at Work, Item 4900 $14.95

It's So Hard to Love You, Item 4962 $14.95

Energy Tapping for Trauma, Item 5013 $17.95

Thoughts & Feelings, 3rd edition, Item 5105 $19.95

Transforming Depression, Item 4917 $12.95

Helping A Child with Nonverbal Learning Disorder, 2nd edition, Item 5266 $15.95

Leave Your Mind Behind, Item 5341 $14.95

Learning ACT, Item 4986 $44.95

ACT for Depression, Item 5099 $42.95

Integrative Treatment for Adult ADHD, Item 5211 $49.95

Freeing the Angry Mind, Item 4380 $14.95

Living Beyond Your Pain, Item 4097 $19.95

Transforming Anxiety, Item 4445 $12.95

Integrative Treatment for Borderline Personality Disorder, Item 4461 $24.95

Depressed and Anxious, Item 3635 $19.95

Is He Depressed or What?, Item 4240 $15.95

Cognitive Therapy for Obsessive-Compulsive Disorder, Item 4291 $39.95

Child and Adolescent Psychopharmacology Made Simple, Item 4356 $14.95

Call **toll free, 1-800-748-6273,** or log on to our online bookstore at **www.newharbinger.com** to order. Have your Visa or Mastercard number ready. Or send a check for the titles you want to New Harbinger Publications, Inc., 5674 Shattuck Ave., Oakland, CA 94609. Include $4.50 for the first book and 75¢ for each additional book, to cover shipping and handling. (California residents please include appropriate sales tax.) Allow two to five weeks for delivery.

Prices subject to change without notice.